Hinduism
and
Scientific Quest

Contemporary Researches in Hindu Philosophy & Religion (ISSN 0971-9628)

1. Idealistic Thought in Indian Philosophy; by Shuchita C. Divatia (ISBN 978-81-246-0021-4)
2. Karma and Reincarnation: The Vedāntic Perspective; by Muni Narayana Prasad (ISBN 978-81-246-0022-1)
3. Stonemill and Bhakti: From the Devotion of Peasant Women to the Philosophy of Swamies; by Guy Poitevin and Hema Rairkar (ISBN 978-81-246-0059-7)
4. Śaivism: Some Glimpses; by G.V. Tagare (ISBN 978-81-246-0076-4)
5. Advaita: A Conceptual Analysis; by A. Ramamurty (ISBN 978-81-246-0067-2)
6. Mind-Body Dualism: A Philosophic Investigation; by Alpana Chakraborty (ISBN 978-81-246-0071-9)
8. Indra and Other Vedic Deities — A Euhemeristic Study; by Uma Chakravarty (ISBN 978-81-246-0080-1)
9. Brahma-Vāda: Doctrine of Śrī Vallabhācārya; by G.V. Tagare (ISBN 978-81-246-0112-9)
10. The Science of Enlightenment: Enlightenment, Liberation and God — A Scientific Explanation; by Nitin Trasi (ISBN 978-81-246-0130-3)
11. Retrieving Sāṁkhya History: An Ascent from Dawn to Meridian; by Lallanji Gopal (ISBN 978-81-246-0143-3)
12. The Philosophical Foundations of Hinduism; by A. Ramamurty (ISBN 978-81-246-0163-1)
13. The Eternal Hinduism; by Baidyanath Saraswati (ISBN 978-81-246-0249-2)
14. Vedānta and its Philosophical Development; by A. Ramamurty (ISBN 978-81-246-0347-5)
15. Sāṁkhya-Yoga Epistomology; by Mukta Biswas (ISBN 978-81-246-0371-0)
16. A Sourcebook of Classical Hindu Thought; by Arvind Sharma (ISBN 978-81-246-0643-8)
17. A Treatise on Advaita Vedānta; by S. Bhuvaneshwari (ISBN 978-81-246-0707-7)
18. Advaita Metaphysics: A Contemporary Perspective; by Tapti Maitra (ISBN 978-81-246-0747-3)

Contemporary Researches in Hindu Philosophy & Religion; no. 7

Hinduism and Scientific Quest

T. R. R. Iyengar

DK PRINTWORLD
Publishers of Indian Traditions

Cataloging in Publication Data – DK
[Courtesy: D.K. Agencies (P) Ltd. <docinfo@dkagencies.com>]

Iyengar, T. R. R. (T. Renga Rajan), 1962- **author.**
Hinduism and scientific quest / T.R.R. Iyengar.
pages cm. – (Contemporary researches in Hindu philosophy & religion ; no. 7)
ISBN 9788124600771 (Hb)
ISBN 9788124604496 (Pb)

1. Hinduism and science. 2. Science – India. I. Title. II. Series : Contemporary researches in Hindu philosophy & religion; no. 7.

LCC BL1215.S36I94 2018 | DDC 294.5165 23

ISBN: 978-81-246-0077-1 (Hb)
ISBN: 978-81-246-0449-6 (Pb)
First published in 1997
Second impression, 2004
Third impression, 2018

Printed and published by:
D.K. Printworld (P) Ltd.
Regd. Office: "Vedaśrī", F-395, Sudarshan Park
(Metro Station: ESI Hospital), New Delhi - 110 015
Phones: (011) 2545 3975; 2546 6019
e-mail: indology@dkprintworld.com
Website: www.dkprintworld.com

Preface

Human endeavour since times immemorial has been an untiring search, a relentless effort to know the Ultimate — which can be variously termed the Ultimate Reality, Ultimate Presence, Ultimate Consciousness, God, the Absolute, and so on. At the same time, thoughts, ideas, aspirations have persevered to lay hold of, discover the unknown answers to the many questions about life and living that have plagued the human mind and consciousness ceaselessly. Religion and Science, the twin disciplines of knowledge, have actually evolved and grown in — and are an outcome of — this undying human thirst to know, a thirst that is neither satiated nor allows itself to be ignored . These traditions, however, are distinct in more than one way; throughout history, they have run a mostly parallel course in terms of their approach and methodology, among other things. It is, in actuality, undeniable that while the religious-philosophical doctrines and thoughts have embraced the 'idealist' approach that underlines the fundamentally spiritual character of reality and exalts the spirit over philosophical matter, western science and material philosophy on the other hand have espoused the 'materialistic' view and seen matter as the ultimate principle over spirit and mind. But here, it is worthwhile to view the contribution of that storehouse of spiritual-intellectual wealth called Hinduism. Hinduism's age-old contribution to human civilization and culture is by no means restricted to religious, cultural, philosophical and spiritual traditions though it may seem so at first sight; it, in reality, embraces diverse fields and aspects of the scientific as well. Moreover, we find that the very thinking and approach that evolved the spiritual-philosophical truths immersed itself in the scientific exercise to conduct sytematic analyses and emerge with new ideas, concepts and discoveries in the field of science.

All the universal truths, ideas, thoughts, that have come down to us from the Vedic times onwards — and preserved to this day in their original essence — are a repository of a range of deep, penetrating thoughts, a result of intense meditation and speculation to arrive at truths at various levels — the material life and living, the realm of thoughts and the intellect, and at the level of the soul. Thus, in our *Vedas*, the Upaniṣadic treasure-vault of spiritual wisdom, and in the approach and ends of Vedānta, Sāṁkhya and other sources of knowledge, it is not just the immediate needs and concerns of a religious life that are addressed; it is the human life and realm in their entirety that is discussed. They deal with a variety of topics that feature as essential components of scientific study and disciplines. The diverse nature of the scientific areas touched upon and the depth and range of the theories extended are simply astounding, even unfathomable at times. Unfortunately, though much has been written about Hinduism's cultural-spiritual contributions, very little has been done to bring to light its achievements vis-a-vis Science. This book "Hinduism and Scientific Quest" attempts to accomplish precisely this.

Herein, Hinduism's contribution to the scientific discipline or realm is studied with the intention to present a comprehensive, all-embracing picture. I have dealt with a wide spectrum of areas and varying issues — from say, the cosmogony principles, no doubt, a broad topic, to something very specific such as use of science in warfare — discussed in Hinduism's core texts and doctrines.Thus, developments in Hindu thought and traditions pertaining to various modern scientific disciplines — Botany, Medicine, Physics, Chemistry, Horticulture, Physiognomy, Weather Science, etc. — have been traced. These are then compared and contrasted with modern scientific theories and findings. The chapters are arranged in such a manner so as to bring as much material as possible on Hinduism vis-a-vis the study of science and scientific disciplines within the book's scope. Our Vedic ancestors' ideas and views, and Upaniṣadic insight into facts such as the origin of the universe, earth, matter, spirit, soul, human life are thoroughly scrutinised for their scientific wealth. I have specifically underlined the significance of Advaita in modern science as it is not a single state of consciousness but a result of considering the totality of all knowledge.

I have also compared and analysed Science and Religion, as two distinct fields, in relation to one another. Eastern and modern scientific thoughts are discussed, at places, in general before delving into Hinduism's contribution itself and placing it in the right perspective.

I am indebted to all the standard works on the varied aspects of the subject from which ideas have been profusely drawn.

I have much pleasure in sincerely thanking Raja Ramanna and A. S. Ramanathan whose articles in *The Hindu* and *Veda, the Word Eternal* have proved extremely helpful to me.

Thanks are due to my innumerable friends and relatives for helping me in varied ways in completing the work. Last but not least, I have to acknowledge my gratitude to my parents (Thirumalai A.S. and Ambujam) who have rendered their ungrudging help and cooperation over the last few years and have aided me immensely in this work.

Immense thanks are due to the publishers M/s D.K. Printworld, but for whose untiring zeal, enthusiasm and tenacity, this work would have remained in my dreams only.

I shall consider myself well-rewarded if this book proves to be of great benefit to those for whom it is meant.

Criticisms and suggestions for improvement are welcome.

Madurai **T.R.R. Iyengar**
Oct., 1996

Contents

1

Introduction

"The most beautiful and the most profound emotion we experience is the mystical." Declares Einstein, perhaps the greatest scientist of this age of science.

What, then, is this "mystical element", so highly eulogised by him?

"It is the source of all true science", is the emphatic answer of the same great scientist.

"Oh, science only?" One may be justifiably tempted to ask.

"Of all true happiness also", it must be answered, "for all of us who hanker after it."

But, as it is, its promise is much more than that. Its scope is all-comprehensive.

The unfailing source of all true humanitarian endeavour, of the exalted and transcendent feeling of oneness experienced by the sage and the man of wisdom, it is the source of intuition and perception of the *yogī*. It is also mirrored in the flash of genius in every field and walk of life. "Whatever in this world is of extraordinary calibre power, beauty and of any quality whatsoever is only invested with an infinitesimal particle of My glory", announces the Lord in the *Gītā*.

It is an intense realisation of this mystical presence that has led people, in all ages and climes, to face self-effacement and martyrdom in the name of God, country or scientific truth. An inadequate grasp of it has driven others to impose untold sufferings and persecutions on their fellow men. It is an irresistible urge to communicate to others, an exaltation in the touch of the beyond, a consciousness of the "supreme and living presence", that induced these fanatics to persecute others. It is a certain indefinable feeling of intimacy and identification which we, in the rarest moments of our lives experience in everything beside us. The seventeenth-century German philosopher Spinoza called it 'substance' or 'God'; the nineteenth-century scientist Ludwig Helobach proclaimed it to be nothing more than nature, the ancient Indian *Vedānta* variously termed it as *Brahman*, *ātmā*, *sat* or *saccidānanda* or reality-consciousness, 'Bliss Absolute'. The reality that is one is variously named by the wise *ṛṣis*.

Both science and religion, the temporal and the celestial pursuits of man, we are assured by the wise of our age, ultimately aim at this 'reality', though in different spheres. Science relentlessly pursues after it in the laboratory laboriously through experiment and minute observation of nature in all its aspects. Yet it only falters, nevertheless fortuitously "stumbling upon the rock of this truth". Religion grows ecstatic over it, feeling certain of its presence, through intuition and self-realisation. According to *Vedānta and Modern Physics* by Srimat Puragra Parampanthi, "Twentieth century science today touches the realm of Advaita Vedānta and shakes hands with the monistic idealism."

The general traditional approach to this fundamental and ultimate reality is twofold. One is the 'idealistic view', the belief that reality is fundamentally spiritual or mental, and that spirit existed prior to philosophical matter — held by all religions and philosophical schools. The other is "materialistic view", the view that matter is the ultimate principle, and that spirit and mind are only a consequence of matter — held by the early western scientists and all materialist philosophers.

All the religions of the world, barring Hinduism and Buddhism are purely monotheistic and authoritarian. They have only arrived at the oneness of God, and not yet of God and man, nor of God, man and the whole of creation. They explain the relationship of man to God by the belief that "man is made in the image of God", the very reverse of the doctrine of 'anthropomorphism'. And this is based on the theory of 'revelation' that the truth, is only revealed to the prophet and the original saints. Nor is there any place in this scheme for rational explanation of the workings of the 'world', except that it is the 'will of God' that things are so ordained in the universe.

Confucious is the only teacher who never talked about God and His mystic relation to man and creation, and only concerned himself with propagating "good conduct and the good of the world". Buddha is also said to be silent on metaphysical matters, but, we may be sure, he was only against the rituals of Hinduism. The great religion bearing his name, which prevails in half the world today, is not more than a secular movement of social reform aimed at Vedic sacrifice and ceremonies.

Philosophy, whether old or new, cannot be said to have solved this problem quite satisfactorily. The western philosophers of the last century and of India after the advent of Buddha and Śaṅkara were all 'Idealist' believers in spirit as opposed to matter. Bergson's creative evolution is only a protest against the blind mechanism of struggle as propounded by Darwin. *Elan Vital* is the intuitive life-principle which perpetually evolves and creates new forms of activity and consciousness in man. It is still unable to comprehend his consciousness of divinity, though it did not prevent him from believing in God and a personal faith. Alexander's emergent evolution gives us a growing picture of the universe with life, consciousness and values emerging successively, making God only "the final result", "not the source and spirit creative of the Universe, present in the whole process as also its final goal".* William James's, 'Radical Empiricism' and 'Pragmatism' only takes us to 'Materialism', 'Pragmatism', 'Sensationalism', 'Pluralism' and Ultimately to 'Naturalism'. Bertrand Russell is a "scientific humanist endeavouring to explain moral values and intuition in terms of evolution". He is a believer in "instinct", which makes him declare that "man's morals in the mass . . . do as much harm as they dare and as much good as they must.** While to the man of Divine Realisation, to the one

* *Hinduism* by D.S. Sarma on Dr. Radhakrishnan.

** Dr. Radhakrishnan's Introduction to *Among the Great* by D.K. Roy.

who has fully sublimated his human nature to the mystical presence, morals are only the means of achieving the highest and maximum good, minimising if not totally eliminating evil.

It is claimed that the nineteenth-century scientists Darwin and Huxley established in their "theory of monistic materialism, the universal substance — a substance with two forms, two aspects, a material and a spiritual at one and the same time, a substance of which matter and spirit are two components, seemingly a synthetic view no doubt; but as admitted by the claimants themselves, it only succeeded in solving", the deep abyss between the animal and the vegetable kingdoms' by the discovery of the single cell 'protoplasm* and was yet unable to formulate the relation between organic and inorganic matter. The difference between life and non-life still remains a 'carefully guarded secret'.

With the advent of the nuclear theory in modern physics, the conception of matter, has no doubt, been totally revolutionised. From the concept of pure atoms and 102 elements of the last century, matter has now become "monistic", and is regarded as only a form of energy, a product of electrons and protons,** which are the negative and positive units of electric charge. The electrons, which were thought formerly to consist of particles came to be considered later as consisting of both "waves and particles". James Jeans observes:

---

* Protoplasma is composed of granules which are made up of water, acid, carbon and nitrogen.

** This is not all. The atom consists of an equal number of electrons and protons (their effects thus neutralized), with all the protons and half the number of electrons contained in the atom packed in its central point called the Nucleus (almost the whole mass of the atom is concentrated here), and the remaining electrons distributed in different orbits of various distances encircling the nucleus, a very large part of the atom being only empty space. The different kinds of atoms and substances are distinguished from one another by the different sets of orbits around the nucleus. This mystery of space element and different orbits is unaccounted for in science. Thus either the conception of matter is not absolutely material or its claims to be the 'Sole Truth' of the universe are unsubstantiated.

> A full discussion of these results made it clear that matter could not be interpreted either as waves or particles or even waves plus particles . . . which in some of its aspects reminds us of particles and in other remains us of waves.

He also says that matter and radiation may not constitute two distinct and non-interchangeable forms of waves. The two may be interchangeable, one passing into another. But Planck's theory, in the words of the same authority, "asserted that radiation was as atomic in its structure as matter." Added to it, Heisenberg's theory of indetertion, that the electron in complete isolation can never be known, asserts that by the very act of contacting the constituents of matter through some given media, the material condition of these constituents is disturbed. These mixed properties and this highly abstruse speculation about matter remind us of the theory of *pañcīkaraṇa* in the Hindu *Vedānta*. According to it, though there are five elements in nature — water, earth, fire, air and ether, yet each element is only held as a compound of all the five elements in their original or pure state in certain propositions. Thus a unit of the earth element contains only half of pure earth with the other half made up of the other four elements, one-eighth each. If the particle property of the electron may be taken to be that of the earth element, the wave-property that of air or water or of both, and radiation that of fire, then the true nature of matter must lie somewhere between these elements, with the 'indeterminacy factor' to be attributed to the last element. *Ākāśa*, is regarded as their ultimate principle. And this *ākāśa*, which is regarded as the inferior or material aspect of *Brahman* or *sat*, the ultimate truth. If we are led to this conclusion by science, we are no less thankful to these scholars, who only arrived at their conclusions after the relentless search of truth, than to the philosophers and saints who reached the same conclusions in a different way.

We are thus forced to the conclusion that 'Reality' still remains one-sided, either as "monistic idealism" or monistic materialism without an integral comprehension of both. The ultimate reality as expounded by Dr. Radhakrishnan is "absolute idealism" with life emerging from matter, mind from life, the sense of values, or as the efficient and material cause of the universe. 'One *sat*', with life and non-life as only conscious and unconscious forces in one progressive evolution from atom to man and to his divine awareness, is not yet an established doctrine or proven fact either in religion, philosophy or science.

Einstein, in his not yet fully established "unified field theory" claimed to show that every form of nature — planets, stars, electricity, light, the very particles inside the atom — obey the same basic natural laws. But 24 pages of his equations which make up this theory are yet to be validated. Einstein and most of the present-day scientists are theists, believers in a supreme power of harmony and intelligence. They believe in God

> ". . . who reveals Himself in the orderly Gods harmony of the universe." — Einstein

> "The material world, which has been taken for a world of blind mechanism, is in reality a spiritual world seen very partially and imperfectly." — J.B.S. Haldane

> "The universe looks more like a great thought than like a great machine." — Jeans

> "The man who regards his own life and that of his fellow creatures as meaningless is not merely unfortunate but almost disqualified for life." — Einstein

> "Religion and natural science are fighting a joint battle in an incessant never-relaxing crusade against scepticism, against dogmatism, and against superstition; and the rallying cry in this crusade has always been, and always will be, On to God."
> — Max Plank

But even this grudging and limited comprehension of Reality is not a result of scientific research. It is a "process of conceptualisation" belonging to the domain of philosophy* — "hard thinking and the bold sweep of imaginative power", and as even Einstein suggests, "by giving

---

* *Advaita Vedanta and Modern Physics* by P. Parampanthi.

free rein to imaginative flights — processes closely resembling the intuitive Sadhana of the yogi which play a major part today in bridging the wise chasm between the scientific axioms and their verifiable consequences."

"The man who regards his own life and that of his fellow creatures as meaningless is not merely unfortunate but almost disqualified for life."

It is to the immortal glory and credit of B. Spinoza that he could glimpse this synthetic reality, this harmonious fusion of both matter and spirit — a conception basically adopted by the modern scientists.

> I do not know what I may appear to the world; but to myself I seem to have been only like a boy playing on the seashore, and diverting myself in now and then finding a smoother pebble or a prettier shell than ordinary, whilst the great ocean of truth lay all undiscovered before me. — Issac Newton

> I give myself over to my rapture. The die is cast. Nothing I have ever felt before is like this. I tremble my blood leaps. God has waited 6,000 years for a looker-on to His wisdom is infinite, that of which we are ignorant is contained in Him, as well as the little that we know. — J. Kepler

> Neither is mind material, nor is matter mental; neither is the brain process the cause, nor is it the effect of thought; nor are the two processes independent and parallel. For there are no two processes and two entities; there is but one process, seen now inwardly as thought, and now outwardly as motion; there is but one entity; seen now inwardly as mind, now outwardly as matter, but in reality an inextricable mixture and unity of both. — Durant on Spinoza in *Story of Philosophy*.

Ancient Hindu culture as portrayed in the earlier *Upaniṣad* and the *Veda*s bears glorious and ample testimony to this view. The ultimate reality is expounded therein in two stages — *ākāśa* as the end of all matter, and *Brahman* as the end of both matter and spirit, *annum* and *prāṇa* as they are called. It is this mystic principle, *sat* or *saccidānanda* as it is also — designated which goes further than the materialistic view, and the substance or God of even Spinoza, and truly supplies the lost link between spirit and matter, between Godhead and Cosmic life, between the one and the many as "a vast Truth-conscious light, all-comprehensive, all originating, all-fulfilling" the consciousness that "sleeping in the stone, feels in the plant, senses in the animal, and thinks in man."

The sages of India, who comprehended the truth, had declared that the usual means of knowledge adopted in the field of science and art do not prevail here. As Reality is conceived to transcend both the physical and mental planes, means which enable one to go beyond the five senses and the mind are proposed to be employed. The faculty of the sixth senses — intuition, 'self-revelation in utter silence'* attainable by the power of purity aided by 'faith or grace' is invoked. Parampanthi observes: "As admitted, Einstein and other great scientists have only unconsciously adopted an amount of this very faculty, when they reached their extraordinary conclusion on natural phenomena." It is therefore, an ungruding and unreserved adoption of the *saccidānanda* in life displayed in the sublimation of the three principal faculties of man — will, cognition and feeling; an organic and integral *sādhanā*; a pure and detached life of service; a life of utter simplicity and devotion, that is imperative in the realisation of the *sat* — the ultimate and final comprehension of both matter and spirit.

Every science is based on some postulate. The postulate of Hindu philosophy (particularly in *Śaiva* philosophy) is that something cannot come of nothing or that something can become nothing. As something and nothing are incompatibles, the truth of this postulate will be easily conceded. If it is so easily accepted, it may be asked why it should be made a postulate. The reason is that there are others who admit the reality of the material universe, but maintain creation *ex nihilo*. The existence of such philosophies necessitates the enunciation of the postulate and the explanation of its implications.

The disappearance of water by evaporation or electrolysis, and the

---

* *Aurobindo the Divine Master* by Suddhananda Bharati.

appearance of dew drops on leaves lead an ignorant man to the belief that something can become nothing and something can come of nothing. Similarly, the evolution of the universe, may be taken even by better informed people to be an instance of something becoming nothing and coming from nothing. To understand the involution and evolution of the universe it is enough to understand the processes of the evaporation and electrolysis of water. We know that, in neither case has water become nothing, but that it has turned into vapour in the one case, and into hydrogen and oxygen in the other. In both cases what really happens is only a change of relationship between the particles that go to make up the water. When it becomes vapour, the distance between the particles increases; and when it splits into gases, the atoms that form the water molecules form molecules of their own. This is true of every kind of change in the universe. When the universe undergoes evolution, the relationship between the particles in it undergoes change, but things neither disappear altogether nor come from mere nothing. *Śaiva* philosophy regards the world as something real and not as an illusion.

Since change takes place only in the relationship of the components of a substance, it follows that whatever has no components cannot undergo change. According to the old view of chemistry, an atom was indivisible and it was therefore not expected that an atom had components. In the year to come even these may be resolved into more minute components. It is safe to assume that a point can be reached beyond which there can be no further analysis. The component or components obtained by such ultimate analysis cannot have any further components and will not therefore be subject to any change. This leads us to the principle "that whatever is further unanalysed cannot undergo any change." This is the first corollary of the postulate. Again, since there can be no change in them, they have always been and will always be what they are. That is, they are external. This gives us the second corollary of the postulate.

When a thing changes or becomes another, it does so under the action of a force that produces the change in the relationship of its components. These forces also are governed by the postulate of the existence of the material cause and of the efficient cause of every phenomena and are therefore essentially deterministic. The fundamental principles of this philosophy are derived from its postulate and the corollaries.

We may start with the assumption that the universe has been undergoing evolution. In the course of this evolution, living beings have been variously adapting themselves to varying environments. There must be a power in them which makes this variation possible. Again, the varying nature of the adaptation shows that the power is not mechanical, but intelligent. This power is called 'Religion'. It must be possessed by some intelligent being. This Being is usually called God. Since He leads all souls to perfection, He must be an all-loving Being.

The essence of all living beings is the soul. But there is difference of opinion as to what this essence is. Some attribute to the soul knowledge, desire and energy. Some postulate a free-will in addition to them. The soul so understood is an indefinite and complex conception and cannot therefore receive scientific treatment. If one man invests the soul with certain adjuncts and another man with other adjuncts, the two men use the same word to denote two different things and cannot find means of agreement. The right course is to use the word to denote the essence of a living being, divested of all its adjuncts. It then becomes a single thing that cannot be analysed any further.

Since living beings are numberless, souls also are numberless. We see that a living being knows, desires and does. Therefore, the soul must have the ability to know, to desire, and to do. But we see that the knowledge of a living being, say a man, changes. This change must be due to the change in the quantity of the energy of knowing. Since the soul is an elementary being, it cannot undergo change. Therefore the energy of knowing is not a characteristic of the soul. Besides, if it belonged to the soul, it would be definite in quality and strength or degree and could never change. But we see that it does change. Therefore the power or the energy is not the soul's and must be supplied to it by something else. Just as an engine is a mechanism that can move, but moves only when power is supplied to it, so the soul has the ability to know, and begins actually to know only when the power of knowing is supplied to it. The desire of a living being also changes both in degree and in kind. Therefore the power of desiring cannot be the soul's. It can similarly be shown that the power of doing also is not the soul's. So, we see that the soul has the ability to know, to desire, and to do, but not the energy or power necessary for the activities. The energy must therefore be supplied to it by something else.

That which supplies the energy to the soul is called *māyā*. It supplies not only the energy but also the tools necessary for using the energy, namely the physical and the mental powers. It also gives the soul embodied and mental power of the world to live in, and things in the world to enjoy. All the worlds are products of *māyā*. These worlds are constantly undergoing change and are either in the process of formation or in the process of disintegration. In other words, they are evolving. The word *māyā* itself means that which (*mā* =) involves and (*yā* =) evolves. The body, the mind, and the energy have all come from *māyā* and are therefore ultimately not different from one another. As *māyā* cannot be further resolved it must be eternal.

But the knowledge that the soul receives through the products of *māyā* is limited and often leads either to doubt or to error. Just, as in dim light, a snake is mistaken for a piece of rope or is held in suspense as being either a snake or a rope, so, with the little knowledge that we derive through *māyā*, we often mistake wrong for right or are in suspense regarding the true nature of a thing. This limitation of knowledge must be due to some other cause or factor.

This cause or factor is called *āṇava*. *Āṇava* constricts the soul's abilities to know, to desire and to do, and does not allow energy to have its full scope. But certain products of *māyā* exert a force in opposition to it and allow a gradually increasing flow of energy according to certain principles. When the soul gets a little knowledge, it become conscious of itself, identifies itself with the body, and commits endless blunders. The most pathetic feature of its blunders is that it is hardly ever aware of them. False pride is one of the first products of little knowledge, but when a person is actuated by it he feels he is quite in the right. The consequence is that the person does not realise for a long time that pride is his bitterest foe. *Āṇava* is thus the root cause of the soul's blunders and consequent misery. *Māyā* gives limited knowledge through the senses and the intellect, and assists the soul in its struggle with *āṇava*.

The acts of the soul appear as thoughts, words, and deeds. Right actions are those that are good to the self and to others. Such acts naturally cause happiness. Wrong acts are those that are bad to the self and to others. As they break harmonious relationships, they cause pain. Right actions are sometimes accompanied by immediate pain; and though a wrong act may give immediate pleasure, it ultimately leads to misery. The pain and pleasure due to right deeds and wrong deeds respectively are not necessarily experienced immediately after the deeds are performed, but reach the soul as circumstances permit, sometimes much long after the deed. Murderers are sometimes arrested several years after the murder and then punished. The effects of these actions, manifested as pain and pleasure produce a tendency in the souls to prefer the right and avoid the wrong. This tendency is coupled with the knowledge received during the effects of *āṇava*. When *āṇava* is completely overcome, the soul becomes free and reaches the final goal.

2

Cosmogony

Ideas of the East

The *Nāsadīya* and the *Puruṣa Śūktas** are indeed the most famous passages of the *Ṛgveda*, included in the tenth or last *maṇḍala* and considered to belong to the celebrated *Sūkta* period. The *Ṛgveda* itself

---

* In praise of the person (*Puruṣa-Sūkta*)

Thousand-headed, thousand eyed
ye, thousand footed, The person
Pervading, who, the universe everywhere
Doth yet surpass is far,
All this the person, all that was,
And all that will be
Of immortality, the Lord Supreme
He transcends by matter still
All this, the universe, His glory;
He's greater far than this.
The beings, all but constitute His one foot;
His three the Heaven immortal.
By three feet He rose infinite high,
His fourth projected here.
By that His pervasion in each and all.
Inanimate object and living;
By that is projected the cosmic form,
The person greater far than this
The person, born from front He excels the earth
From the rear, His own form. →

is the most ancient book not only in the Indian languages but even in the whole world. To the Hindu, it is the revealed book in a much more original and sweeping sense than even the other *Veda*s and the *Upaniṣad*s, in so much as they are either adaptations of it to a

---

→

The great gods and seers wise — they assembled all,
And held the mighty sacrifice psycho-cosmic.
They piled on the altar herbs, ghee and oblations too,
And poured them into the flame flaring high.

Spring became their ghee;
    Summer their fuel;
The directions formed the meters seven,
    And again faggots twenty-one
The mighty shining gods bound and tied
    The person to His post;
They sprinkled Him, the first born One,
    With holy water;
They worshipped Him with flowers
    And offered Him their incense;
They made Him, the cosmic person, their animal;
    Him they did promptly offer

From that sacrifice supreme
Sprung the beings all;
From that beasts and animals,
Cows, horses and goats;
From that the Vedas came,
Rk, Saman and Yajus

Of the person so projected in their mind,
Aye, what was His face, His arms, thighs and feet?
The Holy Brahman was His face,
His arms the princely Ksatra;
His thighs, the Vaisya judicious,
His feet the Sudra faithful formed.
The moon rose from the cosmic mind,
Fire from His mouth,
From the navel the sky,
The Heaven from His head,
From feet the earth,
From ears also the directions.

So it is the gods their sacrifice held,
And so the Dharmas emanated;

particular theme — *Karma Kāṇḍa* or musical note as the *Yajus* or *Sāma* — or explanation, exposition and interpretation, as in the *Upaniṣads*. The *Nāsadīya* is so-called because it begins with *na asat*, i.e., no non-existence. This *Sūkta* is regarded by many scholars as the

---

→
Even so the perfect ones here itself,
To Heavenly spheres do attain

Borne by waters, the earth and herbs,
All life came forth;
Yet in the beginning, all from the deigning Lord,
The Lord, holding within Himself all, took to body,
From the Person the gods,
From Him all mortal life

I know this Person great and infinite,
Splendrous as the sun and beyond all darkness,
Knowing Him thus one crosses death,
To go beyond there's none other way than this

The progenitor of worlds moves inside of everyone
Unborn, yet to form manifold He takes;
His origin do the steady wise know;
Into Him the worlds dissolve at their end

Great Gods Self-luminous and supreme
Who shinest glorious for the gods,
Dost them good for ever,
And wast their first born One,
I bow to Thee
The gods who brought Thee forth
Thee they praise and sing.
The knower all the gods
And goddesses wait upon.

Obeisance, obeisance to Thee a thousand times
Goddess wealth and wealth earth. They queens,
Day and night Thy all embracing arms,
The starry firmament They jewelled cloak,
The twin-gods, Aswins Thy lips,
Which sing, "god unto all".

O spirited universe,
Grant us Thy vision supreme;
O, deign to grant us
All for Thy service

father of the *Upaniṣads* in that it presents their whole theme in a nutshell, and is generally cited for the speculative sublimity of the Vedic thought. It announces, in the most significant terms, the integral Vedic conception of all matter and spirit. The question of all questions is posed here, "What is the beginning of this universe?" and it is answered by asserting that there is no absolute beginning to the universe at all, but only a progressive manifestation of spirit in matter; and the end of a progressive return of matter to spirit in a never-ending cycle. In other words, *Brahmaṇ* is the cause, the sole efficient and material cause, the creator of the world as well as the substance out of which it is created. And this *Brahman* is not dead, inert matter, but the eternal self-conscious entity; the omniscient and the omnipotent; the "one alone" without a second — "breathing by itself without air" and with nothing beyond nor anything beside."

Prof. Vartak says the *Veda*s contain the Ultimate truth. *Nāsadīya Sūkta* postulates that

1. Non-existence was not, nor existence then;
Nor air,* nor the Supreme One — the sky.
Did it pervade at all? Where? For whose joy?
This deep undivided water — was it there?

2. Death was not nor immortality then;
Nor day, nor night, nor any visible sign;
The sole ONE (that was) breathed by itself without air;
Beyond that** was nothing, nor anything beside.***

3. Then was darkness rolled in darkness;
All this was water — the sole expression.
The perfect ONE that was (is) by the ignoble dressed
He was born, by austerity, as his glory.

4. At first the seed psychic (WILL) it was;
It became desire to break into many.

---

* The active principle — *Rajas* in the original.

** In the sense of superior to that.

*** Any other thing, either equal or inferior to it.

The existent is to the non-existent related;
Nor realised the Supreme wise of yore.

5. Verily a ray it was of the Supreme One,
That filled across and kissed above and below.
It became great and productive;
Its inherent power spread behind, its glory before.

6. Who knows, who can tell us sure —
Whence came this cosmos? Whence its projection?
The Gods too doubtless came only later on.
Aye. Who knows how came this all?

7. This whole projection, — whence it was
Whether borne, it was,* or not at all**
The presiding deity of all in the supreme, the sky,
Perhaps He knows it, perhaps he does not.

Ṛgveda; *Nāsadīya Sūkta*

The ultimate reality of all matter, as given out here, is *ākāśa*, the sky or the scientist's ether. (verse 1 and 7) The *ākāśa* is only a "Ray of the Supreme One" or "The dress of the Perfect one become by the austerity of the Supreme one as 'His glory'". The great *Sāṁkhya* doctrine of material evolution attributed to Kapila — the real source for Darwin's modern scientific theory of natural and biological evolution — borrowed from the material of the Greek philosophers Plato and Pythagoras, whose indebtedness to the *Sāṁkhya* doctrine is so well-known, is only a corollary from this *Sūkta*. But what the *Saṁkhya* did not even envisage but only left in doubt, the *Nāsadīya* had quite triumphantly affirmed and advocated. The ultimate oneness of all matter and spirit***

* Borne or held by the Supreme Spirit.

** The basic question in the above is whether this whole projection or creation has come out from the supreme spirit and is being held by it or not.

*** It is remarkable to note that the conception of the ultimate Reality has been one-sided and partial as held by both science and philosophy: science has held a materialistic conception till recently when, with the discovery of the electron, neutron or light wave, it came nearer to the realm of idealism, while philosophy has maintained dualistic, spiritual conception all through →

so triumphantly declared in such lines (as "the existent is to the non-existent related" and "the perfect one is by the ignoble dressed"), is what had fallen from the *Sāṁkhya*'s pride of place with its dualistic and multiple conception of many *puruṣas* and one *prakṛti*. Non-existence is regarded by this passage as the causal state of the Existent One and 'Visible Creation' as the inferior cover or dress of the original substance. And likewise death and immortality, light and darkness, etc. are merely relative terms brought into currency since the start of the cosmic evolution.

In the first verse, the *Sūkta* traces the origin of the existent Universe to its non-existent, literally invisible, subtle cause. As this cause is not manifest and, comprehended physically, it is termed 'non-existence'. In the same sense all negative terms — darkness, night and death — are treated as subtle forms or cause of the positive ones — light, day and life. The one that exists beyond death and life and manifests through light and darkness, night and day, etc. is revealed as the 'Sole Being' in the second verse. In the third, this 'Sole Being, Perfect and One' is expounded as being 'dressed by the ignoble'. It is also hinted that by *tapas* or asceticism, heat or activity produced by the very act of thinking or being, the Sole one became transformed into what is termed 'His Glory'. This process of creation from the psycho-metaphysic point of view is further traced in the next verse. His very *tapas* is called 'His first psychic seed'—will or desire. By desire the 'One' broke up into many. This is the creation, the individual and the collective cosmos and all lifeless matter, poetically termed 'His glory'. But all this, the many, the glory and the creation, is only the One and nothing else. Lest one may miss this central note of the *Sūkta*, the oneness and the absolute oneness of *Brahman* and the Universe, matter and spirit, we are once more reminded, in very significant terms, that "the Existent is to the Non-existent related". The fifth stanza characterises all this as a "Ray

---

→

the ages in the West and in India. In the latter times, this ancient integral conception of the *Nāsadīya* has been asserted by the Jewish German philosopher Barucha Spinoza, in the fifteenth century, and triumphantly reclaimed by the saint-patriot-humanist, Śrī Aurobindo from the *Vedas* and the *Upaniṣads*.

of the *Brahman*", only one beam of light issuing forth out of the full effulgence, which spread on all sides and became productive. This one Ray is the *ākāśa* or Sky and is the integration of all matter.

In the last two stanzas, the *Sūkta* speculates in a lofty philosophic mood on the origin and process of creation. It throws out the gods (Indra, Varuṇa, Agni and Sūrya, etc. of the earlier *Saṁhitā*) as they are unable to reveal the secret.

It is remarkable how the *Sūkta*, indicates, both in the beginning and at the end, in the form of speculation, the limitation of all human speech and endeavour to define the Ultimate. It takes recourse to negative terms as a less offensive way, even as later the *Upaniṣad* speaks in the language of *neti neti*.

The moral lesson of thc *Sūkta* is that we have to comprehend the Reality as an entire unity only. To attempt to strip the spirit naked of all body and to hope to gain access to it, as is proposed in all philosophies which shut out the world and treat all matter as an unreality, is not only a folly and a mistake, the extensive damage of which cannot be repaired in life, afterwards, but a very impossibility itself. For the spirit is the inward essence, of which the body is a mere extension in time and space.

The *Nāsadīya*, while thus explaining how the one perfect *Brahman* becomes the cosmos and creation, does not seek to explain why all this process should take place at all. It cuts short the whole question in the beginning itself by saying that "all this was water—the sole expression". By one process the *Brahman* or spirit evolves into matter, the cause into effect, and by another, matter involves or gets back into spirit, the effect into the cause. Buddhism resolves all this into *śūnya* or Nothing and all questioning is violently put an end to. The orthodox *Vedānta* states that the *Brahman* or the perfect, also qualified as the *saccidānanda* —absolute existence, absolute consciousness and absolute bliss—degrades and deforms into temporal life, little fragments of knowledge and fleeting sensual joy. This impermanent and inconstant, this fragmentary and piecemeal obtaining of the *saccidānanda* is all the negation and limitation we experience in life and the universe in the form of death, ignorance and misery. A spiritual sublimation, a peace that passeth all understanding, a truly inward joy attained through suffering and experience, a wise and intuitive comprehension or moral order of the universe and an ungrudging wholesome surrender to its reign is, perhaps, the possible solution which we can expect and need.

Securely establishing its background and basis in *Māyādvaita*, the message announces itself in the *Nāsadīya Sūkta*. The announcement of this great truth — the oneness of matter and spirit — is made here in two phases or stages. The first stage is *ākāśa* as the integration and the ultimate of all matter, and the second is *Brahman* as the fulfilment of both matter and spirit. It is this very great idea that the sage Yājñavalkya expounds* in *Bṛhadāraṇyaka Upaniṣad* to the lady-seer, Gārgī in the court of King Janaka.

While it is all to its glory that the *Nāsadīya* has proclaimed it in no uncertain and ambiguous terms, the next stage of the Reality itself, the practical side of it, is expounded in two phases by the *Puruṣa Sūkta*, also of the *Ṛgveda*, which most picturesquely portrays how the integrated reality becomes the conditioned, partial and manifest reality in the form of creation or cosmos and the *Īśa Upaniṣad* which teaches how this partial reality integrates with the full, how the individual cosmos is fulfilled in the universal *Brahman*.

AGE OF THE EARTH

Professor Holmes writes regarding the age of the earth in his great book *The Age of Earth* as follows:

> Long before it became a scientific aspiration to estimate the age of the earth, many elaborate systems of the world chronology had been devised by the sages of antiquity. The most remarkable of these occult time-scales is that of the ancient Hindus, whose astonishing concept of the Earth's duration has been traced back to *Manusmriti*, a sacred book.

---

* He said, "O Gārgī, it is the *ākāśa* (unmanifested ether) which pervades that which they say, is above and below the earth as well as between them, and which was, is and will be." "What pervades the unmanifested ether?" He said, "O Gārgī, the knowers of *Brahman* describe it verily as the *akṣara* (the Absolute)."

According to this venerable compilation of law and wisdom, the whole past and future of the world is but a day in the eternal life of Brahmā — a day of 4,320 million years, throughout which finite beings are created out of the Infinite. The day of Brahmā is divided into 14 great cycles, each lasting 308,448,000 years together with a final 'twilight' period of 1,728,000 years at the close of which, when Brahmā's night begins, the finite is destined once more to merge into the infinite. At present the world is in the seventh of these cycles and according to the Hindu calendar recorded in the *Viṣṇu Purāṇa* it is now 1,972,949,048 years since the earth came into existence. By a curious coincidence this characteristically precise assessment is of the same order as the 200 million years, which has recently been the most widely favoured estimate for the age of the expanding universe.

When the Hindu calculation of the present age of the earth and the expanding universe could make Professor Holmes so astonished, the precision with which the Hindu calculation regarding the age of the entire Universe was made would make any man spellbound. Since the introduction of the theory of relativity by Einstein, space, time, and mass have been considered relative. There is nothing which can be called absolute. Time, space cannot be separated and the astronomer looks both outward in space and backward in time; for the light reaching the earth from many of the stars is not of today but of millions of years back. We are seeing the stars when the light left them millions of years ago and it is quite possible that some of those stars might have ceased their existence at present.

Therefore Einstein describes the Universe as a space-time continuum having four dimensions — three of the space-time. Einstein has shown that the properties of the space-time continuum are disturbed wherever there is matter and motion. A star, a comet or a galaxy, says Lincoln Barnett, distorts the geometry of the space-time through which it moves just as a fish swimming in the sea agitates the surrounding water. Space becomes bent or curved in the region of matter — hence the paths of the planets are the results of moving through space distorted by the Sun. As we have already seen the space-time continuum is distorted by the material bodies in it; if the space is curved in the region surrounding the heavenly matter in the universe it must produce a similar effect on the overall curvature of the curvature of the whole space-time continuum. The universe must be regarded as a closed system 'finite but unbounded' and no longer infinite as it used to be supposed *prima facie*. It is beyond one's imagination to visualise a finite universe; but there is nothing so mysterious about it. The surface of the earth, for example, is finite but unbounded. As per the theory of Einstein there is reason to believe that the universe is of such a size and shape that a beam of light travelling at 1,86,000 miles/second, would return to its source after about 200 million earth years. (One million is equal to one million and the figure comes to 200,000,000,000,000). As this figure is nothing but the circumference of the Universe using the formula Pi x D (Diameter) = Circumference, we can calculate the diameter of the universe.

$$\text{Pi} = 22/7$$

$$\text{Diameter} = \frac{200{,}000{,}000{,}000{,}000 \times 7}{22}$$

$$= 636{,}363{,}636{,}363\ 7/11$$

$$= \text{about } 63{,}636{,}363{,}636$$

$$= 364 \text{ light years}$$

(One light year is the distance travelled by light in one earth year at the rate of 186,000 miles/second and is equal to 5.88 million million miles).

In the *Purāṇas* the universe was considered to be a big globe, hence the name *Brahmāṇḍa* God, who is the Lord of everything is described as *Koṭi Brahmāṇḍa Nāyaka* meaning "the lord of the innumerable cosmic spheres". The age of the Universe is given in terms of the life span of Brahmā. In Hindu chronology, there are two scales — one the earth scale, and the other, the divine scale. The same as per astrology and other allied occult subjects is as follows :

6	*prāṇas*	=	1 *vighaṭikā*
60	*vighaṭikās*	=	1 *ghaṭikā*
60	*ghaṭikās*	=	1 *ahorātra*
15	*ahorātras*	=	1 *pakṣa*
2	*pakṣas*	=	1 *māsa*
12	*māsas*	=	1 divine day

30	earthly years	=	1 divine month
360	earthly years	=	1 divine year
4800	divine years	=	1 *kṛta-yuga*
3600	divine years	=	1 *tretā-yuga*
1200	divine years	=	1 *kali-yuga*
12000	divine years	=	1 *divya-yuga*
1000	*divya-yugas*	=	1 *udaya-kalpa*
2000	divine years	=	1 full day of Brahmā
30	such days of Brahmā	=	1 month of Brahmā
12	such months of Brahmā	=	1 year of Brahmā
100	such years of Brahmā	=	1 life span of Brahmā

By the end of this period the entire universe, galaxy, nebula star, perishes. This period of Universal Dissolution lasts for another such life span of Brahmā and on completion of the same, a new creation of everything commences again. This phenomenon is cyclic and has neither beginning nor end. Applying this vast time scale let us calculate the age of Brahmā in terms of earthly years.

1 Brahmā (day)	=	86,40,000,000 earthly years
1 year of Brahmā	=	86,40,000,000 x 360 earthly year
1 life span of Brahmā	=	86,40,000,000 x 360 x 100
	=	31,10,40,000,000,000

According to Einstein's theory, the age of the universe is about 200 billion years

1	billion	=	1,000,000 x 1,000,000
200	billion	=	1,000,000, x 1,000,000 x 200
		=	200,000,000,000,000

A comparison of both these figures clearly shows the precision with which the Hindu calculation was made. According to the Hindu calculations we can estimate the present age of the entire Universe. At present Brahmā has completed his 50 divine years of life and is in the 51st year.

1 divine year	=	86,40,000,000 x 360 earthly year
50 divine years	=	86,40,000,000, x 360 x 50
	=	155,520,00,000,000 earthly years

By 1959, 1,972,949,060 earth years have been completed. Hence the total age of the universe at present comes to 1,55,520,00,000,000 plus 1,972,949,060 which is equal to 155,521,972,949,060 earth years.

While the *Taittirīya Upaniṣad* was able to quote the following verse about the Brahmā as:

> Brahmā is verily, Intelligence, and Eternity. Whosover does both realise this Brahmā abiding in the Akasa enshrined in the innermost recesses of his self, realiseth what all he doth desire, in communion with that Brahma. From this Atma did evolve the Akasa; from Akasa emanated Vayu; from Vayu arose Agni; from Agni Ap (water); from Ap arose Prithvi (or Prithivi). From Prithvi were born the Osadhis (Cereals). From Osadhis was derived Anna (Food). And Purusa (Man) is an evolute of Anna. And thus Purusa is verily the quintessence of Anna (Food).

ORIGIN OF UNIVERSE

The most ancient cosmogonic speculations of the West might be cited from the tablets found in the library of Asshurbanapal in Assyria. Apart from the profound influences which these Assyrian cosmogonic theories exercised on the creation thories of the later Jews these Assyrian theories themselves remain. They seem to trace their origin from a more ancient Sumerian text from which Asshurbanpal was copied and translated from the libraries of lower Chaldea. There are six tablets now, the extent of which summarise certain theories on creation. The first tablet commences with the description of a time when there was neither heaven nor earth, neither planets nor the gods, when a primeval expanse of water extended everywhere. Presiding over this dreary water expanse were two divinities, Male and Female, called Aps and Tiamat, the two primordial principles through whose union the gods were created. But Tiamat, after having given birth to the gods, conceived a hatred for them, and begot a huge horde of monsters to aid her war against her own progeny, the gods. She made Kingsu the commander of the monster legion who struck terror into the hearts of the gods, An and Ea. Finally the gods elected Marduk as their

Generalissimo, after having put his powers to a severe test. The new general of the gods then led the fray against Tiamat, accompanied by the seven winds which he had created. After a fierce battle he slew Tiamat into two halves, like a fish that is cut. From one of these halves he made the firmament, and from the other the solid earth below. In this creation myth, the gods have been identified with the stars of the constellations of the Zodiac, and Marduk with the sun who dries up the vast expanse of the primeval waters, and causes the emergence of the earth and the growth of vegetation. This Assyrian creation myth bears striking resemblances to the Egyptian creation myth, where Shu, the son of Amman-Ra, the god of the air separated his sister Nut from Keb.

The cosmic scheme of the ancient Phoenicians has been transmitted to us by Sanchroniathan. At the beginning of all things, was a dark and windy air, or a thick breeze, and turbid chaos resembling Erebus; and these were unbound, and for long ages had no limit. When this wind became enamoured of its own first principle and an intimate union took place, that connection was called Pothos; and this was the beginning of the creation of all things. But it knew not its own production; and from its embrace with wind was generated Mot, which some call Mud, and others the putrefaction of water mixture. And from this sprung all of creation, and the generation of the Universe.

Confucius, the great Chinese philosopher, seems to follow the ancient traditions of his nation in his cosmogonic speculation. According to him, before heaven and earth were born and before chaos was divided, there was fire and water; and the sediment of water formed the earth. The grosser part of water congealed, as it were, and hence it is that the ranges of hills resemble the waves of the sea. The coarsest sediment of water thus became the earth; and the purest portion of fire became the wind, thunder and lightning, the sun and the stars. 129,600 years is normally considered one year, the duration of a creation. Then followed the Deluge or the Great Cessation, when there were cataclysmic changes; the vast expanses of water changed position, mountains were obliterated, men and all things were destroyed. It was because of such terrible cataclysms that shells of snails and pearls of oysters were found at the summit of lofty mountains. Thus, after the Deluge follows a fresh creation.

Ideas of the West

From the Far East, let us again proceed to the west, this time to a consideration of the cosmogonic ideas led by Diodorus. According to this ancient historian, there were two schools of thought with regard to the world order. According to one school, the world had neither beginning nor even shall have an end; likewise, mankind also has been eternally existent. Others, on the contrary, regarded the world as being created at first, and people created at a later date in creation. According to the latter, the primeval air, in a continual agitation, churned as it were, into the lightest and grossest parts. Of the lightest components of the air arose the firmament. The grossest, not the gross—but part, coupled with humidity, became water. And then, out of the vast seas and on the spreading earth, arose living creatures. The cosmogonic scheme of the ancients is well expounded by Euripides in the following verse:

> A mass confused
> Heaven and earth once were
> Of one form; but after separation
> The men, trees, beasts of earth
> With fowls of the air
> First sprang up in a generation

Menelippe of Euripides; passing on to the Orphic cosmogony, considered that Chronos and Adrastea produced a gigantic egg which divided into midst. The upper part of the egg formed the sky, and the lower part the earth. Out of the egg came planes, the shining God who contained in himself the germs of the other gods.

It is amazing to find that the Greek cosmogony resembles the Upaniṣadic as expounded by the *Chāndogya Upaniṣad*:

> In the beginning there was Non-Being. It then transformed itself into Being. It grew into a vast egg. For a year it remained so, and then it broke open. One part of the broken shell was of silver; the other of gold. The silver part became the earth, while the golden part became the heaven. The thick membranous part of the egg became the mountains. The thinner membranes became the clouds. The arteries of the egg

> became the rivers of the world. The fluid within became the oceans, while that came out of the egg was the sun, whose advent was greeted with great acclaim.

The similarity between the Greek and the Upaniṣadic idea of the cosmic egg cannot be an accident.

The *Veda*s gave the world the sublime Hymn of Creation. It quotes that:

> Non-being then existed not nor being;
> There was no air, nor sky that is beyond it
> What was concealed? Wherein? In whose protection?
> And was there deep unfathomable water?

This stress on water — "without distinctive marks, this all was water" — is repeated in the *Upaniṣad*s. Prominent in their teaching, says Hume, is a 'cosmogonic theory' which was advanced among the early Greeks by Thales and which was also the widely prevailing Semitic idea, namely, that the original stuff of the world was water. Thus in the *Bṛhadāraṇyaka Upaniṣad*, we find it stated that "in the beginning this world was just water." "It is just water solidified that comprises this earth, that comprises the atmosphere, that is the sky, that is gods, and men, that is animals and birds, grass and trees, beasts, together with worms, like flies and ants; all these are just water solidified." In the later *Kaṭha*, a more philosophic theory of the world-ground was added on to this older theory that water was the primal entity: "*Ātman* was born of old from the waters." Somewhat similar combinations of the earliest and later theories are made in the *Aitareya Upaniṣad* where *ātman*, after creating the waters, "from the waters drew forth and shaped a person", from whose members the different parts of the world and of man emanated.

So much for the mythologic explanations of cosmogony as advanced by the nations of antiquity. On this question of cosmogony the historian's history of the world ventures the remark that "the answers that the ancients gave to this ever present question were various, but they had vagueness". The various cosmogonic theories might be apparently various but are essentially the same. All the ancient systems recognise some Divinity as the agency that ordained the present cosmos, and brought about the evolution of the universe out of the primordial stuff. There are, no doubt, variations in details. But the fundamental idea is the same. As for the charge of vagueness — that, instead of being a defect, is really their cardinal merit. No one, not even in this day of advanced scientific knowledge could pretend to assert, with any degree of certainty, when exactly the cosmos was evolved. Such an attempt to fix the age of the cosmos in dogmatic terms would be worse than folly, since man appeared in the cosmic theatre long after the cosmos itself came into existence. Hence the human mind can never assert anything with regard to what proceeded its own existence by aeons. At best, it could only summarise, and all summations must perforce be vague. If the cosmogony of the cultures of the pre-Christian era was 'various and vague' there is at least one cosmogonic system of antiquity which not merely claimed to be the creational fact, but went so far as to fix the time of creation of the earth almost to the split second. This is the Hebraic cosmogony as expounded in the first two chapters of Genesis in the Old Testament:

> In the beginning God created the heaven and the earth.
>
> And the earth was without form, and void, and darkness was upon the face of the deep. And the spirit of God moved upon the face of the waters.

These two opening verses of the chapters on the Genesis sum up as it were, the beginnings of the cosmos. A comparative study of this with the more ancient cosmogonic scheme would show that, instead of the pagan divinities that presided over the creation, it is God that created the world. Further according to this system of cosmogony, whatever the more ancient cultures had to say with regard to the cosmos was pure myth, whereas its own cosmogony was the highest fact. And moreover, instead of the 'vagueness' of the earlier systems, the Mosaic cosmogony substituted a precise period of cosmic evolution, compressing the entire process within a period of six days.

> And God saw everything that He had made and, behold, it was good. And the evening and the morning were the sixth day.
>
> And the work of creation being over, He rested on the seventh

day from all his work, which he had made.

However, in the Mosaic system, the whole world just as we know, was formed in the course of six days — unless the days of the Genesis bear a different connotation from the accepted connotation of the word. And though the Genesis itself is silent with regard to the exact date of the creation of the earth, later theologicians have ingeniously fixed the date of birth of the earth. Archbishop Ussher, in the seventeenth century fixed the date as 4004 BC. Later theologicians however, not being content with the specifications of the year alone, added further refinements to their date-scheme and specified 9 a.m. of the 23rd October, 4004 BC as being the exact hour, correct to the second, fixed in accordance to the present G. M. T. Christian theology has, therefore, succeeded in substituting extreme precision instead of the 'vagueness' of the pagan cosmogonies. While we must certainly admire the daring and ingenuity of the theologicians, we cannot but look askance at this cosmogony, not merely in the light of the hoary cosmogonies of the pre-Christian cultures, but also in the light of the modern scientific cosmogony as well. Nevertheless this cosmogonic dogma of Christian theology held a dominate place in Mediaeval thought even as late as the last century, due to the influence that Christian theology has had on contemporary thought. It was, however, only in the latter half of the last century that the overwhelming advances of science slowly but surely knocked the bottom out of this Hebrew cosmogony, till then regarded as the incontrovertible truth with regard to creation.

Although the chapter of Genesis in the Old Testament does not give us any inkling as to the mighty events that preceded creation, later theology has set forth a mighty sequence of events that preceded creation of the earth or of the starry universe — all space was totally void of anything; and this primeval space was an immense sphere of infinite radius. Divided equatorially, this sphere could be conceived as being made up of the two hemispheres, the upper hemisphere constituting the Empyrean or the Heaven, and the Lower hemisphere being the domain of Chaos. Heaven, the abode of God, is only a celestial replica of the earth, with plains, hills and valleys, inhabited by myriads of the sons of God, such as the Seraphim, the Cherubim and the lesser orders of the Hierarchy, Arch-angels, Princes Powers and Intelligences —

Angels, progeny of Light,
Thrones, Dominations, Princedoms, virtues, powers
Paradise Lost, Book V

And beneath the crystal floor of Heaven, enclosed in the lower hemisphere rages chaos :

— a dark
Illimitable ocean, without bound,
without dimension; where length, breadth and height
And time and place are lost. Where eldest Night
And Chaos, ancestors of Nature, hold
Eternal Anarchy, amidst the noise
Of endless wars, and by confusion stand
For Hot, Cold, Moist and Dry, four champions fierce,
Strive here for mastery, and to battle bring
Their embryon atoms.
Paradise Lost, Book II

Thus both the Empyrean and Chaos have been co-existent in infinite space, for immemorial aeons according to seraphic standards. But at last some mighty event occurs to break the grand monotony of Heaven, an event that vouchsafed to posterity a chronicle of

How first began this heaven which we behold
Distant so high, with moving fires adorned
Innumerable; and this which yields or fills
All space, the ambient Air, wide, interfused,
Embracing round this florid Earth; what cause
Moved the creator, in his holy zest
Through all eternity, so late to build
In chaos; and, the work begun, how soon
Absolved. *Paradise Lost*, Book VIII

One day, God summons His celestial Hierarchy and presents to them His only begotten son, and commands them

bow
All knees in Heaven, and shall confess Him Lord.
Paradise Lost, Book VIII

But one among the Arch-angels and his confederate, later to be known in earthly annals as Lucifer and Beelzebub, conspire to disobey the mandate of God. War breaks out in Heaven, Lucifer and Beelzebub and their hordes are vanquished; the crystal floor of heaven opens, and the rebel horder is hurled through the floor of heaven, down, down into the bottomless chaos, and they keep hurtling through chaos, for a period of nine days and nine nights, until Hell, preordained, and situated at the Antarctica of Universal space, receives them; and there they lie confounded for another period equivalent to

> Nine times the space that measures day and night
> To mortal men. *Paradise Lost*, Book VIII

And by the time the fall ends the hordes recover from their stupor; lo, the world has been created by the Son of God who

> in his hand
> He took the golden compasses, prepared
> In God's eternal store, to circumscribe
> This universe, and all created things.
> One foot he centred, and the other turned
> Round through the vast profundity
> And said Thus far extend, thus far thy bounds,
> This be thy circumference, O world
> Thus God the world created, thus the earth
> Matter unformed and void darkness profound
> Covered the abyss; but on the watery calm
> His brooding wings the Spirit of God outspread
> And vital virtue infused, and vital warmth
> Throughout the fluid mass
>
> *Paradise Lost*, Book V

Out of this circumscribed globe marked out in chaos arises the starry firmament, the earth with all its birds of the air and the beasts of the wild and finally Man, all in the six days

> And . . . . hanging in a golden chain
> This pendent world, in bigness as a star
> Of smallest magnitude
>
> *Paradise Lost*, Book II

is situated almost below the floor of heaven. Thus between the Empyrean above and Hell below hangs this starry universe.

Vedic Cosmogony

In the *Encyclopaedia Britannica,* Vol. 6 B page 578, this science of cosmogony has been defined as

> the branch of astronomy which tells of the evolutionary behaviour of the universe and the origin of its various characteristic features. While early cosmogony was limited to the origin of this planetary system only, modern cosmogony embraces other galaxies, planetary system in general and the origin of the chemical elements which constitute this universe.

But Vedic cosmogony goes far beyond this and tells us how this universe came into being, and who made it and which Divine forces played their part in this creation. It also describes the condition of the universe, as it was before this creation. It also tells us about the primordial root matter. "What was it, and how was it, and the cause of changes brought about in it" — up to the creation of the universe as we find it now. Maurice Materlinck says,

> It is possible to find in our human annals, words more majestic, more full of solemn anguish, more august intones, more devout and more forcible than these.

It surpasses all that has been written or said, and goes further than we shall ever dare to go.

Again in another place, we have —

> From His fervour, risen to its height natural and moral laws emanated. There was darkness and thence the bellowly flood of Salil arose, and from that, the calculation of time began, day and night followed, the creator produced in due order — the sun, the moon, the earth and the heaven and this middle region of air, and the region beyond as in previous creations. — *Ṛgveda*

A.C. Bose writes:

> The process of creation is a spiritual Act of God, through a sacrifice, in which Absolute reveals His splendour.
>
> There was primordial matter and the force of God was acting on it and giving it motion. God's cosmic forces were working throughout. There are such numerous verses in the Vedas — telling us that God creates this earth and heaven. Juan Mascaro, a Spanish scholar of the Vedas writes we have in these verse the dawn of spiritual vision and also the doom of human though in these sublime songs of creation. They tell us of the beginning of things.

Not only this, *Veda*s go further and tell us in detail that primordial matter first existed in the smallest forms of *paramāṇu*s (smallest particles) which were invisible and inert. This matter was then in a state of equilibrium, the three qualities of the matter were *rājasic*, *tāmasic* and *sāttvic* (Protons, Electrons and Neutrons). When matter has *sāttvic* qualities, these qualities, are dormant. When the force of God acts, motion is given to these *paramāṇu*s and these qualities begin their work — particles rotate, mix with other particles. This state is called *mahat*. The next stage is that of *ahaṁkāra* (uniting of particles of different elements, then *tanmātra*s are formed — ten senses, five gross elements, and four *antaḥkaraṇa*s (mind, *cit*, intellect and ego). These are made of finer particles of matter. These 24 elementary things are from all the objects and substances, organic and inorganic, in this world. This process is explained by Sage Kapila in *Sāṁkhya Śāstra*. The 25th thing are souls — which on entering the bodies of human beings become born as youthful men and women in the beginning. All objects and substances which are material are made of these five elements in fine or gross form. The *Veda*s also tell us the characteristics of these five elements — ether, air, agni, water and earth. Ether is invisible, all-pervading and inert; it does not exist in molecular form but is always as *paramāṇu*s. Air is invisible — weightless, it has motion; Agni is visible as well as invisible, it has form, it gives heat and light, it is weightless. Water has form, it becomes invisible in gaseous form, it solidifies as snow, it is loose, it is smooth, it flows — it has velocity, it has weight. The principle of ether is sound, the principle of air is touch, the principle of Agni is colour and form, the principle of water is taste and the principle of earth is smell. All other substances are made of these. Vedic science does not admit the existence of any other element while modern science counts more than a hundred. All these are compounds and mixtures of the five elements according to the *Vedas*.

Vedic cosmogony recognizes the existence of several natural forces. It calls them *Devas*. They are also called powers of God, hence they are divine. *Vedas* name them as *prāṇa* or cosmic force or as *Marut* (electric and magnetic force). Those Divine powers have their own functions. They are God's force formed by Him at the beginning of creation and they carry on their functions till the existence of creation. Those gods also find mentioned in Greek mythology. In this way, the field of Vedic cosmogony is even wider than the field of modern science. Modern science is also now nearing the acceptance of an intelligent, all-powerful agent as creator, maintainer and master of the Universe. The movements of these planetary systems and their existence, workings, functions and effects are all well regulated and this cannot be possible unless they are controlled by some all knowing, all powerful designer and master. In this way, modern cosmogony is coming to admit the existence of God as creator of the universe.

The cosmic unit of time, according to Hindu mythical astronomy, is the *kalpa* or a day of Brahmā, the creator. Brahmā creates in the morning; and at night the three worlds, *ākāśa, bhūmi* and *pātāla* (earth, heaven and hell) are reduced to chaos, every being that has not obtained liberation retaining its essence which takes form according to its *karma* when Brahmā wakes up in the morning. Thus the eventful days and nights pass on till Brahmā reaches the hundredth year of his life when "not only the three worlds but all planes and all beings, Brahmā himself, *devas*, *ṛṣis*, *asuras*, men, creatures and matter" are all resolved into *mahāpralaya* (the great cataclysm). After hundred years of chaos another Brahmā is born. Lest the reader should become apprehensive of his own longevity it may be added that a *kalpa* or day of Brahmā is equivalent to 4,320,000,000 years. The day of Brahmā is divided into 1,000 *mahāyugas* of equal length each consisting of four *yugas* as stated earlier in this text. The period of each *yuga* is given below:

Yugas	*Years*
Kṛtayuga	1,728,000
Tretāyuga	1,296,000
Dvāparayuga	864,000
Kaliyuga	432,000

According to Hesiod, the Greek poet, the mythical history of his country consists of five ages. In the beginning the Olympians under Kronos created the race of the Men of Gold. In those days men lived like gods, with unalloyed happiness. They did not toil with their hands for earth brought forth her fruits without their aid. They did not know the sorrows of old age, and death to them was like passing away in a calm sleep. After they had gone hence their spirits were appointed to dwell above the earth, guarding and helping the living. The Gods next created the Men of Silver, but they could not be compared in virtues and happiness with the men of 'the elder age of golden peace'. For many years they remained mere children and as soon as they came to the full strength and stature of manhood they refused to do homage to the Gods and fell to slaying one another. After death they became the good spirits who live within the earth.

"The Men of Bronze followed springing from ash trees and having hearts which were hard and jealous so that with them 'lust and strife began to gnaw the world'. All the works of their hands were wrought in bronze. Through their own invention they fell from their high estate and from the light they passed away to the dark realm of King Hades, unhonoured and unremembered." "After the Heroes came the Men of Iron — the race of these wild days. Our lot is labour and vexation of spirit by day and night, nor will this cease until the race ends, which will be when the order of nature has been reversed and human affection turned to hatred." The fourth age, the age of Heroes, is considered to be an interpolation. Hesiod's scheme it seems had only four ages.

The manner of destruction of the world at the end of the *Kaliyuga* is differently described in the Hindu mythology.

The *Sāṁkhya* Cosmology

Here are two words, the microcosm and the macrocosm, the internal and the external. We get truths from both of these by means of experience; there is internal experience and external experience. The truths gathered from internal experience are psychology, metaphysics and religion; from external experience, the physical sciences. Now a perfect truth should be in harmony with experience in both these words. The microcosm must bear testimony to the macrocosm, and the macrocosm to the microcosm; physical truth must have its counterpart in the internal world, and the internal world must have its verification in the outside. Yet as a rule we find that many of these truths are constantly conflicting. At one period of the world's history the 'internals' became supreme, and they began to fight the 'externals'. At the present time, the 'externals', the physicist, have become supreme and they have put down many claims of the psychologists and metaphysicians. So far as my little knowledge goes, I find that the really essential parts of psychology are in perfect accordance with the essential parts of modern physical knowledge. It is given to every individual to be great in every respect; it is not given to the same race or nation to be equally strong in the research of all the fields of knowledge. The modern European nations are very strong in their research into external psychical knowledge, but the ancient Europeans were weak in their research into the internal part of man. On the other hand, the Orientals have not been very strong in their researches in the external physical world, but have excelled in their research into the internal, and therefore we find that some of the oriental theories are not in accordance with occidental physics, neither is occidental psychology in harmony with oriental teachings on this subject. The oriental physicists have been criticised by occidental scientists. At the same time each rests on truth, and, as we stated before, real truth in any field of knowledge will not contradict itself, the truths internal are in harmony with the truths external.

We know the present theories of the cosmos according to the modern astronomers and physicists, and at the same time we know how they hurt the old school of theologians, and how every new scientific discovery that is made, is a bomb thrown into their houses, and how they have attempted in every age to put down all research. In the first place, let us go over the psychological and scientific ideas of the Orientals as to cosmology and all that pertains to it, and we shall find now wonderfully it is in accordance with all the latest discoveries of modern science and when there is anything lacking, we shalı find that it is on the side of modern science. We all use the word nature, and Hindu philosophers called it by two different names, *prakṛti* which is almost the same as the English word nature, and the more scientific name, *avyaktam* from which everything proceeds, out of which come atoms and molecules, matter and force, and mind and intellect. It is startling to find that the philosophers and metaphysicians of India ages ago stated that mind is but matter in a finer form; for what are our present materialists striving to do but to show that mind is as much a product of nature as the body? And so is thought; and we shall find by and by that the intellect also comes from the same nature which is called *avyaktam*, the undifferentiated.

The ancient teachers define *avyaktam*, as the equilibrium of the three forces, one of which is called *sattva,* the second *rajas* and the third *tamas*. *Tamas* the lowest force, is that of attraction; a little higher is *rajas*, that of repulsion. These are held in perfect control or balance, by the *sattva*. There is no creation, no modification; but as soon as this equilibrium is lost, the balance is disturbed and one of these forces gets stronger than the other. Then change and motion begin and evolution of all these goes on. This state of things is going on cyclically periodically; that is to say, there is a period of disturbance of the balance, when all these forces begin to combine and recombine, and this universe is projected; and there is also a period when everything has a tendency to revert to the primal state of equilibrium and the time comes when a total absence of all manifestations is reached. Again, after a period, this state is disturbed, the forces tend to project outward and the universe slowly comes out in the form of waves; for all motions in this universe are in the form of waves, in successive rises and falls.

Some of the old philosophers taught us that the whole universe settles down for a period; others maintained that this settling down applies only to systems. That is to say, while our system here, this solar system will quieten down and go back into that undifferentiated state, there will be millions of other systems going the other way. I should rather follow the second opinion, that this quietening down is not simultaneous over the whole universe, but that in different parts, different things are going on. But the principle remains the same, that all we see, the *prakṛti* herself is progressing in successive rises and falls. The stage of going back to the balance, to the perfect equilibrium is called the end of the cycle. The whole *kalpa*, the evolution and the involution, has been compared by theistic writers in India to the outbreathing and inbreathing of God; God as it were, breathes out of the universe, and it returns into Him again. When it quiets down, what becomes of the Universe? It still exists, only in finer form as it is called in Sanskrit *kāraṇa*, the causal state. Causation time and space are still there, only they are potential. This return to an undifferentiated condition constitutes involution. Involution and evolution are eternally going on, so that when we speak of a beginning, we refer only to the beginning of a cycle.

Ancient Hindu Views about Ākāśa and Prāṇa

The most extraneous part of the universe is what in modern times we call gross matter. The ancient Hindus called it the *bhūtas*, the external elements. One of these, according to them, is the cause of the rest, for every other element is produced out of this one, and this element has been called *ākāśa*. This is somewhat similar to the modern idea of ether, though not exactly the same. *Ākāśa* is the primal element out of which every gross thing proceeds, and along with it there is something else called *prāṇa*; we shall see what it is as we go on. The *prāṇa* and the *ākāśa* exist as long as creation lasts. They combine and recombine and form all gross manifestations until at the end of the cycle all these subside and go back to the unmanifested form of *ākāśa* and *prāṇa*. There is in the *Ṛgveda*, the oldest scriptures in existence, a beautiful passage describing creation, which is most poetical; when there was neither aught nor naught, when darkness was rolling over darkness, what existed? And the answer is given; It (the Eternal one) then existed without motion. *Prāṇa* and *ākāśa* were latent in that Eternal one, but there was no phenomenal manifestation. This state is called *avyaktam* which literally means 'without vibration'. At the beginning of a new cycle of evolution, this *avyaktam* beings to vibrate, and blow after blow is given by *prāṇa* to the *ākāśa* causing condensation and gradually through the forces of attraction and repulsion, atoms are formed. These in turn condense into molecules and finally into the different gross elements of which every object in nature is composed.

We generally find these things very curiously translated; people do not go to the ancient philosophers or to their commentators for their translation and have not learning enough to understand for themselves. They translate the elements as 'air', 'fire' and so on. If they would go to the commentators they would find that they do not mean anything of the sort. The *ākāśa* by the repeated blows of *prāṇa* produces the vibratory state of the *ākāśa*, which in turn produces gaseous matter. The vibrations growing more and more rapid generate heat, which in Sanskrit is called *tejas*. Gradually it is cooled off and the gaseous substance becomes liquid *āpa*, and finally solid, *pṛthivī*. We have fist *ākāśa* vibrating, then comes heat, then it becomes liquefied, and when still more condensed it appears as solid matter. It goes back to the unmanifested condition in exactly the reverse way. The solids will be covered into liquid and the liquid into a mass of heat, that will slowly go back into the gaseous state, then disintegration of atoms will begin and finally the equilibrium of all forces will be reached, when vibration will stop and thus the cycle of evolution, which in Sanskrit is called *kalpa*, will be at an end. We know from modern astronomy that this earth and sun of ours are undergoing the same transitions, this solid earth will melt down and become liquid once more, and will eventually go back to the gaseous state.

Prāṇa cannot work alone without the help of *ākāśa*. All that we know of it is motion or vibration. Every movement that we see is a modification of this *prāṇa*, and everything we know in the form of matter, either as form or as resistance, is a modification of this *ākāśa*. The *prāṇa* cannot exist alone or act without a medium, and in every state of it whether as pure *prāṇa*, or when it changes into the other forces of nature, as gravitation, it can never be separate from *ākāśa*. You have never seen force without matter or matter without forces; what we call force and matter are simply the gross manifestations of the two, and these when superfine, the old philosophers have called, *prāṇa* and *ākāśa*. *Prāṇa* you can call in English, life or vital energy, but you identify it with the spirit *ātman*. Thus creation is a product of *prāṇa* and *ākāśa* and it is without beginning and end; it cannot have either, for it is eternally going on. The next question that comes is rather a fine one. Some European philosophers have asserted that this world exists because I exist, and if 'I' do not exist, the world will not exist. Sometimes it is expressed thus — if all the people in the world were to die, and there were no more human beings, and no animals with powers of perception and intelligence, all manifestations would disappear. It seems paradoxical, but gradually we shall see clearly that this can be proved. But these European philosophers do not know the psychology of it, although they know the principle; they have only a glimpse of it.

Let us consider another proposition of these old psychologists, which is rather startling, that the grossest elements are the *bhūta*s, but that all gross things are the result of fine ones. Everything that is gross is composed of a combination of fine things, so the *bhūta*s must be composed of certain fine particles, called the *tanmātra*s in Sanskrit. I smell a flower; in doing so, something must have come in contact with my nose. The flower is there. I do not see it move towards me; but without something coming in contact with my nose how can I have the smell? That which from the flower comes into contact with my nose are the *tanmātra*s, fine molecules of that flower, so fine that no diminution will be perceived in the flower, even if we all smell it the whole day. So with heat, light, sight, and everything. These *tanmātra*s can given again, which will be subdivided into atoms. Different philosophers have different theories about the dimensions of atoms but we know these are only theories, so we leave them out of discussion. Sufficient for us that everything gross is composed of things that are very minute. We first get a gross element, which we feel externally, and composing them are the fine elements, which our organs touch, which come in contact with the nerves of the nose, eyes and ears. The eternal wave which our organs touch, which come in contact with the nerves of the nose, eyes and ears. The eternal wave which touches my eyes, I cannot see, yet I know it must come in contact with my optic nerve before I can see the light. So with hearing, we can never see the particles that come in contact with our ears, but we know that they must be there. What is the cause of these *tanmātra*s? A very startling and curious answer is given by our psychologists — self-consciousness. That is the cause of these fine materials, and the cause of the organs. What are these organs? Here is the eye, but the eye does not see. If the eyes did see, when a man is dead and his eyes are still perfect, they would still be able to see. There is some change somewhere; something has gone out of the man and that something, which really sees and of which the eye is but the instrument, is called the organ. So the nose is an instrument, and there is an organ corresponding to it. Modern physiology can tell you what that is, a nerve centre in the brain. The eyes, ears, etc. are simply the external instruments. Thus the organs, *indriyas*, as they are called in Sanskrit are the real seats of perception.

What is the use of having one organ for the nose, and one for the eyes, and so on? Why will not one serve the purpose? To make it clear to you: I am talking and you are listening, and you do not see what is going on around you because the mind has attached itself to the organ of hearing and has detached itself from the sight organ. If there were only one organ, the mind would see and hear and smell at the same time, and it would be impossible for it not to do all three at the same time. Therefore it is necessary that there should be separate organs for all these centres. This has been borne out by modern physiology. It is certainly possible for us to see and hear at the same time, but that is because the mind attaches itself partially to both centres, which are the organs. What are the instruments? We see that these are external and made of the gross materials. Here they are eyes, nose and ears, etc. Of what are the organs made? They are made of finer materials and are internal things because they are the centres. Just as this body is composed of gross material for transforming *prāṇa* into different gross forces, so these finer organs behind are composed of finer materials, for the manufacture of *prāṇa* into finer forces of perception. All these organs or *indriyas* combined plus the internal instrument *antaḥkaraṇa*, are called the finer body of man — the *liṅga śarīra*.

It has a real form, because everything material must have a form. Behind the *indriyas* is the *manas*, the *citta* in *vṛtti*, what might be called the vibratory or the unsettled state of the mind. If you throw a stone into a calm lake, first there will be vibration, and then resistance. For a moment the water will vibrate and then it will react on the stone. So, when any impression comes on the *citta* or mind stuff, it vibrates a little. This state of the mind is called the *manas*. Then comes the reaction, the will. There is another thing behind this will which accompanies all the acts of the mind, which is called egoism, the *ahaṁakāra*, the self-consciousness, which says 'I am' and behind that is what is called *mahat*, the intellegence, the highest form of nature's existence. Behind the intellect is the true self of man, the *puruṣa*, the pure, the perfect, who is alone the seer, and for whom is all this change. The *puruṣa* is looking on at all these changes. He himself is never impure; but by implication, by what the Vedāntists call *adhyāsa* or reflection, he appears to be so — as when a red flower is held before a piece of crystal, the crystal will look red or with a blue flower the crystal will look blue and yet the crystal itself is colourless. There are many *puruṣa*s each pure and perfect, and it is all these various divisions of gross matter and fine matter that are imposed on them and make them appear variously coloured.

Why is *prakṛti* doing all this? *Prakṛti* is undergoing all these changes for the enjoyment and the benefit of the self, so that it will realise its free nature. This immense book which we call the universe is stretched before man so that he may read; and come out as an omniscient and omnipotent being. I must here tell you that some of our best psychologists do not believe in a personal God in the sense in which you believe in him. Kapila denies the existence of God as creator. His idea is that a personal God is quite unnecessary; *prakṛti* is sufficient to work out all that is good. He repudiated the so-called 'Design' theory of the universe. A more childish theory has never been advanced. But he admits a peculiar kind of God. He says we are all struggling to get free, and when man become free, he can, as it were, melt away into *prakṛti* for the time being, to come out at the beginning of the next cycle an omniscient and omnipotent being and be its ruler. In that sense he can be called God. Thus you and I and the humblest beings will be Gods in different cycles. Kapila says, there can be such Gods in a temporal God, but an eternal God, eternally omnipotent and eternally ruler of the universe can never be. If there were such a God there would be this difficulty; He must either be bound or free. A God who is perfectly free would not created; there would be no necessity. If He were bound, He would not create because He could not. He would be weak himself. So in either case, there cannot be an omnipotent or omniscient eternal ruler. So wherever the word God is mentioned in our scriptures — the *Veda*s, Kapila says, it means those perfected souls who have become free. The *Sāṁkhya* system does not believe in the unity of all souls. *Vedānta* believes that all individual souls are united in one cosmic Being called *Brahman*; but Kapila, the founder of the *Sāṁkhya,* was dualistic. His analysis of the universe, so far as it goes, is really marvellous. He was the propounder of Hindu evolutionalists, and all the later philosophical systems are simply an outcome of his thought.

According to this system, all souls will regain their freedom and their natural rights, which are omnipotence and omniscience. Here the question may be asked, whence is this bondage of the souls? The *Sāṁkhya* says, it is without beginning; but if it be without beginning, it must also be without end and we shall never be free. Kapila explains that this 'without beginning' means 'not in a constant line'. *Prakṛti* is without beginning and without end, but not in the same sense as is the soul, because *prakṛti* has no individuality, just as a river every moment gets a fresh body of water, and the sum-total of all these bodies of water is the river, and yet the river is not a constant quantity. Similarly everything in *prakṛtis* is constant changing but the soul never changes. Therefore as *prakṛti* is always changing, it is possible for the soul to come out of its bondage. One theory of the *Sāṁkhya* is peculiar to this psychology. The whole of the universe is built upon the same plan as one single man or one little being; so, just as I have a mind, there is also a cosmic intelligence and egoism, them the *tanmātra*s and the organs, and then the gross elements. The whole universe according to Kapila is one body, all that we see are the grosser bodies, and behind these are the finer bodies, and behind them a universal egoism and behind that a universal intelligence; but all these are in *prakṛti* — all these are manifestations of *prakṛti*, not outside of it. Each one of us is an art of that cosmic consciousness.

Just as there is a sum-total of intelligence out of which we draw what we require, so there is a sum-total of mental forces in the universe out of which we are drawing eternally, but the seed for the body must come from the parents. The theory includes heredity and reincarnation too. Material is given to the soul out of which to manufacture a body, but that material is given by hereditary transmission from the parents. The theory includes heredity and reincarnation too. Material is given to the soul out of which to manufacture a body, but that material is given by hereditary transmission from the parents. We come now to the proposition that in this process there is an involution and an evolution. All is evolved out of that indiscrete *prakṛti*; and then is involved again and becomes *avyaktam*. It is impossible according to the *Sāṁkhyas*, for any material thing to exist, which has not as its material some portion of consciousness. Consciousness is the material out of which all manifestations are made. The elucidation of this comes in our next sub-heading, and I will show how it can be proved. I do not know this table as it is, but it makes an impression: it comes to the eye, then to the *indriyas*, and then to the mind; the mind then reacts and that reaction is what I call "the table". It is just the same as throwing a stone into a lake; the lake throws a wave against the stone; this wave is what we know. The waves coming out are all we know. In the same way the fashion of this wall is in my mind; what is external nobody knows; when I want to know it, it has to become that material which I furnish. I, with my own mind have furnished the material for my eyes; my mind has furnished the material in search of something outside with the occasion, the suggestion and upon that suggestion I project my mind, and it takes the form of what I see. The question is the same thing. Because we all have a part of this cosmic mind. Those who have mind will see the thing, and those who have not will not see it. This goes to show that since this universe has existed, there has never been a want of mind, of that one cosmic mind. Every human being, every animal, is also furnished out of that cosmic mind, because it is always present and furnishes material for their formation.

Prakṛti and Puruṣa

So far the contribution of Hindu gods and goddesses' to the origin of the universe and their mythology has been discussed *prakṛti* and *puruṣa* with respect to *Sāṁkhya* philosophy are discussed. *Prakṛti* has been called indiscrete or inseparate by the *Sāṁkhya* philosophers and defined as a perfect balance of the materials in it; and it naturally follows that in perfect balance there cannot be any motion. All that we see feel, and hear is simply a compound of motion and matter. In the primal state, before this manifestation, where there was no motion but perfect balance, this *prakṛti* was in limitation. Again, according to *Sāṁkhya,* atoms are not the primal state. This universe does not come out of atoms, they may be the secondary or tertiary state. The original matter may compounds into atoms, which in turn compounds into greater and greater things, and as far as modern investigations go they rather point towards that. For instance, in the modern theory of ether, if you say ether is also atomic that will not solve the proposition at all. To make it clearer, say that ether is composed of atoms; and we know that ether is everywhere, interpenetrating, omnipresent, and that atoms are floating, as it were in ether. If ether again is composed of atoms, there will still be some space between two atoms of ether. What fills up that? And again there will be another space between the atoms of that which fills up this space. If you propose that there is another ether still finer, you must still have something to fill that space, and so it would be *regressus ad infinitum*, i.e., what the *Sāṁkhya* philosophers call *avavasthā* — never reaching a final conclusion. So the atomic theory cannot be final.

According to the *Sāṁkhya*, this *prakṛti* is omnipresent, one omnipresent mass of matter in which are the cause of everything that exists. What is meant by cause? Cause is the more subtle state of the manifested state, the unmanifested state of that which becomes manifested. What do you mean by destruction? It is reverting to the cause; the materials out of which a body is composed go back into their original state. Beyond this idea of destruction, any idea such as annihilation, is absurd. According to modern physical sciences, it can be demonstrated that all destruction means that which Kapila called ages ago 'reverting to the causal state', going back to the finer form. You know how it can be demonstated in a laboratory that matter is indestructible. Those of you who have studied chemistry will know that if you place a candle and a caustic pencil inside a glass tube, and let the candle stay but then take the caustic pencil out of the tube and weigh it you will find that the pencil will weigh exactly its previous weight, plus the weight of the candle — the candle becomes finer and finer, and goes to the caustic. So that in the present stage of our knowledge, if any man claims that anything becomes annihilated, he is only making himself absurd. It is only uneducated people who would advance such a proposition and it is curious that modern knowledge coincides with what those old philosophers taught.

The ancients proceeded in their inquiry by taking up mind as the basis; they analysed the mental part of the universe and came to certain conclusion, while modern science is analysing the physical part, and it also has came to the same conclusions. Both analyses have led to the same truth. You must remember that the first manifestation of this *prakṛti* in the cosmos is what the *Sāṁkhyas* called *mahat*. We may call it universal intelligence — the great principle; that is the literal meaning. The first manifestation of *prakṛti* is this intelligence, not consciousness. Consciousness is only a part of this intelligence, which is universal. It covers all the grounds of consciousness, sub-consciousness and super-consciousness. In nature, for instance, certain changes are going on before your eyes which you see and understand, but there are other changes so much finer that no human perception can catch them. They are from the same cause, the same *mahat* is making these changes. There are other changes beyond the reach of our mind or reasoning, all these series of changes are in this *mahat*. This is understood better when applied to the individual. Out of this *mahat* comes the universal egoism, and these are both material. There is no difference between matter and mind, save in degree. It is the same substance in finer or grosser form; one changes into the other, and this exactly coincides with modern psychological research. This substance called *mahat* changes into the material called egoism, the fine state of matter, and that egoism changes into two varieties. In one variety, it changes into the organs. Organs are of two kinds, organs of sensation and organs of reaction. They are not the eyes or nose but something finer — what you call brain centres, and nerve centres. This egoism becomes changed, and out of this material are manufactured these centres and these nerves. Out of the same substance, egoism is manufactured; another fine form the *tanmātras*, fine particles of matter; those, for instance which strike your nose and cause you to smell. One cannot perceive these fine particles, one can only know that they are there. The *tanmātras* are manufactured out of the egoism, and out of the *tanmātras*, or subtle matter, is manufactured the gross matter — air, water, earth and all the things that we see and feel.

These are all cosmic things. The universal extension of matter, unbroken, one substance, undifferentiated which is the first state of everything, and which begins to change just as milk becomes curd; and that is changed into another substance called *mahat*, which in one state manifests as intelligence and in another state as egoism. It is the same substance, only changed into the grosser matter called egoism. Thus is the whole universe itself built as it were, layer after layer, first as undifferentiated *prakṛti* and that changes into universal egoism and that changes into universal sensible matter. Matter changes into universal sense-organs, again changes into universal fine particles, and these in turn combine into universal fine particles, and these in turn combine and become this gross universe. That is the cosmic plan, according to the *Sāṁkhyas* and what is in the cosmos or macrocosm must be in the individual.

Take an individual man. He has first a part of undifferentiated nature in him, and that material nature in him changed into *mahat* — a small particle of the universal intelligence and small particles of the universal intelligence in him become changed into egoism — a particle of the universal egoism. The egoism in turn becomes changed into the sense-organs, and the *tanmātras*, and out of the latter combining, he manufactures his world, his body. This is the first stepping stone to *Vedānta,* and it is absolutely necessary to know, because this is the basis of the different systems of philosophy of the whole world. There is no philosophy in the world that is not indebted to Kapila, the founder of this *Sāṁkhya* system. Pythagoras came to India and studied this philosophy and carried some of these ideas to the Greeks. Later it formed the Alexandrian school, and still later formed the basis of Gnostic philosophy. Thus it became divided into two parts; one went to Europe and Alexandria, and the other remained in India and became the basis of all Hindu philosophy, for out of it, the system that of Vyāsa was developed. This was the first national system that the world saw, this system of Kapila. Every metaphyisician in the world must pay homage to him. This most ancient of philosophers, is mentioned even in the *Vedas*.

To return again to the microcosm man. As we have seen, he is build on exactly the same plan. First the nature is indiscrete or perfectly balanced, then it becomes disturbed, and action sets in and the first change produced by that action is what is called *mahat* — intelligence. Now you see that this intelligence in man is just a particle of the cosmic intelligence — the *mahat*. Out of it comes self-consciousness, and from this the sensory and the motor nerves, and the finer particles out of which the gross body is manufactured. There is one difference between Schopenhauer and the *Vedānta*. Schopenhauer says, that desire or will is the cause of everything. It is the will to exist that makes us manifest, but the Advaitists deny this. They say it is intelligence. There cannot be a single particle of will which is not a reaction. So many things are beyond will. It is only something manufactured out of the ego, and the ego is a product of something still higher, the intelligence, and that is a modification of indiscrete Nature or *prakṛti*.

It is very important to understand this *mahat* in man — the intelligence. Intelligence itself is modified into what we call egoism, and this intelligence is the cause of all these changes which result in producing the body. This covers all the grounds of subconsciousness, consciousness and super-consciousness. What are these three states? The sub-conscious state is what we find in animals, and call instinct. This is nearly infallible but very limited. Instinct almost never fails. An animal instinctively knows a poisonous herb from an edible one, but its instinct is limited to one or two things, it works like a machine. Then comes the higher state of knowledge, which is fallible, makes mistakes often, but has a larger scope, although it is slow, and this you call reason. It is much larger than instinct, but there are more dangers of mistaken instinct, though there are more dangers of mistakes in reasoning than in instinct. There is a still higher state of the mind of the super-conscious, which belongs only to the *yogīs*, men who have cultivated it. This is as infallible as instinct, and still more unlimited than reason. It is the higher state. We must remember that as in man this *mahat*, is the real cause of all that which is manifesting itself in various ways, covering the whole ground of sub-conscious, conscious and super-conscious states, the three states in which knowledge exists

— so in the cosmos, this universal intelligence, *mahat*, exists as instinct, as reason and as super-reason.

Theory of Knowledge

Now comes a delicate question, which is always being asked. If a perfect God created the universe, why is there imperfection in it? What we call the universe is what we see, and that is only this little plane of consciousness or reason and beyond that we do not see at all. Now, the very question is an impossible one. If one takes up only a bit of a mass and looks at it, it seems to be imperfect because we make it so. How? What is reason? What is knowledge? Knowledge is finding associations. One goes into the street and sees a man, and knows it is a man. One sees many men, and each one makes an impression on the mind, and when one sees this man, one calmly refers to one's store of impressions puts this new one with the rest, pigeon-holes it and is satisfied. When a new impression comes and it has associations in one's mind, one is satisfied, and this state of associations is called knowledge. Knowledge is therefore, pigeon-holing one experience. With the already existing fund of experience, and this is one of the great proofs that one cannot have any knowledge until one has already a fund in existence. If one is without experience, or if, as some European philosophers think, the mind is a *tabula rasa*, it cannot get any knowledge, because the very fact of knowledge is the recognition of the new by comparison with already existing impressions. There must be a store already to which to refer a new impression. If a child is born into this world without such a fund, it would be impossible for him to get any knowledge. Therefore the child must have been in a state in which he had a fund, and so knowledge is eternally going on. It is mathematical experience. This is very much like the Spenserian and some other Western philosophies. They have seen that there cannot be any knowledge without a fund of past knowledge and that therefore the child is born with knowledge. They have found out the truth that the cause enters into the effect, that it comes in a subtle form in order to be developed. But these philosophers say that these impressions with which the child comes, are not form in order to be developed. But these philosophers say that these impressions with which the child comes are not from the child's own past, but were in his forefathers and have come to the child by hereditary transmission. Very soon they are going to find this theory untenable, and some of them are even now giving hard blows to the idea of heredity. Heredity is very good, but incomplete. It only explains the physical side. How would you explain the influence of environment in according with it? Many causes produce an effect, and environment is one of them. On the other hand, the Hindu philosophers say that we make our own enviornment, because as our past was, so we find out the present. In other words, we are what we are here now, because of what we were in the past.

Knowledge is pigeon-holing a new impression with an old impression — recognising a new impression. What is meant by recognition? Finding its association with a similar impression that we already have. Nothing further is meant by knowledge. If that be the case, it must be that one has to see the whole series of similars in the process. Suppose one is to know a pebble; to find its association, one will have to see the whole series of pebbles similar to it. But with the universe one cannot do that, because in our reasoning we see only one perception of it, and can neither see on this side or on that side of it and refer it to its association. Therefore the universe seems unintelligible, because knowledge and reason are always finding associations. This bit of the universe cut off by our consciousness is a startling new thing, and we are not able to find its associations. Therefore we are struggling with it and we think it is so horrible, so bad — sometimes we think it is good, but generally imperfect. The universe will be known only when one finds its associations. One shall recognise them when one goes beyond the universe and our little self-consciousness and then alone will the universe stand explained. Until we do that all our fruitless striving will never explain it — because knowledge is the finding of similars, and this conscious plane gives us only a partial view of the universe. So with our idea of the universal *mahat* or what in our ordinary everyday language we call God. All that we have of the idea of God is only one perception, a partial view of Him and all the rest is cut off and covered by our human limitation. "I, the universal, so great am I that even this universe is a part of Me." That is why we see God as imperfect, and we can never understand Him, thus it is impossible. The only way to understand Him is to go beyond reason, beyond self-consciousness.

When one goes beyond the heard and hearing, the thought and thinking, then alone will one come to Truth. Go beyond the Scriptures, because they teach only up to *prakṛti*, up to the three qualities of which it is composed and out of which evolves the universe. When we go beyond them we find the harmony, not before.

So far it is clear that this macrocosm and microcosm are built on exactly the same plan and of this microcosm we know only one very small part. We know either the sub-conscious, not the superconscious. We know only the conscious. If a man says 'I am a sinner' he is foolish, because he does not know one part of himself; he is most ignorant about himself; he knows only one part of himself because knowledge covers only one part of the mind he is in. So with this universe it is possible to know only one part through reasoning, but *prakṛti* comprises, the whole of it, the sub-conscious, the conscious and the super-conscious, the individual *mahat* and the universal *mahat* with all their subsequent modifications, and these lie beyond reason.

What makes *prakṛti* change? We have seen up to the point that everything in nature, *Prakṛti* itself, is *jaḍa*. It is working under law; it is insentient. Mind, intelligence and will all are insentient. But they all reflect the sentiency, the chit of some Being who is beyond all this, and whom the *Sāṁkhya* philosophers call *puruṣa*. This *puruṣa* is the unwitting cause of all these changes in *prakṛti* — in the universe. That is to say, this *puruṣa,* taking Him in the universal sense, is the God of the universe. It is claimed that the will of the Lord created the universe. This is very good as a common daily expression, but that is all. How could it be will? Will is the third or fourth manifestation out of *prakṛti*. Many things exist before it; and what created them? Will is a compound, and everything that is a compound has its production out of *prakṛti* — will itself cannot create *prakṛti*. It is not simple to say that the will of the Lord created the universe is illogical. In the will of man, will covers a little portion only of self-consciousness. It moves our brain, some say. If it did you could stop the action of the brain, some say. If it did you could stop the function of the heart, it is not the will. Who moves the heart? It is not the will because if it were, you could stop it at your will. It is neither will that is working your body, nor the universe. But it is something of which will itself is one of the manifestations. This body is being moved by a power of which will is only a manifestation. This body is being moved by a power of which will is only a manifestation, in one power of which will be a part of the body. So, in the universe here is will, but that is only one part of the universe.

The whole of the universe is not guided by will; that is why we do not find the explanation of it in will. Suppose, one takes it for granted that the will is moving the body, and then complain. One had no right to take for granted that it was the will. In the same way if one takes the universe and thinks it is will that moves it and then find that things do not coincide, it is one's fault. This *puruṣa* is not will, and it cannot be intelligence because intelligence itself is a compound. There cannot be any intelligence without some sort of matter. In man, this matter takes the form which we call brain. Wherever there is intelligence, there is what we call brain. Wherever there is intelligence there must be matter in some form or other. Thus intelligence being a compound, what then is this *puruṣa*? It is neither intelligence nor *buddhi* but yet it is the cause of both these; it is His presence that sets them all vibrating and combining. *Puruṣa* may be likened to some of those substances which by their mere presence promote chemical reaction, as in the case of cyanide of potassium which is added when gold is being smelted. The cyanide of potassium remains separate and unaffected, but its presence is absolutely necessary for the success of the process. So with the *puruṣa*. It does not mix with *prakṛti*; it is not intelligence or *mahat* or any one of its modifications but the self, the pure, the perfect. " I am the witness and through my witnessing *prakṛti* is producing all that is sentient in *prakṛti*? producing all that is sentient and all that is insentient."

Whence then is this sentiency in *prakṛti*? Its basis is in the *puruṣa* and it is the very nature of the *puruṣa*. It is that which cannot be expressed or understood, be expressed or understood, but which is the material of all that we call knowledge. This *puruṣa* is not consciousness, because consciousness is a compound but whatever is radiant and good in this consciousness belongs to it. Sentiency is in the *puruṣa* but the *puruṣa* is not intelligence not knowing — it is the very condition in which knowledge is possible. The *cit* in the *puruṣa*, plus *prakṛti* is what is known to us as intelligence and consciousness. All the joy and happiness, and light in the universe belongs to the *puruṣa*, but it is a compound because it is that *puruṣa* plus *prakṛti*. Wherever there is any happiness, wherever there is any bliss, there is one spark of that immortality which is *puruṣa*. This *puruṣa* is the great attraction of the universe; untouched by, and unconscious which is unconnected with the universe; yet it attracts the whole universe. In this world insentiency that *puruṣa* alone is sentient. This is the *puruṣa* of the *Sāṁkhyas*. As such it necessarily follows that this *puruṣa* must be omnipresent, for that which is not omnipresent must be limited. All limitations are caused and that which is caused must have beginning and end. If the *puruṣa* is limited, it will die, will not be final, will not be free, but will have been caused. Therefore if not limited, it is omnipresent. According to Kapila, there are many *puruṣa*s, not one. An infinite number of them —you are one, I am one, each is one; an infinite number of circles, each one is neither born nor dies, which is running through this universe. It is neither mind nor matter and the reflex from it is all that we know. We are sure if it be omnipresent, it knows neither death nor birth. *Prakṛti* casts her shadow upon it, the shadow of birth and death, but it is by its own nature eternal. So far we have found the theory of Kapila wonderful. When question were asked to Kapila, he was able to explain the questions which were still unanswered by other personalities. The questions were who created *prakṛti*, but Kapila was able to explain with certain points. He says that *prakṛti* was uncreated and it is omnipresent. Yet all the glory really belongs to Kapila and it is very easy to give a finish to a building that is nearly complete.

3

The Upaniṣadic Conception of Creation and Modern Science

The *Ṛgveda* in the tenth *maṇḍala* makes the following declaration which forms the genesis of the Upaniṣadic conception of creation:

In the beginning there was neither naught nor aught,
Then there was neither sky nor atmosphere above,
What enshrouded the universe?
In the receptable of what was it contained,
Was it enveloped in gulf profound of water?
Then was there neither death nor immortality
Then was there neither day nor night nor light nor darkness,
Only the existent One breathed, calmly, self-contained,
Naught else than him there was — naught else above, beyond.
Then first came darkness hid in darkness, gloom in gloom
Next all was water, all a chaos indiscreet,
In which the One lay, void shrouded in nothingness.
Then, turning inwards, he by self-developed force grew,
And in him desire, the primal germ of mind
Arose, which learned men, profoundly searching, say
Is the subtle bond connecting entity
With nullity. This ray that kindled dormant life,
Where was it then? Before? Or was it above?
Were the parturient powers and latent qualities
And fecund principles beneath, and active forces

That energised aloft? Who knows? Who can declare
How and from what has sprung the universe? The gods
Themselves are subsequent to its development.
Who, then, penetrates the secret of its rise?

According to the *Ṛṣi*s also, this beautiful universe has not been existing always. There was a time without a trace of it; it was so to speak a void enveloped in darkness. The supreme Being, the Eternal Entity without a second, was the light of that darkness. In the languages of the *ṛṣi*s:

> The Real alone existed before creation as the one supreme God without a second. He meditated and having meditated created all this that exists. From Him were born life, mind, all the senses, the heavens, the air, the light, the water and the earth that contains all. As a spider gives out and takes in its thread or as a plants grow on the earth or as hairs comes out from a living person. So do all senses, all worlds, all *deva*s, all being come forth from that self, the undecaying one. *Brahman* became enlarged through meditation. From it was produced food. From matter came *prāṇa*, the sensorium, truth, the five elements, the worlds and in the worlds the imperishable fruit. From Him, who is all-knowing and all-perceiving, whose penance consists in knowledge, were produced this lower *Brahman*, name form and primal matter. As sparks, similar to the undecaying one also return to it.

The *Sat*, the Supreme Being, who in the beginning abided in His own undifferenced unity, decided to 'become many and grow and grow forth' and according mused in Himself the scheme of the cosmos and with His contemplation, has projected into being all that is. By and from His will-power everything came into existence. Thus, according to the *Ṛṣi*s, the Supreme Being is both the efficient and the material cause of the Universe. The proximate explanation of creation therefore lies in the impelling will force, inner fervour, intense abstraction and desire, the primal germ, the subtle bond that connects entity with nullity.

The *Sat* is the vast image of the Supreme *puruṣa* described in the *Ṛgveda*, whose 'one footstep are the heavens' from 'whose mind is the moon', from 'whose eye the sun', from whose interior are the skies and from whose head the heavens, from whose mouth the *Brahman*, from His arms is the kṣatriya, from whose feet the śūdra. In the same strain, the *Muṇḍaka Upaniṣad* describes the immanence of God in the universe, when it says "Heaven is His Head, the sun and the moon are His eyes, the quarters His ears, the uttered *Veda*s His speech, air is His breath and the world His heart. Out of his two feet has come out the earth. This Person is the Inner self of all creatures." Thus the Supreme Being is the source and substance, soul and life and form of creation. But we do not know the process of His manifestation. It is mysterious. The *ṛṣis* say that, by an act of sacrifice, the Supreme Being imposes on Himself what is called self-limitation and the manifested universe is but the outcome of this self-limitation. And in this mysterious process of the spirit's self-unfolding we find that gradual growth and not primal maturity is stamped on all objects subject to time and space. Slow developments and not miraculous spasms of creative power are universal. Not by an arbitrary fiat of will, not by a paroxysm of energy, but by orderly unending growth, by the graduated operations of the law of evolution which must have started trillions and trillions of years ago and which involved and involves a long series of processes by which successive stages of development have been reached from the simple to the more complex does the Supreme Being convert Himself into this wonderful, variegated world of silent and insentient objects.

From Him was first born the inorganic universe, not the illusory, imaginary, unreal, but the solid, substantial, real universe — a universe of stupendous adjustments, in which each object in space and each event in time could be understood only in the light of the whole of the universe of space, peopled by millions and millions of heavenly bodies, countless, systems profusely scattered at enormous instances over an immense void, and so arranged and distributed in relation to one another and in accordance with the requirements of profound mathematics as to secure the safety of one and all; glorious galaxies of suns, planets, satellites, comets — quietly, submissively, mechanically yet majestically, moving and rushing in marvellous harmony and with unerring precision, without clash or conflict in their appointed orbits, to the march of celestial music, in strict obedience to the hidden system of eternal laws implanted in them.

From Him was next born organic nature which shines in His divine radiance with all the charm and beauty of the vegetable kingdom and acts in conformity with His ordinances. From Him next came the denizens of the animal kingdom from the tiniest worm to the towering elephant endowed with consciousness. All these act instinctively in harmony with his laws—laws exhibiting a unity which is characterised by an admirable correlation of structure to environment and of organ to function, by the mutual interdependence of animal and vegetable life and the continuous self-adjustments of part to part and change to change, and above all by the ingenious contrivances which minister to the prospective harmony of nature.

We thus see that in the process of God's evolution, all inorganic nature is a pathway of forces working towards the consummation of that which we call life. The rocks, the seas, the atmosphere are the prior requisites which make the fragrant flowers, the precious fruit. These in themselves are ends; but they are also means. For without them, the air could be filled with no buzzing and twittering life, the surface of our globe could give support to beasts and creeping things, the sea would be empty of the vast shoals that crowd its depths. The plants furnish the great laboratory which prepares food for these. 'Only' says Dr. Martineau, a modern Western sage, "that unlike our chemist's apparatus and processes, their experiments are all silent, their alembics all sweet, their products the grace and beauty of the world, this conscious life, itself an end, is in turn, in a thousand ways, means towards human life. And within the scope of this human life, the appetites, the affections, the sentiments, in ascending scale, step after lead up to the final realisation of the ideal of the conscience".

Marvellous, miraculous, is the birth and growth of human life. Once perceptible only as a mere dot of protoplasmic substance, but through direct action and intimate watch moving mysteriously into outer growth and inner development, till the world vies with amazement that it should have come out in the wondrous form of a self-conscious individual with infinite possibilites. How ceaselessly, how abundantly, God's creative is in evidence — every desire and prompting anticipated and provided for; the milk preceding the child, the sun-shine awaiting the eye, the breeze in readiness to refresh the boy and all the affinities and associations with the entire environment brought into immediate touch and relationship and made to subserve the designs and indicates of His province.

Not only is God's own love thus evident in the shaping and unfolding of the human life, but He has also planted it in the heart of man. God has so made the world that all mutual service and interdependence of human beings tends to involve the aroma of friendship and the affection of heart, and so to suffuse life with a beauty nothing else could give. Suppose for a moment that God had made the world of mankind without this mystery of love. Suppose each man and woman beholding the faces, hearing the voices of others, but with ever the light of mutual kindness in the eye. Imagine all the range of motive which springs from our affections for each other. What dreariness life would be. And yet God might so have built up the world. He might have implanted in us all the necessary instincts to carry the world along without affection in any human heart. He has not done so. He has given us friendship, sympathy, affection, love. Hence it is that the *ṛṣis* have stated that "we not only come into life in love but continue to live in love and are finally resumed into love."

The Scientific Conception of the Universe

Let us see what science has to say about the story of the Universe. It tells us that in the beginning, that is, before there was any organised universe at all, a thin semi-gaseous and semi-liquid substance evidently diffused throughout space, gradually thickening at certain centres. This thickening is, it says, the first step in the starting of evolution. Who or what caused the thickening, science has no answer as already stated. The essential idea of matter is that it is inert, remains in its present condition for ever, unless disturbed by some external agency. As the only spontaneous agent we know of is the self-conscious free-will, the will of a Supreme Being must be regarded as what has brought about the first thickening of the centre.

The aforesaid thickening, says science, produces a marvellous rotatory motion. The rotary motion, in its turn, transforms the centres each into a globe, which revolves on its axis with immense velocity and prodigious heat. These globes are the suns, the innumerable galaxies of stars which light up the sky radiating light and heat, and of which our sun is one. This rotatory motion next leads on to smaller masses being flung off from each central sun and these, though first forming rings like the present ring of Saturn, gradually also become globular with motion round their own axis, as well as motion round the central sun. These are the planets of which our earth is one. These planets again in many cases fling off further films which formed into moons having a treble motion, rotation round their own axis, motion round their parent planets and with their planets motion round the central sun. Of these our moon is one.

Thus the first great stage running through millions and millions of years shows the primitive world-stuff gradually parcelled out into stars and systems, moving with perfect orderliness through the universe. And in each system, the various members settled down to their ordered orbits in circulation around the central sun. Even the wayward comets are caught into this system or that and compelled to move through a settled orbit as obediently as the moon. Besides, every sun revolves on its own axis and is moving through space accompanied by its family of planets, just as our own sun is moving towards the constellation, Hercules. And so to the human spectator, ever since he began to reflect on the marvels of the nightly skies, the heavens have always been the very symbol and type of order and harmony. Next comes the cooling of the afore-mentioned sundry bodies by radiation of their heat into space by degrees which has brought, is bringing and will bring each for a period to a temperate heat, such as that now enjoyed by our earth. Thus after many an aeon, those elements which the earliest science of man enumerated — fire, air, earth and water, appear on the scene of our globe. Then the formation of mould and soil and slime.

Then comes the most important stage in evolution. Science sees atoms of inorganic matter shifting into such marvellous combinations at last to constitute that mysterious protoplasm, the physical basis of life, an absolutely new beginning in the process of evolution. Why should just this combination of atoms should suddenly put on that entirely new set of characteristics which we call life. Science can form no sort or kind of guess. There is a great chasm between inorganic and organic which no bridge of scientific thought can span. No Newton can ever make intelligible according to mechanical causes the germination of a single blade of grass. The scientific man meeting at every step of his progress this strange apparition of life, cannot account for how, whence or what it is and is awed and bewildered. Life is a mystery and will ever remain a mystery to the mere mechanic. In other words, science confesses the fact of life to be inexplicable. Professor Lionel Beals says:

> There is mystery in life — a mystery that has never been fathomed, and which appears greater the more deeply the phenomena of life are studied and contemplated. In living centres — far more central than centres seen by the highest magnifying powers — which the understanding may tend, proceed changes of the nature of which the most advanced physicists, and chemists, fail to afford us the conception. Nor is there the slightest reason to think that the nature of these changes will ever be ascertained by physical investigation, inasmuch as they are certainly of an order totally distinct from that to which any other phenomena known to us can be relegated.

> Between the living state of matter and its non-living state there is an absolute and irreconciliable difference; that so far from our being able to demonstrate that the non-living passes by gradations into or gradually assumes the state or condition of the living, the transition is sudden and abrupt and the matter already in the living state may pass into the non-living condition in the same sudden and complete manner. The formation of bioplasm direct from non-living matter is impossible even in thought; except to one who sets absolutely at naught the facts of physics and chemistry.

Dr. Annie Beasant thus reasons:

> If from the blind clash of atoms and the hurling forces, there

> comes no explanation of life and of Mind, if these remain *sui generis*, if they loom larger and larger as cause rather than as effects, who shall blame the searcher after Truth, when, failing to find how Life can spring from force and matter, he seeks whether life be not itself the centre and whether every form of matter may not be the garment where with veils itself an Eternal and Universal life?

Onward in the march of evolution, the aforesaid lifegiving protoplasmic matter, mysteriously goes on building itself up into more and more highly organised forms in the vegetable kingdom, from the simplest sea-weed to the mighty royal oak, till at last it becomes the seat of consciousness, a still more inexplicable and unprecedented phenomenon. This consciousness — sustaining life substance, says science, next branches out and pushed along the line of progression till all the varieties of the animal kingdom are formed from the simplest skin-bag in the ocean slime — through the mollusca and crustacea and the vertibrates, up to the regal man himself — by far the most mysterious product of evolution, the crown and glory of creation, who is conscious of his selfhood, of his distinction from all the universe around him and who is of a self-determining, self-estimating and self-directing will and self-contained capacity of thought, saying to himself 'I am I'.

*Ṛṣi*s says in the *Upaniṣad*s that they can prove the simple motions at the beginning, and that it is only reasonable to believe that it is so right on to the end. 'Give us' say they, "those thickening at certain centres of the primeval universal, glowing world-stuff and centres of earth, which we can show that the rotation and the sun-making and the planet-making and the moon-making must follow by the primary laws of motion, and so the universe, even as it is could not help being evolved, if only you give it time. Suppose that unconscious matter is itself endowed with certain energies and forces which act automatically without the presence of will. Supposing all this is granted, who or what brought about the thickening of the primeval glowing world-stuff? How did the evenness turn to unevenness? We must have some power there to start the evolution. Evenly spread fluid that had been lying evenly spread from all eternity — even supposing it had existed from all eternity, and had never been created — could not by sudden spasm gather into knots and nuclei unless some power other than itself were applied to it. Push God back and back, if you will, but at the outset, for the first start of the stupendous evolution, we must have divine volition or our even fluid will remain even and unorganised for ever and ever. Divine volition is therefore the first requisite in the process of evolution as held by our *ṛṣis* — Ṛgvedic and Upaniṣadic."

And there are at least two more hitches or hurdles. No science can, as we have seen already, explain the evolution of organic from inorganic matter. Life as stated above is an absolutely new beginning. Who or what gave the magic touch to the first lump of protoplasm made of the ancient elements of carbon, nitrogen, hydrogen and oxygen for its renewal from surrounding matter which we call life? Most certain it is that whatever else we make or unmake, life is not, cannot be our own making. We cannot keep it. Its growth does not depend upon our will. Its changes are unconscious, involuntary. Nature swarms with life. The earth teems with life. The seed of life — the principle of life, appears to be everywhere. The transparent air is filled with beings which the microscope renders visible. And finally, after this vegetable life had become common on the earth, by what possible process did it suddenly become the seat of that quite new and unprecedented thing which we call consciousness? This too was clean new beginning and no possible laws of motion or of matter can as much as begin to account for it. Stamp matter, then, with what endowments we will, there are at least these three points where we can, by no possibility, get rid of the divine will force which is the beginning of the whole process of evolution, the beginning of life and the beginning of consciousness.

There are indeed certain deep and ingenious speculations which strive to smooth away these hitches by supposing that both life and consciousness have been in some dim way inherent in the universe from all time, and that the building up of the vegetable and animal kingdoms is but the development and specialisation of the vague life-power which lies in all things. This new world of consciousness in bird and beast, and in man himself, is but the brighter blaze in higher organisms of the dim consciousness which stirs even in the humblest atom of inorganic matter. But even if we were to allow this somewhat strained speculation, we should still have to recognise what is called a 'hitch', — the appearance of one who is a person consciously distinct from all the universe around. And this sense of being a separate self, a person distinct in consciousness from all other beings is the assurance and conviction that lies deepest, clearest and most secure in the heart of everyone of us.

Nature seems always to be working with increasing interdependence and harmony — animal dependent on vegetable, vegetable on animal, grass feeding the flocks, insects fertilising the flower, man dependent on the trees of the wood, and the flocks and herds, the flocks and herds themselves dependent on man, and now in historic times, men themselves becoming ever more and more dependent on each other — the artisan dependent on the husbandman, the husbandman on the artisan; the artist supplying the highest pleasures of the man of affairs, the man of business supplying the necessities of the artist; the wheat growing countries feeding the coal-producing countries, the coal and iron nations creating all the implements of civilisation for the populations of the grain lands. So that the progress of that little bit of the universe, the earth, which is intimately known to us, turns out to consist in the ever-increasing complexity of its elements, and the beautiful interdependence of those elements. So that it looks as if the Great power lying at the back of all and ruling over all, which we call God and the *ṛṣis* called *Brahman* found divine delight in this universality of dependence and service between all the individual atoms of the world which He created.

By no manner of means could the philosophers, above referred to, explain how the universe came to be a universe — a single, magnificent, complicated system, characterised by a marvellous unity in variety. Certainly the atoms could not, as humorously observed by Dr. Flint, have taken counsel together and devised a common plan and worked it out. Granting for argument's sake that all the atoms of matter are eternal, it is still beyond all expression improbable that these atoms with these forces, would give rise to anything entitled to be called a universe without a presiding Mind. It is a million to one that they would never produce the simplest of the regular arrangements which we comprehend under the designation of nature, or the lowest of vegetable or animal organisms; a trillion to one that they would never produce a solar system, the earth, the vegetable or animal kingdom or human history. No number of material atoms, although eternal and endowed with mechanical forces can explain the unity and order of the Universe and therefore the belief in their eternal existence does not free us from the necessity of believing in a single intelligent cause, a supreme mind to move and mould, combine, and adjust the ultimate atom of matter into a single, orderly homogeneous system. Here again the progress of science has not more convincingly and completely disproved the once prevalent notion that states that the universe was created about six thousand years ago, than it has convincingly and completely established that the hitches mentioned above, and various transformations and activities involved in the process of the evolution of the universe can be solved. In passing, I may state that physical science has also established that what we call matter is essentially force and nothing but force, that the whole material world is ultimately resolvable into forces; that all its force are but manifestations or outgoings of One will force. If so, the whole material world is not only dependent on will but on One supreme Mind. This will is not only the cause and controlling power of nature, but its substance also. Every atom, every molecule is not therefore self-existent but must in what is ultimate in it, bear the impress of a supernatural power and wisdom and reflect the glory of a Supreme Being and proclaim its dependence on Him. According to the *ṛṣis* also, the great secret, the final mystery of the universe is that the substance of all is one and that substance is not matter but God's great and glorious spirit.

History of the Evolution of Human Life

From the above digression, we shall revert to the history of the evolution of human life and trace the further ascent of man in the process of God's creation. Measured by physical size, man is too puny as compared to those gigantic orbs that people limitless space. But judged by the powers that are deposited in his bosom, man is the very crown of creation. Infinity is enshrined in every human soul — God does truly regenerate, reproduce, recreate Himself in every human spirit. How wonderful are the powers that He has treasured in each soul — not merely to take the measurements of time and space, but scale the heights and sound, the depths of time and so to probe into the very centre and gauge the whole circuit of space as to surpass and outreach time and space the power to look ahead and after is granted to man because he is truly and verily His child. This offspring of God, known and honoured, cherished and exalted as man — the possessor of that mystic eye which can pray into the sealed secrets of creation is wonderful. What the rest of God's creation accepts and obeys as law, he spells out and embraces as the rule of life. Above all, this marvellous human atom, looking forth from his planet, has measured and weighted the gigantic celestial bodies, traced their orbits through the heavens, divined the processes by which they grew from dusty nebulae into glowing sun or life-blessed planet. He has tracked the subtle proteus from form-to-form and made it now fly with his messages, and carry him from corner-to-corner of the globe with inconceivable speed. Starting as a speck, then a living cell, a germ, growing as a miracle, then a self-unfolding shape, a fininshed figure, a hope incarnate, developing on the wings of God's inspiration, this wonderful being, known as man, has been every minute living proof of God's divine glory.

Process of God's Evolution

The process of God's evolution does not stop with the production of the merely self-conscious and free-willed man. God's creative and controlling power, His ceaseless causal energy goes on, from the first thickening of the primeval fluid world-stuff expanding step by step, thrill by thrill, vibration by vibration, movement by movement till it manifests itself in the God-like being of the poet and the prophet, the saint and the martyr, the philosopher and the sage, the philanthropists and the patriot. This steady progress, stage by stage, through means after means, on and ever on towards a noble end, so wondrous in its adjustments and adaptations, is the mark, not so wondrous in its accidental clash of purposeless, mindless atoms, not of mere chance or dead matter or blind force, but of His conscious self-determining will which sees the end from the beginning and weaves the ages as a work upon the loom evolving successively matter out of nothingness, the pleasure garden of an earth out of a blazing furnace, life out of the lifeless, animal and vegetable, humanity out of animalism, and divinity out of humanity. Thus it is borne in upon us quite irresistibly that in the immense evolution under the stress of His living energy, there has been guiding design from first till now — an increasing purpose running through the ages.

In the glory of God's creation, no two living creatures are ever exactly alike. Twins are often mistaken to be alike only through the superficial nature of observation. For each one has a distinct mark in look, in department, in voice, in gesture. His gracious attention is always individual, attention focused on the unit, not merely spread over the type. Likewise no two souls are quite alike, each one rounded out in the fulness of its individuality. Else, God's very capacity to create worlds will look exhausted. But wonderful is the Divine mother's fecundity and infinite variety within the bounds of general uniformity.

So science is struggling hard to unravel the mystery of creation; let us see with what success. It has proved beyond all doubts the indestructibility of matter. It has analysed the human minds and believes in its unextended immaterial nature. It has no definite answer about the nature of our souls. As regards a creator, it is either sceptic. So far as this aspect of its researches is concerned, the result is not at all satisfactory. But in course of time it may be expected to define more clearly its ideas respecting mind, soul and god.

Let us, however, see whether science at any time will be able to know all about the universe. All scientific researches are based upon ordinary sense-perception, which holds the outer universe to have an independent existence, i.e., something with an independent mind. Whether we are conscious of it or not, it exists. It also holds that we derive all our knowledge about it through our sense-organs and garner them in our minds. Now, it is also a fact that the Universe is infinite in every way, for we can never imagine the limit in space in which it is located. If we start in a railway train with incredible velocity to find out the end of space in any direction whatever, it will not be possible for us to come to the limit even at the end of several years; for there will remain space enough to travel still further. Material particles being both infinitely scattered and indestructible, as well, although sometimes it may remain in a manifested and sometimes in an unmanifested condition. But it is always eternal and infinite in its nature.

Now, as regards our phsyical self, we are merely three and a half cubits in length. With regard to our mental self also, we are limited. We know many things, indeed, but there are many more things that we do not know. Hence our minds are circumscribed on all sides by impassable walls of ignorance. But it may be argued that the mind has an infinite potential for knowledge; its power for expansion is infinite. That may be, but we must hold that as it stands at present, it is finite. Suppose it knows all about this world of ours in one day. Still, even after the lapse of a million years, its knowledge about the Universe must remain limited, since there will remain innumerable worlds still unknown, peopling the infinite bosom of space.

We first come across the name of a perfected and all knowing sage in the *Śvetāśvatara Upaniṣad*, one of the principal Vedic texts. In describing the all-powerful and all-gracious nature of God, this *Upaniṣad*, says: "He saw Kapila, the most ancient among the all-knowing sages, and first of all infilled him with powers." Thus Kapila was the first *ṛṣi* or all-knowing and perfected being. He was a man, for he was born like all ordinary mortals. How was it possible for him to become all-knowing? We have seen that it is not possible for any man to know all. Kapila, like others, found out that the objects which make up the Universe are innumerable objects. But, he said, really there are only two objects. It is only when we look at the Universe through ignorance, through a wrong method of perception, that it appears to be a collection of innumerable entities. Otherwise there are only two entities—*prakṛti* and *puruṣa*, i.e., matter and spirit. These two are the uncreated, self-existent and primary beings. When they are combined together, the combination and *prakṛti* number only twenty-four. The innumerable permutations and combinations of these first principles have brought this Universe into existence.

Chemical science has found out that there are at present 102 elements, but it is not certain whether these will continue to be regarded as such. Most of them may be found as compounds. Kapila's science is not empirical. It is perfectly certain and positive about the number of its first principles; so that it appears to a superficial enquirer to be dogmatic. He has given very clear and irrefutable proofs to establish the validity of his affirmation. He was the first to find out the phenomenal nature of the Universe and analysed it in three ways. What is a phenomenon? It has got three factors — Spirit (*adhyātma*), Matter (*ādhibhūta*), the illumining principle which unifies the former two (*ādhidaiva*). The Universe can only be perceived by the subjects, the knower, i.e., there must be a subject and an object to make a perception possible. Now in order to look at the universe there must not only be the knower and the object, but also the illumining and unifying principle. If I wish to look at the picture in darkness, I cannot. There must be a light between men and picture-object, and the light is the illumining principle. In the case of the eyes, the illumining principle is the light; of the tongue, water, of the nose, earthly particles and so on. Thus the universe can be known only by the help of the unifying principle standing between it and myself. So there are three factors to make a phenomenon possible — *puruṣa* and *prakṛti*, self and not-self, spirit and matter, and that which unites these two — in other words, the *adhyātma*, *ādhibhūta* and *ādhidaiva*.

Matter and Spirit

Further, I think of the Universe only by means of mind. Now let us see where the universe actually exists. It exists in me. This is exactly what Kapila first pointed out. The visible universe exists in the seer; for the seer alone can see; the knower alone can know. He also answered the question whether it is desirable to have the universe continue to exist for our enjoyment. It is an undeniable fact that we are so constituted that it does not seem possible for us to do away with it. We are born with the idea that it is a reality. We seem to depend upon it for our food and other wants, for our happiness, nay for our misery; they bring us innumerable births and deaths and accompanying troubles. So we must get rid of the very idea of the universe. He has also shown the means of doing so. We have seen that according to him the universe is not an infinite entity; he has numbered the factors composing it. Therefore it can be got rid of. It is a compound and not an element. Separate the components and it dissolves and disappears. Matter and spirit only remain. This is what is called the condition of salvation, *mokṣa*. It is the contact with matter that you appear to yourself as finite, although you are infinite. This is not desirable. Who would wish to lose his infinite power? If there is a chance of my becoming the lord of the universe should I not claim it? How many are the candidates for acquiring limited powers. Much more should everyone be a candidate for infinite power. You cannot know that you are limitless unless you separate your connection with the limited. Matter is limited, and so also must every material body be. Matter is defined to be that which is limited, and spirit to be that which is limitless. So if you wish to know that you are infinite, have no connection with matter. Do not think that your three and a half cubits of height constitutes your whole being.

This is Kapila's great philosophy. He was the first to point out that the mind is not spirit or self. Western philosophies identify the mind with the soul, and seat it in the brain. Kapila pointed out that it is as much material as the living organism. Mind is that which thinks, feels and wills. This is the Western definition of it. But there can be no thought, feeling, or will without a corresponding object; you know that there can be no transitive verb without matter; hence it is material. It has consciousness, because it is permeated by the self. We all know that there are two sorts of matter, the unconscious or dead, and the conscious or living. Dull, dead matter is naturally conscious. But this living organism of course is conscious, and yet we do not call it spirit. Similarly though the mind has consciousness, we call it material because it is inseparably connected with matter. Hindu philosophers, without any exception, look at the mind just as they look at this living body, and regard it as one of the several organs through which the *puruṣa* or the Self comes in contact with the world. Hence it is called the sixth sense-organ. We have five kinds of sensation through the five senses. These sensations are named in the *Sāṁkhya* system of *tanmātra*s. Mind, as the sixth sense, enables us to think, feel and will. The illumining or unifying principle of each sense must stand between the self and the Universe.

Now the universe is generally believed to be space and Time. Time is made up of present and future. The five senses are able to perceive the present universe. The Universe of the past and the future is conceived by the mind. Thus the senses and the mind are the six intervening agencies through which alone the soul is able to unite itself with *prakṛti*. What are the results of this union? Knowledge, perception and sensations. And these are called phenomena. Therefore it is not a simple and self-existent entity. It is a compound. The moment it is split up into its factors it vanishes. Then it is only spirit and matter. But spirit knows not only its own existence, but also that of matter. Hence the conceptions of both matter and spirit as well as of their countless unions, the phenomena or the universe — all exist in the spirit of the self.

Kapila's philosophy enables you to understand clearly how the universe has come into existence. The primary categories, *puruṣa* and *prakṛti* or spirit and matter, are in themselves inactive. Spirit is inactive because it is infinite. That which is finite can have motion from one place to another, but the infinite has no outside, and hence where can it go? There is another reason for its inactivity or peaceful calmness. Being perfection itself, and thus having no want, it needs no activity. It is the feeling of want that actuates a man to work for its removal. *Puruṣa* is wantless, and hence he is quiet. *Prakṛti* or matter also is inactive; being inert and unconscious, it has no power to go from one place to another. Out of these two inactive entities, how has this incessant activity, this universe, come into existence? The Universe is all notion. How can it spring from two motionless cause? How can it ever come into existence? In answer to this question, Kapila gives a very fine and apt illustration. The lame man cannot walk, the blind man cannot see; but if the lame man gets on to the shoulders of the blind man, both can go wherever they like. Similarly, spirit, united with matter, produces all these countless activities that go by the name of the universe.

Spirit again is infinite. Now suppose a rich man has been imprisoned and forced to live on thin gruel alone. Would he not rebel against such a sort of life and struggle hard to free himself from it? Such is the case with everyone of us. We are all infinite, but by some irresistible power we have been imprisoned in this material and mortal body. Hence life has become a constant struggle to throw away this unbearable limitation or bondage. Everyone aims at a higher or more expanded form of life. For instance, the poor man wants to become rich, the rich richer.

Infinite power potentially exists in us. Some unaccountable, irresistible and foreign power has deprived us of our glory and imprisoned us in this filthy dungeon of a body. So we naturally resent this and strive to break through this finite shell.

The universe is full of activities — creative, preservative and destructive. Kapila has thus explained how two inactive principles produce activity. But who brought them together? In answer Kapila says 'None'. The combination or union is from time without beginning. Thus he finds no necessity to believe in the existence of an eternal god, because none is required to bring about the union; we become free, no Divine help being needed. He has written a few aphorisms to show the non-existence of God. He says in one of them, "The existence of God cannot be proved". He brings the reason in the next aphorism, which says, "For God cannot be either free or not free." A free, perfect and infinite God would have no desire to create, preserve and destroy. If he is not free, He is imperfect and finite, and can have no power to create. Thus there cannot be an external God. This is putting one on the horns of a dilemma. When we attribute to God the power to bring together and harmonise all contradictions in Himself, as when we say that He is finite and infinite, active and inactive simultaneously, this argument falls to the ground. Moreover, Kapila says that the union of *puruṣa* and *prakṛti* is beginningless. Now can we imagine knowledge without a knower, activity without an actor, and spirit cannot come together without a unifier. If this union is beginningless and infinite, so also must be the unifier which is another name for God. Through His infinite and inconceivable power which goes by the name of *māyā*, He brings about this union. 'I make the souls forget their true nature by means of *māyā* as a divine'. *Māyā* limits even the limitless. None can go beyond it. Only those who surrender themselves to His mercy can cross over it.

Thus even from Kapila's philosophy we may arrive at an eternal god. He also holds that without a creator, a preserver and a destroyer, creation, preservation and destruction are not possible. So for each cycle there should be a Brahmā, a Viṣṇu and a Śiva. But this system upholds the plurality of souls, and so he does not believe in one permanent Brahmā, Viṣṇu and Śiva. According to him, these are posts that are filled by a fresh set of qualified souls in each cycle. He does not believe in the permanency of the person although he holds the post to be permanent. But as there cannot be more than one infinity, there cannot be more than one *puruṣa*. Hence God must be absolutely one and eternal, of whom Brahmā, Viṣṇu and Śiva are different manifestations, so we cannot separate creation, preservation and dissolution. Whatever is created must continue to exist for some time, and then disappear. Thus from Kapila we learn that the Universe of phenomena is actually existing in the self or the knower. It cannot, does not know its own existence; whereas a phenomenon must be known in order to be a phenomenon.

We also arrive at the same conclusion even if we study the problem from the modern scientific standpoint. Where does the Universe exists? It is localised in space and time. Are they self-existent or themselves localised somewhere? It is an undeniable fact that they exist only in your waking condition, and not when you sleep soundly. When a man like R.P. Van Winkle in the story sleeps even for several months, he does not know where he has been lying or how long. So space and time exist in your waking condition, i.e., they exist when you are conscious or in other words in your consciousness. Now your consciousness is confined inside your body; for outside it, in other words, in your consciousness, the world exists. Hence the universe is inside your body, which is pervaded by the self. So the whole cosmos is in yourself. Immanuel Kant has also pointed out that space and time are the two forms of the sense and the mind; they do not exist apart from them. There is another way of arriving at the same conclusion. Suppose a big cannon is fired two miles away from you, there being nothing intervening between it and yourself. You see the flash, and you know that almost simultaneously with the flash, the roaring sound is there. But you do not hear it. There is no sound for you. You hear it a few seconds after the sound for you. You hear it a few seconds after the actual occurrence. Nowhere does the sound take place? In the cannon or in the ears? The auditory nerves within the ears carry the vibration to the brain centre which carries it to the mind, and that to your centre, which is yourself; and then you hear it. So the sound exists inside yourself, and not in the cannon outside. Similarly touch, taste and smell exist inside your senses or in yourself. And so the Universe, which is but an aggregate of innumerable sensations of form, taste, and smell, exists inside your body, in your mind or in your own consciousness, not outside. There is no such thing as space or time outside you.

There is another method of arriving at this conclusion. You know that every object of inference exists in the mind. There are two ways of looking at the universe—*pratyakṣa* and *anumāna*. Or yonder hill, you see the smoke alone directly, and you infer that there must be fire along with it. This knowledge of the fire is not based upon your direct perception through your eyes. The fire exists only in your mind. So is every matter of inference. How far does our direct perception extend? We see the beautiful birds winging their way through the air in all directions; we see the sun during the day, and the shining starry world in the nights. Even beyond these there must be space; that is what we infer. The space beyond is conceived as made up of various concentric sphere, one surrounding the other which go by name of *janaḥ, mahaḥ, tapaḥ* and *satyam*. Of these we are able to see directly only this side of *svarga* or heaven, while the other outer spheres are invisible to us; we simply infer their existence. Now whatever is inferred, is in the mind. So all the outer spheres are in the mind. But all the inner spheres, which make up the visible universe are inside the outer. So the visible universe must be inside the mind or in yourself.

Again, who illumines all these? The sun. What illumines the sun? The eyes; for an eyeless man has no sun. What illumines the eyes? The mind. What illumines the mind. The self. So the whole universe is illumined by yourself. But for you, there can be no universe. Thus you see that you cannot localise it outside yourselves; the whole of it exists in your own minds in your own selves. But at present conditions are such that we are forced to regard it as outside ourselves. When we have already known, there is a possibility of our knowing all about the universe since it exists in our consciousness.

The eternal and infinite creation, about which we learn from ancient history, geology, astronomy and all other sciences. Where does this universe exist? My little universe exist in my own little mind, self. It cannot exist in mind or knower, as the existence of a phenomenon is only possible in consciousness. This we have already seen. Now the eternal creation is an unbroken series of countless phenomena running on throughout all time, and so it must be in an eternal and infinite mind or self, which is God. Hence this creation goes by the name of *Īśa-sṛṣṭi* or God's creation. When the finite man of three and half cubits in length will gradually get rid of this wrong notion about himself with the increasing light of wisdom, when, disentangling himself from the meshes of his little body and mind, he will merge his pure self in the infinite self of god — then alone will the truth shine upon him, the idea of limitation and fear of death will cease to trouble him, and he will lose himself in the ocean of eternal peace and bliss by realising his perfect and infinite self.

The sense of causation is one such involuntary intuition and is inseparable from the human mind in all phases of life and is universal. Even undeveloped minds such as those of children are conscious of it. If we see a painting, we know there is a painter. If we hear, we know there is a musician. If we read a book, we know that there is a human writer. When we see a vessel spreading her canvas and majestically riding on the billows of a stormy sea, we conclude that she has a pilot on board. The work or products necessarily involves a worker or producer. Therefore, when we see works or products infinitely beyond the power of man, then we know that the power resides in someone else who is super-human. In the same manner, we cannot observe the glories of the firmament above us, its infinite extent, its beauty, and the imperishable ever-progressive soul within us, and the marvellous skill with which every plant and animal and individual self has its wants cared for, and yet fail to see that there must be a Supreme Being. We cannot receive good without thinking of a bestower of good. We cannot rest in the sense of bounties from an unknown hand. Man would become restless and enfevered to find out the benefactor. Gratitude demands expression, enforces search for the giver. Hence the ceaseless life — long search and pursuit of the *ṛṣis* in quest of the Supreme Being through various spiritual *sādhanās* and their eventual success in discovering Him and their immersion in His Bliss. They were satisfied when they preached to thousands about the truths they discovered and shared with them the truths they discovered and found themselves in bliss and enjoyment. Even as the flower blossoms not for its own pleasure, even as the stream flows not for its own benefit, even as the tree stands not for its own comfort, even as the mountain stands not for its own majesty; the lives of *ṛṣis* are not meant solely for their own advancement but as a source of strength to the whole of humanity. They accordingly went forth, each one of them, in ecstatic raptures as the humble instruments of the Supreme Wielder of the destinies of mankind, proclaiming to the world:

> I have discovered the sweet God. I have seen the Great spirit. Listen to me, ye sons of Immortal Bliss, even who live in the heavenly abode. I have found the Ancient one; I have known the Supreme Being whose light shines forth from beyond all darkness and knowing Him alone you shall be same.

The Supreme Being proclaimed by the *ṛṣis* is a Being whose existence had no cause, no beginning and can have no end and whose non-existence is impossible, inconceivable and unthinkable. The whole nature of this unoriginated Being or the aggregate of His attributes is uncaused and must be necessarily and immutably what it is, so that He cannot have any attribute or modification of His attribute. Whatever are the attributes of the unoriginated Being, He possesses each of them unlimitedly. In whatever manner the Supreme Being exists or is present anywhere, He exists in the like manner or is present everywhere. He is one individual uncompounded substance, identically the same everywhere and to which our ideas of the whole and part, magnitude and quantity, cause and effect, time and space, are not applicable. He possesses intelligence and power unlimited and all other moral attributes that are in themselves absolute perfection. The *ṛṣis* announce that there is in the universe but one unoriginated Being who must therefore be the original fountain of all existence and the First cause of all things, that all things owe their existence ultimately to the power of the First cause operation according to His free will; that creation is only the coming out of what already existed potentially in the First cause; that the Supreme Being, the *Brahman*, the Almighty God, the first cause and author of all things, is a Being of infinite goodness, wisdom, mercy, justice, truth and all other moral perfections such as becoming the supreme author and governor of the Universe. What is more, as the efficient and personal first cause, the Supreme Being, say the *ṛṣis* is *sarvantaryāmī*, dwells, secretly in all objects, sentient and insentient, animating the myriad forces in nature and brightening its whole face with a heavenly beauty.

The first cause, announce the *ṛṣis*, is a free cause, a will, a spirit, a reason, a consciousness. The universe is a universe; that is to say, it is a whole, a unity, a system. The first cause of it, therefore, in creating and sustaining it, must comprehend, act on and guide it. The complex and harmonious constitution of the universe must accord to the divine idea of creating reason.

The universe is not, therefore, a chaos, formed by chance, but ordained, ruled and controlled with obvious purpose by a power infinitely greater than our own, and by a mind exhibiting infinitely greater wisdom and knowledge. Everything grows or comes out of something else. In other words, every event is preceded by something from which power flows forth, shaping, making and controlling that event, as our act of will shapes and makes and controls the blow of the fish or the tramp of the foot. It is a fundamental and primary fact of our nature that we cannot help thinking of all phenomena as caused and controlled by power of this kind coming from some source or other.

But unfortunately we have got into the habit of using the word 'cause' in a very loose way. And chiefly we create confusion by talking of the laws of Nature themselves as if they were causes. We ask why gas which escapes is smelt so quickly all over the room, and we reply that it is caused by the diffusion of gases; we ask why the cannon-ball that is fired off curves upwards and in a few hundred yards actually strikes the ground; and the reply is that it is caused by the law of gravitation. But that is altogether a confused and confusing use of the word cause. The phenomenon is explained by the law, but it is not caused by the law. For what is a law of nature? It is simply the avowal that certain phenomena always happen in a certain way. And it is a law of Nature that any two masses tend to approach each other with a force which varies inversely as the squares of their distances. But that is not the cause of the apple falling to the ground, or the sea following the rising and settling of the moons; it is only for explanation of these things. Each dropping of an apple and each rise or fall of the tide is just one more act which goes to make up the boundless mass of facts which we gather up and bind together purely and solely for convenience of thought, under one law — the law of gravitation.

We want to know the cause of this very wide spread fact that bodies do move towards one another in the way stated in the law of gravitation, and stating the law does not bring us a hair's breath nearer to the cause. There must be something or other like the influx of will-power into our muscles, when the surface of the sea moves towards the ground according to the moon's movement when the apple moves towards the ground and when two drops of water lying close together on a perfectly smooth horizontal sheet of glass are unable to rest close together, and actually move up to each other and coalesce in one big drop instead of two small ones. There is a pull somewhere like the pull we give when we ring the door bell. Who or what pulls them? Does the moon pull the sea, the earth the apple, one drop the other drop? No, moon and earth and drop are simply masses of matter. The mind cannot form the idea of their pulling without for the moment thinking them as alive and exercising will-power. But they are not, so far as we know alive. They have so far as we can judge, no will-power. Who or what pulls them? We are compelled to believe that apart from the big or small masses of matter themselves, there is in every case what we call a force, that is, a power like our will-power which does the pulling — only that it always does the pulling according to the same laws, whether with big masses or little mass, whether on earth or in the sun or through the vast forces which seem so empty, lying between the world masses which are scattered through the heavens.

What then is, this wondrous force? We do not actually observe it in the external world at all. What we perceive is only the following of one event by another. But we believe that this succession is impossible without an active conscious force behind it. This impels us to see that the most important principle of physical science, the law of universal causation, is really the revelation, the mode of working, of an eternal, unchangeable, self-conscious and self-determining spirit in nature which must necessarily possess intellect and will, intelligence and motive.

Again the picture which modern science draws of the universe is indeed surpassingly sublime. It says that the universe is filled with force which glows through every atom of matter — solid, liquid, gaseous, throughout the infinite area of the boundless whole. The things which naturally give us the highest conception of force and majesty are the grand bodies that march so ceaselessly through the heavens — the tidal movements of oceans from end to end of the globe, or the fall of huge masses under the power of gravity; but all this energy nothing in comparison with that which is found to lie in the atoms. It is the nature and force of the atom that gives shape to the crystal, quality to the acid or alkali, colour, odour, softness or hardness to substances. It is the atoms that build up every individual body from a drop of water to a whirling sun.

Take the minutest particle of matter which the eye can see. That itself is a whole universe of energy. Within its bounds, molecules are vibrating, moving from one side to another with inconceivable velocity all the time. And the like is going on in every particle of matter from here away to the most distant star whose light takes several millions of light years to reach us. Imagination reels before the effort to conceive this tremendous force pulsating with one beat from end to end of the universe, if there were any ends at all. But it gives us the firm conception in response to the sense of causality in us that every individual motion be the outcome of causality, be it ever so minute. It is in fact, the direct expression of a power akin to the will-force which we know in ourselves. Does this not give us a truly transcendent idea of God as the Supreme Force that fills and penetrates and binds every atom of matter in the universe? This leads us also to the inescapable philosophical conclusion that He, without whose mandate even an ant could not pass out of existence and not a sparrow would fall to the ground, whose conscious energy concentrated in every particle of the ant's body, in every feather of the sparrow, in every thread of down on each feather and in every chemical atom in each thread, for whose care no mote floating in the sun-beam is too minute, cannot be heedless of the human soul looking forth with wonder at the heaven of heavens or indifferent to the heart that approaches Him in reverent love and prayer.

It is this sublime truth which *ṛṣi* Yājñavalkya declared when he described the Supreme Being in the *Bṛhadāraṇyaka Upaniṣad* as "The one who dwells in the earth and the heaven within the earth and within the heaven, whom the earth and the heaven do not know, whose body the earth and the heaven are, and who pulls the earth and the heaven within." The *ṛṣis* further goes on postulating likewise in greater detail the immanent, binding and pulling power of God in eleven other natural phenomena viz. in the water, the fire, the sky, the air, the sun, the moon and stars, the ether, the darkness, the light, then in the individual self, finally in the eight organs, viz. the breath, the tongue, the eyes, the ears, the mind, the skin, the knowledge and the seed.

In other words, fire, air, earth and water, thunder, lightning, rain and wind, herb, shrub, plant and tree, insect, bird, beast and man are all aglow with His pulling power and vitalising presence. Every object, every being is His temple, to which all the departments of science, open up a high road. Steam and electricity, light and heat, ether and sound, directly reveal Him. The force of gravitation, is only a beautiful vista through which He is described. The movements of the rolling plants above reveal Him as a mighty architect who holds those stupendous orbs in His Hand. In the movements of the winds, we distinctly feel the His breath as he rides over the whirlwind and shakes the universe by His power. The more we study the mathematics and the mechanics of physical forces, the move vividly do we see Him, the great mathematician and mechanics, who has constructed this wondrous mechanism. Every department of knowledge leads us into His immediate presence. The whole universe becomes His *sanctum sanctorum*, the holy of holies, in which we always worship and adore Him as the everlasting light, the author and giver of life, the maker of all suns, the fountain-flood of all truth, wisdom, love and righteousness, the eternal unchangeable one. We likewise commune with Him as the god of Astronomy, and Meteorology, the god of Mathematics and Mechanics, as the god of Electricity and Magnetism, the god of winds and tides, the God of light and sound, the god of agriculture and manufacture — in fact, as the all-comprehending, all-penetrating, all-sustaining, all-ordering, all-harmonising, all-unifying personal providence who animates and regulates directs and guides, controls and quickens everyone of life's manifold spheres.

Again, in reply to searching questions put to him in the court of King Janaka by Vacakanavi Gārgī, an enlightened lady philosophical enquirer, regarding ether, *ṛṣi* Yājñavalkya says; "Ether is woven like warp and woof in the *akṣara,* the Imperishable Being". He then describes the invisible and intangible nature of this Being and winds up by glorifiying His sovereignty.

On account of the importance of the matter, I am inclined to reproduce below the questions of the enquirer and the answers of the *ṛṣi* (*Bṛhadāraṇyaka Upaniṣad*):

> Gārgī said : "O Yājñavalkya, as the son of a warrior from the Kasis might string his loosened bow, take two pointed foe piercing arrows in his hand and rise to do battle. O have risen to fight thee with two questions. Answer me these questions."
>
> Yājñavalkya said : "Ask, O Gārgī" she said : "O Yājñavalkya, that of which they say that it is above the heavens, beneath the earth, embracing heaven and earth, past, present and future, tell me in what is it woven, like warp and woof?." Yājñavalkya said : "That of which they say that is is above, the heavens, beneath and future, that is woven like warp and woof, in the ether (ākāśa)." She said : "I bow to thee, O Yājñavalkya, who has solved me that question. Get thee ready for the second". Yājñvalkya said : Ask, O Gārgī." She said : "In what then is ether woven like warp and woof"? He said : "O Gārgī, the brāhmaṇas call this *akṣara.* It is neither coarse nor fire, neither short nor long, neither red nor fluid; it is without shadow, without darkness, without air, without ether, without attachment, without taste, without smell, without eyes, without ears, without speech, without mind, without light, without breath, without a mouth, without measure, having no within and no without; it devours nothing and no one devours it. By the command of the *akṣara* the Imperishable, O Gārgī, sun and moon stand apart. By the command of that *akṣara* O Gārgī, heaven and earth stand apart. By the command of that *akṣara*,

> O Gārgī, what are called moments, hours, days, and nights, half months, months, seasons, years, all stand apart. By command of the *akṣara*, O Gārgī, some rivers flow to the east from the white mountains, others to the west or to any other quarter. Whatsoever, O Gārgī without knowledge that *akṣara*, offers oblations in this world, sacrifices, and performs, penance for a thousand years, his work will have an end, whosoever, O Gārgī, without knowing this *akṣara* departs this world, he is miserable. But he, O Gārgī who departs this world, knowing this *akṣara*, he is a *Brahman*. That *Brahman*, O Gārgī, is unseen but seeing; unheard, but hearing; unperceived, but perceiving; unknown, but knowing. There is nothing that sees but it, nothing that hears but it, nothing that perceives but it, nothing that knows but it, in that *akṣara* then, O Gārgī, the ether is woven, like warp and woof."

Another *ṛṣi*, Śāṇḍilya, the *Chāndogya Upaniṣad* visualises, the Supreme Being as:

> The intelligent whose body is spirit, whose form is light, whose thoughts are true, whose nature is like ether from whom all works, all desires, all sweet odours and tastes proceed; He who embraces all this, who never speaks and is never surprised.

The Scientific Conception of the Universe

Let us see what modern science has to say about ether. It says it is subtler than force, surrounds every particle of matter, penetrates everybody, fills all space and pulsates with life. But we cannot see it. The hardest iron is not impervious to it. The most complete atmospheric vaccum, even the desert voids that reign between star and star, are full of it and the absence of common matter only serves to transmit the etherial waves better. A ray of light passing from sun to the earth is a column of ether in vibration. At every point, ether exerts a force of enormous intensity. In comparison with the bulk of ether, ordinary matter forms but a trifling part of the universe. For, even if we disregard the ether diffused through ordinary matter and interplanetary spaces, and suppose the whole of our solar system to be filled with ordinary matter, the proportion between it and the etherial sphere whose radius is the distance to the nearest fixed star, is said to be only as one to eleven trillions. Though the medium of vision, ether and its vibrations is farther beyond all visibleness than the tiniest molecule and is more tenacious than steel, we move through it constantly without feeling it. So enormous is its pressure, no balance can weigh it. It touches us on every side every second, but no touch of ours can detect it. As Professor Tyndall has said : The domain in which this motion of light is carried on lies entirely beyond the reach of our senses. The waves of light require a medium for their formation and propagation, but we cannot see or hear or feel or taste or smell this medium. How then has its existence been established? By showing that the assumption of this wonderful intangible ether, all the phenomena of optics are accounted for with a fulness and clearness and conclusiveness which leaves no desire of the intellect unfulfilled.

Again what has been stated above is true of that which the science of mechanics rest on — uniform force and rectilineal motion. No eye has seen or shall see it. So also in electricity, magnetism, thermodynamics, the subtle analysis of modern investigation has banished altogether with the former theories of material fluids and substituted the conception of invisible forces. The scientific energies now believed in are not physical things but mental data. Gravity, for example, is not a material entity but the correlate of thought, of motion, the occult cause inferred by the mind where change of place is observed. None of these phenomena is visible to the physical senses. Yet they are not dismissed as mere fictions of the intellect, but believed in as established scientific truth.

Moreover, all the objects that science studies are seen in space. All the events that it traces are known as occurring in time. These two — space and time, are fundamental conditions of all science. Yet, neither space nor time is itself a material thing capable of being perceived by the senses. Shall space and time, then, be set down as figments of the brain?

If science, can, of necessity, make some of the most tremendous unproven assumptions which it is possible to conceive, if science must assume in its experiments the veracity and trustworthiness of man's own faculties, of the senses and the intellect which play their part in making up all the human experiences, and above all, if science may accept the perception and the satisfaction of the reasoning powers of man and also of his memory as good proof of what no observation can discover, why should the *ṛṣi*s, the seers of ancient wisdom, be debarred a similar line of reasoning and argument in asserting that the phenomena of the visible and invisible, the tangible and intangible world could be accounted for only by the existence of the invisible and intangible, that they share the Imperishable Being, in whom the invisible and intangible ether itself is 'woven like warp and woof' — a Being who has no form visible to the eye, whom no one can see with eye and who is revealed through the heart, the understanding and through meditation?

Let us next see how modern science and eminent scientist and philosophers bear surpassingly corroborative testimony to the God-vision of the ancient *ṛṣi*s. For the information of readers not versed in scientific enquires, I may premise by saying that the function of science is to observe, explain, classify and interpret the phenomena of nature and that the method employed in scientific investigation is not different from ordinary reasoning but simply the process of commonsense, critical understanding, carried out with precision, aided by the experience of the inward man. The starting point of all science is in the observation of nature. The various senses — sight, hearing, smell, taste, touch perceive various objects such as, star, rock, water, plant, animal and notice their varied qualities , such as, heat, cold, hardness, softness, perfumes, sounds, forms, etc. These are compared, their likenesses and differences noted. Then classifications are formed — families, species, substances — forces, laws, and as the result of these inductions, general propositions are laid down — the main principle ruling in this inductive process being to classify together the like things, separating them from the unlike and to interpret the unknown by the known, not *vice versa*. And accepting, as we do, the widest possible definition of the term nature, regarding it as inclusive of the domain of mind as well as the domain of matter, we may assert that science has quite properly to do with everything that concerns human life, either in the past or in the present, and whether we call it sensuous or spiritual. Scientific investigation, then, is by no means complete, its discoveries or theories cannot be looked upon as conclusive if it is not so extended as to cover the whole area of human thought and action. What man has thought and done, endured and endeavoured in bygone ages is as truly evidence of the development of life, is of as great value in building up an intelligible and reasonable system of universal truth as are the fossil remains of the flora and fauna of other epochs which the scientist rightly regards as of the first importance. Accordingly, the whole occupation of science, ever since there has been any science at all, has been gathering up the happenings in the universe, showing that they are not irregular, but regular, classifying them, in neat bundles, each with its label bearing the name of some law of nature. That is what true nature and science always is at and it is never at anything else at all. It does a perpetual tiding up of our observations of natural phenomena and it cannot bear to leave any of them lying about unclassified.

It suffices for our present purpose to state that first of all science laid its hands on the notions of planets and showed that they were all regular. But it left comets and meteors alone for a long while; and the kind of narrow religion which has based the evidence of god only on the exceptional, specified by certain events which she called miraculous, could say and did say "yes, the motions of the planets are part of the constitution of the universe and do not need God", but look at the comet's tail measuring millions and millions of miles in length and sweeping across the skies and look at the shower of falling stars. God does not leave the universe alone, you see here His hand. But science presently stretched out her hand and swept them — did them up in bundles, labelled them and showed that they, too, were part of the regular order and not special interferences at all. All that has been the lively and sporting game of science all along, and she keeps steadily filching away all miraculous evidences one after another on which popular religion relied for its existence, and arranging them in her own territory as regular, orderly parts of the universe, till it looks as if the religion which relies on the special interference of God would have nothing left at all, for science will have parcelled out and appropriated the whole area of phenomena as belonging to her domain. This is why blind orthodox religion cries out in angry protest at every fresh advance of science. Every such advance of religion seems to be the substitution of natural forces for the action of God in some fresh sphere. So the progress of science necessarily seems to be a progress towards atheism. As science shows that natural law covers the history of the heavenly bodies, of the earth, of organic life, each of these seems to be taken away from God. And so a false theology has successively fought against the protagonists, particularly of astronomy, geology, biology and execreted them as the enemies of God, and looked upon science as a godless and blind teacher, a sacrilegious intruder upon the domain of revealed truth. And thus among all denominations and phases of religious thought there was more or less suspicion, jealousy and abuse of scientific research and physical investigation. It was also a fact almost equally patent that on the part of science likewise — among many at least of its representatives, there was a similar hostility entertained towards religion and that only all religious organisations but all spiritual faiths and principles were looked upon as their natural foes.

Science and Religion

True religion, wherever it exists, recognises science as divine in all knowledge. It therefore welcomes every scientific discovery which expands man's ideas and vision of the universe and the discoverers are hailed as the prophets and messengers of God. Calumny, persecution, torture will not be their fate, as in days gone by, for daring to denounce, popular, powerful, anointed, religious, scriptural beliefs, such as, the flatness of the earth, the myriad-hooded serpent, Ādiśeṣa supporting the earth, the stationariness of the globe, of the creation of the world.

The eighteenth century was much occupied by a controversy between two schools, the Neptunists, who attributed almost everything to water, and the volcanists, who equally over-emphasized volcanoes and earthquakes. The former sect, who were perpetually collecting evidences of the Deluge, laid great stress on the marine fossils found at great altitudes on mountains. They were the more orthodox and therefore the enemies of orthodoxy tried to deny that fossils were genuine remains of animals.Voltaire was especially sceptical; and when he could not longer deny their organic origin he maintained that they had been dropped by pilgrims. In this instance, dogmatic free thought showed itself even more unscientific than orthodoxy. Bufforn, the great naturalist, in his Natural History maintained fourteen propositions which were condemned by the Sorbonne theological faculty in Paris as 'reprehensible'. These were that the present mountains and valleys of the earth are due to secondary causes, and that the same cause will in time destroy all the continents, hills and valleys, and reproduce others like them. Here 'secondary causes' means all causes other than God's creative flat; thus in 1749 it was necessary to the orthodox to believe that the world was created with the same hills and valleys, and that the same distribution of land and sea, as we find now except where, as in the case of the Dead Sea, a change had been wrought by miracle. Columbus who discovered a new continent need not fear disgrace at the hands of the theologians at Salamanea, because of his inability to adduce support for his theory of discovery in the scriptures of his religion. Copernicus need not surpass his heliocentric theory of the heavens for 36 years and escape persecution only by death. Galileo will not be tortured and compelled to recant his famous declaration that the earth moves. Bruno will not be burnt alive for daring to assert a plurality of worlds. Lyell for his revolutionary geological conceptions and Darwin for his astounding theory of 'the descent of man' will not be execrated as the enemies of God. On the other hand, religion and seience are now regarded as a complement, and supplement the natural friend and ally of each other. The first writer to set forth a modern scientific view in geology was Hutton, whose *Theory of the Earth* was first published in 1788, and in an enlarged form in 1795. He assumed that the changes which have occurred in past times on the surface of the earth were due to causes which are now in operation and which there is no reason to suppose are more active in the past than in the present. Although this was in the main a sound maxim, Hutton carried it too far in some respects, and not far enough in others. He attributed the disappearance of continents to denudation, with the consequent deposition of sediments on the bottom of the sea; but the rise of new continents he attributed to violent convulsions. He did not sufficiently recognise the sudden sinking of land or its gradual rise. But all scientific geologists since his day have accepted his general method of interpreting the past by means of the present, and attributing the vast changes to those causes which were now observed to be slowly altering coast-lines, increasing or diminishing the height of mountains, and raising or lowering the ocean-bed.

It was chiefly the Mosaic chronology that had kept men from adopting this point of view at an earlier date and the upholders of Genesis made vehement onslaughts on Hutton and his disciple Playfair. "The party feeling," says Lyell in his *Principles of Geology*, excited against the Huttonian doctrines, and the open disregard of candour and temper in the controversy will hardly be credited by the reader, unless he recalls to his recollection that the mind of the English public was at that time in a state of feverish excitement. The progress of geology is entangled with that of biology owing to the multitude of extinct forms of life of which fossils preserve a record. Insofar as the antiquity of the world was concerned, geology and theology could come to terms by agreeing that the six days were to be interpreted as six ages. But on the subject of animal life, theology has a number of very definite views, which it was found increasingly difficult to reconcile with science. No animals preyed on each other until after the Fall; all animals now existing belong to species represented in the ark; the species now extinct were, the few exceptions, drowned in the flood. Species are immutable, and each has resulted from a separate act of creation. To question of these propositions was to incur the hostility of theologians.

Modern physical science, one cardinal principle of which is, as stated above, the unity of the whole universe, the latent truth and reality of all persistent forces, has established that the universe is not an eternal quiescene. It is in constant change and constant motion. These changes and motions, are part of a series actually existing and progressing. No matter what intermediate cause there may have been, the mind is not satisfied to stop with any of these but passes farther and farther back seeking the first cause which must some time have first started the series. Now this first cause cannot be matter itself, for matter has no spontaneity of action. The essential idea of matter is that it is inert, as already stated above; remains in its present condition for ever unless disturbed by some external agency. If matter did not observe this law, no science of it would be possible. In whatever condition and position matter originally existed, in that it must always have remained. To start the evolution of the universe, therefore, some external agency possessed of spontaneity, acting upon matter, must be inferred. As the only spontaneous agent we know of is self-conscious free-will, the will of some supreme being must be regarded as The Great First cause.

Lord Kelvin, popularly known as the investigator of nature, was, after a research extending over a period of sixty years, promoted to announce to the world in unequivocal language that "the phenomena of living things, such as a spring of mass, a microbe, a living animal and the natural interdependence of vegetable and animal life and the wonderful design displayed in them, looked and considered as a matter of scientific investigation compels us to conclude that there is a scientific reason for believing in the existence of a creative mind and directing power.

The mathematician, the geologist, the astronomer, the naturalist, the biologist, and the physiologist, among others, are all able to tell us that there are objects in nature which are constricted and regulated in their functions and movements according to definite and immutable laws — laws characterised by super-human wisdom, working not only for particular ends but working together in perfect harmony for the preservation and welfare of the whole universe. They will also tell us that mere chance is absolutely excluded from the operation of these laws, that everything is the result of antecedent cause; that wherever changes or developments occur in substance or organism, they manifestly fulfill some ulterior purpose; and whenever the power to produce such change does not exist in the subject of that change, the power is not it; a motive power must act apart from the substance or organism, a power, which the latter does not possess. And whenever we observe any process of this kind, some mind of intelligence has had that purpose in view and either has furnished the substance or organism with the motive power necessary for the accomplishment of the purpose, or itself works in and through the said substance or organism for effecting the purpose.

The astronomer tells us that in the earth's circuit round the sun, an orbit of about 583 millions of miles, its average speed is between 18 to

20 miles a second, so that in one day of 24 hours, it travels about a million and a half miles. The orbit is not quite an exact circle but elliptical. The sun is not in the centre, therefore the earth must be at one time of its revolution nearer the sun than it is at another. There are two danger of its running wholly away from the sun into space, when it is farthest from it, in spite of the sun's power of attraction to keep it in its orbit. How marvellously these dangers are prevented by the earth simply hastening and slackening its speed to suit the varying conditions. As she approaches nearer and nearer to the sun as in winter, she has to put in greater speed in order to overcome the stronger attraction of the sun. We have to move faster to prevent our falling into the sun. Thereafter in six months time we shall be at our farthest distance from the sun. The sun's pull upon us will then grow weaker and we shall be in danger of flying off our track altogether unless we diminish speed and give the sun time to get a better grip upon us; that saves us from our other peril, and instead of flying off in space, we are bent round and turn the corner in safety.

How marvellous also it is that the earth having completed its circuit round the sun and having travelled at various degrees of speed and been subject to other disturbances on its path nevertheless, turns up at Greenwhich to within the one-hundredth part of a second. The earth being dead matter, its exceedingly sensible behaviour under changing circumstances must be attributed to a super-human mind working it or in it, a mind which understands fully the laws of centripetal and centrifugal motion and imposes those laws upon our planet, as elsewhere, to carry out its purpose of keeping it always in its orbit. Besides, our earth, is so related to the sun and moon that seed time and harvest never fail, and the ebb and flow of tides never deceives us.

The naturalist tells us of the life and economy of the clover plant, revealing the secrets of its marvellous powers of self-preservation and the contrivances for its survival and reproduction. This intelligence and forethought revealed in its organisation and habits far surpass anything which the skill or mind of man could have produced. The clover is so constituted that only bees can fertilise it and the bee is so organised the one of its chief occupations is to gather honey from the clover and by its visits unconsciously to fertilise the clover seeds. Here we have one purpose manifest in the reproduction of the clover which it cannot and does not do by itself. On the other hand, we have another purpose manifest, i.e., the gathering of honey by the bee, which involves the accomplishment of the purpose of reproduction. We know that the bee no more made itself; than the clover made itself and certainly the bee did not make the clover nor the clover made the bee. In other words we cannot posit the power of constructing the organism in the organism themselves, and we cannot ascribe the purpose of fertilising the clover to the bee any more than we can ascribe the purpose of furnishing honey to the clover. We see a double purpose which cannot be traced to the subjects concerned, and which is carried out by a double process which neither of them could originate, much less achieve. We find, therefore, that the adaptation of the bee and the clover to each other's purposes, of which they are not conscious, is the plan and achievement of some intelligent, designing and creative power.

The physiologist tells us that the gastric juice secreted by the stomach dissolves all ailments, but does not dissolve the stomach itself, although the latter is of precisely the same nature as the ailments with which it is nourished, because it is lined with a coating which is not attacked by the gastric juice and which protects the walls which it covers. What could the most perfect art have done to protect the walls of the stomach, but invent a precaution similar to that which exists in reality? And how surprising it is that an organ destined to secrete and use an agent most destructive to itself, is found armed with a protective tunic, which must have always co-existed with it, since otherwise it would have been destroyed before having had time to procure for itself this defence. Does this not display intelligence of a designing and creative mind?

Again, Tyndall gives a very graphic description of the combination of the remarkable arrangements by which the human ear is fitted to be an organ of hearing. Says he,

> Finally, there is in labyrinth a wonderful organ, discovered by the Marchese Corti, which is to all appearance a musical instrument, with its chords so stretched as to accept vibration of different periods, and transmit them to the nerve-filaments

> which traverse the organ. Within the ears of men and without their knowledge this lute of 3000 strings has existed for ages, accepting the music of the outer world, and rendering it fit for reception by the brain. Each musical tremor which falls upon this organ selects for its tensioned fibres the one appropriate to its own pitch and throws that fibre into unisonant vibration. And thus, no matter how complicated the motion of the external air, may be, those microscopic strings can analyse it and reveal the constituents of which it is composed.

Does not this wonderful phenomenon of which the possessor of the ear is absolutely unaware, disclose the existence of a super-human intelligence directing it?

The geologist tells us that inorganic products grow by accretion, by the external addition of one part to another by one force acting upon another. The botanist and the biologist tell us that a vegetable or animal germ, on the other hand, sustains itself by its own power. External objects is a matter which is added to it. It is not mere accretion as in inorganic objects but assimilation, turning of external matter to its own use by the inherent power of the germ. This wonderful process involves selection which directly carries purpose with it and confirms the existence of an intelligent mind behind it.

Furthermore, while in the case of inorganic matter, the cause determines the effect, the parts determine the whole, the present determines the future; in the case of organic matter, it is the effect that determine the cause, the whole that determine the parts and the future that determines the present. The vegetable seed grows into the tree with trunk, branches, leaves, flowers and fruits — members which in their turn sustain in the life of the whole tree and contribute to the production of the seed for the perpetuation of its kind. The animal germ likewise grows into the finished animal body with its complex system of organs, each devoted to a particular function and all contributing to the life and reproduction of the whole. In these instances, we see that what comes last, the completed organism with its various functions is potentially contained in the seed or the germ and determines its whole process of life and growth. But this potential existence of the effect in the cause can mean nothing else than this, that the idea or design of the effect determines or works in the cause and that it can emanate only from an intelligent mind.

Again, from the wise adaptation of means to ends in vegetable and animal life, the physiologist and the anatomist are accustomed to infer certain design and purposes as their explanation and they freely employ this idea of design to assist them in solving the problems of their department. Moreover, from such cases of curious adaptation, as in the life and economy of the clover and the bee explained above. Science has not only affirmed design but also some designer, but unfortunately does not penetrate further to know more about this designer. Religion, however carries on the work employing the same principles of reasoning, argues from the evidence of fitness and contrivance in the world, intelligent design and from the intelligent design, an intelligent designer of supreme power and wisdom equal to the supreme work manifested in the universe of creation.

Botany tells us how the petals twine into one another to constitute the citadel of the future flower and fruit. This says religion, is too handiwork of a deep-sighted genius who, as Plato observes, geometries, everywhere. A certain student of Plato went into a meadow and marvelled to note in countless flowers the same unfailing symmetry in the several parts. He exclaimed: "Plato thou speakest the truth when thou didst declare that God geometries."

Stronger verification, then, than this would hardly seem to be desired of Religion by anyone. Yet, if it is demanded it has a further confirmation. "There is no more convincing proof", says Professor Jevons, "of the soundness of scientific knowledge than that it thus confers the gift of foresight." "Prevision", says Auguste Comte, "is the test of true theory." The astronomer's wonderful prediction of the movements of the planets, the occurrence of eclipses, the return of comets — even as in Leverrier's discovery of Neptune, the existence and movement of a hitherto unknown body — afford the most conspicuous proof of the correctness of the Copernican system and the Newtonian Laws. By mere mathematical calculations one can map out the whole orbit of a planet precisely as the telescope may slowly trace it. Does not this disclose the unerring ways of the Great Geometrician? Once at Dublin, Sir Robert Ball, the great astronomer, concluded through his calculations that the transit of Venus would occur at a particular definite movement. Accordingly, he sets his telescope to the expected region of the sky, though overcast with dense clouds. At the right minute, the weather clears a white and reveals the planet as it floats majestically across the solar disc. Such is the wonderful order and correlation disclosed by astronomy.

The secret underlying the story of blinding of Śukrācārya, the Venus by Lord Vāmana, the incarnation of the Supreme Lord, during the time of Danvendra, Bali Raja who was the then reigning Indra, is that though now we belong to the Northern Indra system, the Devendra, yet 13,13,13,000 years before our earth was towards the Southern Indra star, the Danvendra, with respect to our solar systems and its primary, the *Ṛṣi* star and its primary, the Dhruva star. With respect to the motion of polaris, the Dhruva star, when our earth moves in the northern celestial hemisphere, then the Northern Indra star rules the earth, and when our earth moves in the southern celestial hemisphere, the Southern Indra star rules the earth. After the great deluge, when the earth comes out of the waters and enters in the southern celestial hemisphere, then Raja Bali, the incarnation of the Southern Indra star, the *Jyeṣṭhā nakṣatra*, Antares takes possession on this earth, as a king, and when the solar system moves towards the north again, then comes the turn of the Northern Indra star to take possession of this world. Therefore, Bali, the Danvendra, was ordered to vacate the throne to Devendra as the former's time was over.

Stars of the southern celestial hemisphere are called *dānavas*, and the stars of the northern hemisphere are called *devas*, so that the two Indra stars are known as Danvendra and Devendra respectively.

Śukrācārya was the incarnation of the Venus. And because it is an inferior planet, having its orbit within the orbit of the earth, it cannot go round the earth and receive the light of the sun as does the moon on every full moon day. It can be seen rising but only up to 46^0 when it again returns back towards the sun, on its revolutionary course, fading day by day till at last it is lost behind the disc of the sun. Hence, it is seen as the Morning Star when it rises and sets in the east, and as the Evening Star when it rises and sets in the west. Venus seems to receive light from the earth only on a half-portion, so that it is said to be blind, having only one eye.

The blinding of Śukrācārya by the Lord signifies that the Venus star was self-radiant till then and thereafter, became a planet and was not self-radiant.

More than all, every fibre in a living frame, every hair in the back of a worm, the slenderest line or the faintest tint on a leaf — all are scrupulously designed and attended to in God's government. 'Nothing walks with aimless feet'. Everything has a definite purpose in the ordering of the world. If the globe became lighter by the weight of one grass blade, its orbit would be inconceivably disturbed and the crisis of a clash would at once be introduced into the system of the universe.

Newton, the great discoverer of gravitation, declares:

> It is inconceivable that inanimate brute matter, should without the medium of something else which is not material operate upon and affect other matter without mutual contact. That gravity should be innate, inherent, and essential to matter, so that one body may act upon another through a vacuum, without the mediation of anything else, by and through which their action and force may be conveyed from one to the other, is to me so great an absurdity, that I believe no man who is philosophical has a competent faculty of thinking can ever fall into it.

Referring to 'Force' which brings about a succession of events in 'Nature', Professor Huxley, the celebrated physiologist, who is rightly or wrongly believed by many to be an avowed atheist and sceptic, states — 'Undoubtedly active force is inconceivable except as a state of consciousness, except as something comparable to volition."

Sir John Herschel similarly says:

> In the only case in which we are admitted to any personal knowledge of the origin of force, we find it connected, possibly

> by intermediate links untraceable by our faculties, but yet indispensably connected with volition, and by inevitable consequence with motive, with intellect and with all those attributes of mind in which — and not in the possession of arms, legs, brains and viscera — personality consists.

Kepler, the prince of astronomers, proclaiming his grand hypothesis of the law of the planetary distance in his celebrated work, *The Harmony of Worlds*, touched the zenith of the scientific intellect when, obsessed by the conviction that in tracing out the laws of nature he was thinking of God's thoughts after him, he exclaimed awe-struck:

> O God, I think Thy thoughts after Thee. I think Thee, my creator and Lord that thou hast given me this joy in Thy creation, this delight in the works of Thy hand. I have shown the excellency of Thy works unto men, so far as my finite mind was able to comprehend Thine infinity. If I have said aught unworthy of Thee or aught in which I have sought my own glory, graciously forgive it.

Lyell, the great geologist, concludes both his *Elements of Geology* and *Principle of Geology* by affirming that geological research finds in all directions the clearest indications of a creative intelligence, that as we increase our knowledge of the inexhaustible variety displayed in nature, and admire the infinite wisdom and power which it manifests, our admiration is multiplied by the reflection, that it is only the last of a great series of pre-existing creations, of which we cannot estimate the numbers or limit in times past.

The idea of a creative intelligence and mysterious force making living things behave in their various ways, each according to its kind, has occurred to more than one philosopher. Shaw calls it the life-force and this life force was interpreted over a century ago by Schopenhaur as "The World Will" and as 'Idea and will in Nature'. According to them, nature is no independent power, but it is the work of a super-human something existing as It wishes it to exist, reflecting Its mind and purpose and therefore trustworthy witness of it.

As in the only case where we know force directly in the human constitution, we find it to be an attribute of will and intelligence, an energy and expression of spirit, we must infer in accordance with the general rule of science to interpret the unknown by the known, that force is everywhere else but an energy and expression of a spirit, a conscious power or will, a creative mind, an infinite intelligence. And of what other spirit can it be than of the one infinite and almighty personality whom the *ṛṣi*s proclaimed as *parabrahman*, as *paramātman*, as the self and described and glorified Him in different ways according to their individual perceptions as shown below:

> He from whom the universal world proceeds, who is the Lord of the universe and whose work is the universe, is the supreme being. — *Taittirīya Upaniṣad*

> From His love surely have all these beings been born; by his love created beings are sustained and into His love they proceed and enter. — *Taittirīya Upaniṣad*

> The Supreme Being is the God, who is in fire, who is in water, who interpenetrates the whole world, who is in herbs, who is in big trees. To him we bow down agains and again.
> — *Śvetāśvatara Upaniṣad*

Let us now go back to the testimony of science to the God-vision of the *ṛṣi*s. From what has been stated already it follows that every fact which science can tell the world, every law it can unravel, every force it can trace out has some divine message for man. Every natural phenomenon, be it bacteria in sealed flasks or coloured bands in a spectrum, be it building power of molecule, mimicry of insects, natural selection among animals, has something to tell of God's thoughts and powers and methods of action. Nature then to the religious man constitutes God's oldest Testament, His most direct scripture and His most inspiring revelation. The ideas disclosed in it are God's thoughts; natural laws are divine laws which are the modes of the manifestation of the divine being, the enunciation of His wise designs. Natural history is a chapter of natural theology. The principles of philosophy are the expositions of His profound purposes.

The first writer to set forth a modern scientific view in geology was Hutton, whose *Theory of the Earth* was first published in 1788, and in an enlarged form in 1795. He assumed that the changes which have occurred in past times on the surface of the earth were due to causes which are now in operation, and which there is no reason to present. Although this was in the main a sound maxim, Hutton carried it too far in some respects, and not far enough in others. He attributed the disappearance of continents to denudation, with consequent deposition of sediment on the bottom of the sea; to violent convulsions. He did not sufficiently recognise the sudden sinking of land or its gradual rise. But all scientific geologists since his day have accepted his general method of interpreting the past by means of the present, and attributing the vast changes which have occurred during geological time to those very causes which are now observed to be slowly altering coast-lines, increasing or diminishing the height of mountains, and raising or lowering the ocean bed.

It was chiefly the mosaic chronology that had kept men from adopting this point of view at an earlier date, and the upholders of Genesis made vehement onslaughts on Hutton and his disciple Playfair. "The Party feeling," says Lyell, "excited against the Huttoniam doctrines, and the open disregard of candour and temper in the controversy will hardly be credited by the reader, unless he recalls to his recollection that the mind of the English public was at the time in a state of feverish excitement. A class of further progress of geology is entangled with that of biology, owing to the multitude of extinct forms of life of which fossils preserve a record. Insofar as the antiquity of the world was concerned, geology and theology could come to terms by agreeing that the six 'days' were to be interpreted as six 'ages' — But on the subject of animal life, theology had a number of very definite views, which it was found increasingly difficult to reconcile with science. No animals preyed on each other until after the Fall; all animals now extinct belong to species represented in the ark; the species now extinct were, with few exceptions, drowned in the flood. Species are immutable, and each has resulted from a separate act of creation. To question any of these proposition was to incur the hostility of theologians.

The first biologist who gave prominence to the doctrine of evolution was Lamarck. His doctrines, however, failed to win acceptance, not only on account of the prejudice in favour of the immutability of the species, but also because the mechanism of change which he suggested was not one which scientific men could accept. He believed that the production of a new organ in an animal's body results from its feeling a new want; and also that what has been acquired by an individual in the new course of its life is transmitted to its offspring without the second hypothesis; the first would have been useless as part of the explanation of evolution. Darwin who rejected the first hypothesis as an important element in the development of new species, still accepted the second, through it had less prominence in the system of Lamarck's. The second hypothesis, as to the inheritance of acquired characters, was vigorously denied by Weissmann, and although the controversy still continues, the evidence is now overwhelming that, with possible rare exceptions the only acquired characters that are inherited are those that affect the germ cells, which are very few. The Lamarckian mechanism of evolution cannot therefore be accepted.

Lyell's *Principles of Geology*, first published in 1830, a book which, by its emphatic statement of the evidence for the antiquity of the earth and of life, caused a great outcry among the orthodox, was nevertheless not, in its earlier editions, favourable to the hypothesis of organic evolution. It contained a careful discussion of Lamarck's theories, which it rejected on good scientific grounds. In later editions, published after the appearance of Darwin's *Origin of Species* the theory of evolution is guardedly favoured.

Darwin's theory was essentially an extension to the animal and vegetable world of *laissez-faire* economics, and was suggested by Malthus's theory of population. All living things reproduce themselves so fast that the greater part of each generation must die without having reached the age to leave descendants. The human populations, though their rate of natural increase is slower than that of any other animals except elephants have been known double in 25 years. If this rate continued throughout the world for the next two centuries, the resulting population would amount to five hundred thousand millions. But we find, in fact that animal and plant populations are, as a rule roughly stationary; and the same has been true of human populations. It follows, that if some members of a species differ from others in any way which gives them advantage, they are more likely to survive. If the difference has been acquired, it will not be transmitted to their descendants, but if it is congenital it is likely to reappear in at least, a fair proportion of their posterity. Lamarck's view on is that the giraffe has a long neck as a result of stretching of its neck up to the high branches, and that the results of this stretching became hereditary for giraffe's. The Darwinian view at least as modified by Weismann, is that giraffes from birth, had a tendency to long necks, and were less likely to starve than others; therefore, they left more descendants, which in turn were likely to have long necks — some of them, probably, even longer necks than their already long-necked parents.

Darwin's theory depended upon the occurrence of chance variations, the causes of which, as he confessed, were unknown. It is an observed fact that domestic animals have been greatly changed by artificial selection; through the agency of man, cows have come to yield more milk, race horses to run faster, and sheep to yield more wool. Such facts afforded the most direct evidence available to Darwin of what selection could accomplish. It is true that breeders cannot turn a fish into a marsupial or a marsupial into a monkey; but changes as great as these might be expected to occur during the countless ages counted by the geologists. There was, moreover, in many cases, evidence of common ancestry. Fossils showed that animals intermediate between widely separated species of the present had existed in the past; the pterodactyl for example, was half bird, half reptile. Embryologists discovered that, in the course of development, immature animals repeat earlier forms; a mammalian foetus, at a certain stage, has the rudiments of a fish's gills, which are totally useless and hard to explained except as a surviving feature. Many different lines of argument combined to persuade biologists both of the fact of evolution, and of natural selection as the chief means by which it was brought about. Darwinism was as severe a blow to theology as Copernicanism. Not only was it necessary to abandon the fixity of species and the many separate acts of creation which Genesis seemed to assert; not only was it necessary to assume a lapse of time since the origin of life which was shocking to the orthodox; not only was it necessary to abandon a host of arguments for the beneficence of providence derived from the exquisite adaptation of animals to their environment, which was now explained as the operation of natural selection—but, worse than any or all of these, the evolutionists ventured to affirm that man was descended from the lower animals.

The conception of purpose is a natural one to apply to a human artificer. A man who desires a house cannot, except in *The Arabian Nights*, have it rise before him as a result of his mere wish; time and labour must be expended before his wish can be gratified. But omnipotence is not subject to such limitations. If God really thinks well of the human race — an unplausible hypothesis, as it seems to me — why not proceed as in Genesis, to create man at once? What was the point of the ichtyosaurs, dinosaurs, diplodochi, mastodons, and so on? Barnes himself confesses, somewhere that the purpose of the tapeworm is a mystery. What useful purpose is served by rabies and hydrophobia? It is not answer to say that the laws of nature inevitably produce evil as well as good, for God decreed the laws of nature. The evil which is due to sin may be explained as the result of our free will, but the problem of evil in the pre-human world remains. Barnes accepted the solution offered by William Gillespie that the bodies of beasts of prey were inhabited by devils, whose first sins antedated the brute creation; yet it is difficult to see what other logically satisfying answer can be suggested. The difficulty is old, but nonetheless real. An omnipotent Being who created a world containing evil must Himself be at least partially evil.

To this objection the pantheistic and emergent forms of the doctrine of cosmic purpose are less exposed. Pantheistic evolution varies according to the particular brand of Pantheism evolved; that of Professor J.S. Haldane which we are now to consider, is connected with Hegel, and, like everything Hegelian is not very easy to understand. But the point of view is one which has had considerable influence throughout the past hundred years and more, so that it is necssary to examine it. Moreover, Professor Haldane is distinguished for his work in various special fields, and has exemplified his general philosophy by detailed investigations, particularly in physiology, which appeared to him to demonstrate that the science of living bodies has need of other laws besides those of chemistry and physics. This fact adds weight to his general outlook.

According to this philosophy, there is not strictly speaking any such thing as 'dead' matter, nor is there any living matter without something of the nature of consciousness, and to go one step further there is no consciousness which is not in some degree divine. The distinction between appearance and reality which we considered briefly in Mysticism is involved in Professor Haldane's views, although he does not mention it; but now, as with Hegel, it has become a distinction of degree rather than of kind. Dead matter is least real living matter; human consciousness still more, but the only conceived of complete reality is God, i.e., the universe is conceived divine.

Haldane says "to make mechanistic interpretation the sole basis of our philosophy of life, we must abandon completely our traditional religious beliefs and many other ordinary beliefs." Fortunately, however, he thinks, there is no need to explain everything mechanistically, i.e., in terms of chemistry and physics, nor, indeed is this possible, since biology, needs the conception of the organism. "From the physical standpoint life is nothing less than a standing miracle." "Hereditary transmission . . . itself implies the distinguishing feature of life as co-ordinated unity always tending to maintain and reproduce itself." "If we assume that life is not inherent in nature, and that there must have been a time before life existed, this is an unwarranted assumption which would make the appearance of life totally unintelligible". "The fact that biology bars the door decisively against a final mechanistic interpretation of our experience is at least very significant in connection with our ideas as to religion". "The relations of conscious behaviour to life are analogous to those of life to mechanism". "For psychological interpretation the present is no more fleeting moment; it holds within it both the past and the future". As biology needs the concept organism, so psychology needs that of personality; it is a mistake to think of a person as made up of a soul plus a body or to suppose that we know only sensations, not the external world, for the truth in the environment is not outside us. "Space and time do not isolate personality; they express an order within it, so that the immensities of space and time are within it, as Kant saw."

From this point, we are ready to take the next step, from single personalities to God."Personality is not merely individual. It is in this fact that we recognise the presence of God — God present nor merely as a being outside us, but within and around us as the personality of personalities. "It is only within ourselves, in our active ideals of truth right, charity and beauty and consequent fellowship with others that we find the revelation of God." Freedom and immortality we are told, belong to God, not to human individuals who in any case are not quite real. Were the whole human race to be blotted out, God would still, as from all eternity, be the reality, and in His existence what is real in us would continue to live.

One last consoling reflection: from the reality of God, it follows that the poor ought not to mind being poor. It is foolish to grasp at 'unreal shadows of the passing moment, such as useless luxury.' "The real standard of the poor may be far more satisfying than that of the rich." For those who are starving, one gathers, it will be a comfort to remember that "the only ultimate reality is the spiritual which we denote by the existence of God." The Pantheistic doctrine of Cosmic purpose like the theistic doctrine, suffers, though in a somewhat different way, from the difficulty of explaining the necessity of a temporal evolution. If time is not ultimately real — as practically all pantheists believe, why should the best things in the history of world come later rather than early? Would not the reverse order have done just as well? If the idea that events have dates is an illusion, from which God is free why should He choose to put the pleasant events at the end and the unpleasant ones at the beginning? I agree with Dean Inge's view which is expressed in *Outspoken Essay*, Volume II as

> We magnify the problem of evil by our narrower moralism, which we habitually impose upon the Creator. There is no evidence for the theory that God is a merely moral being, and what we observe of His laws and operations here indicates strongly that He is not thinking this question unanswerable.

The emergent doctrine which was expressed by Alexander is that dead matter, living matter, and mind, have appeared successively and continue. The term is called emergence. Life emerges from matter and mind from life. A living being is also a material being, but one so fashioned as to exhibit a new quality which is life . . . And the same thing may be said of the transition from life to mind. A mindful being is also a living being but one of such complexity of development, so finely organised in certain of its parts, and particularly in its nervous system, as to carry mind — or if you please to use the word, consciousness.

He goes on to say that there is no reason why this process should cease with mind. On the contrary, it suggests a further quality of existence beyond mind, which is related to mind as mind to life or life to matter. That quality I call deity, and the being which possesses it is God. It seems to me, therefore, that all things point to the emergence of this quality, and that is why I said that science itself, when it takes the wider view requires deity. The world, he says is "striving or tending to deity" but "deity has not in its distinctive nature as yet emerged at this stage of the world's existence." He adds that, for him God, "is not a creator as in historical religions, but created."

There is a close affinity between Alexander's views and those of Bergson's *Creative Evolution*. Bergson holds that determinism is mistaken because, in the course of evolution, genuine novelties emerge, which could not have been predicated in advance or even imagined. There is a mysterious force which urges everything to evolve. For example, an animal which cannot see has some mystic foreboding of sight and proceeds to act in a way that leads to the development of eyes. At each moment something new emerges, but the past never dies, being preserved in memory — for forgetting is only apparent. Thus the world is continually growing richer in content, and will in time become quite a nice sort of place. The one essential thing is to avoid the intellect, which looks backward and is static; what we must use is intuition, which contains within itself the urge to create novelty.

Various difficulties make the philosophy of emergent evolution unsatisfactory. Perhaps the chief of these is that, in order to escape from determinism, prediction is made impossible and yet the adherents of this theory predict the future existence of God. They are exactly in the position of Bergson's shell-fish, which wants to see although it does not know what seeing is. Alexander maintains that we have a vague awareness of deity in some experiences which he describes as 'numinous'.

The feeling which characterizes such experiences is, he says "the sense of mystery, of something which may terrify us or may support us in our helplessness, but at any rate which is other than anything we know by our senses or our reflection." He gives no reason for attaching importance to this feeling or for supporting that, as his theory demands, mental development makes it become a larger element in life. From anthropologists one would infer the exact opposite. The sense of mystery of a friendly or hostile non-human force, plays a far greater part in the life of savages than in that of civilised men.

Indeed, if religion is to be identified with this feeling every step in known human development has involved a diminution of religion. This hardly fits in with the supposed evolutionary argument for an emergent Deity.

The argument in any case, is extraordinarily thin. There have been, it is urged, three stages in evolution; matter, life and mind. We have no reason to suppose that the world has finished evolving, and there is therefore likely, at some later date, to be a fourth phase — and a fifth and a sixth and so on, one would have supposed. But no, with the fourth phase evolution is to be complete. Now matter could not have foreseen life, and life, could not have foreseen mind, but mind can, dimly, foresee the next stage, particularly if it is the mind of a Papuan or a Bushman. It is obvious that all this is the merest guesswork. It may happen to be true, but there is no rational ground for supporting it. The philosophy of emergence is quite right in saying that the future is unpredictable, but having said this, it at once proceeds to predict the future. People are more unwilling to give up the word 'God', than to give up the idea for which the word has hitherto stood. Emergent evolutionists, having become persuaded that God did not create the world, are content to say that the world is creating God. But beyond the name, such a God has almost nothing in common with the object of traditional worship.

With regard to cosmic purpose in general in whichever form, there are two criticisms to be made. In the first place, those who believe in cosmic purpose always think that the world will go on evolving in the same direction as hitherto in the second place, they hold that what has already happened is evidence of the good intentions of the universe. Both these propositions are open to questions.

As to the direction of evolution, the argument is mainly derived from what has happened on this earth since life began. Now this earth is a very small corner of the universe, and there are reasons for supposing it by no means typical of the rest. Jean considers it very doubtful whether, at the present time, there is life anywhere else. Before the Copernican revolution, it was natural to suppose that God's purposes were specially concerned with the earth, but now this has become an implausible hypothesis. If it is the purpose of the cosmos to evolve mind, we must regard it as rather incompetent in having produced so little in such a long time. If it, of course, possible that there will be more evolution of mind later on somewhere else, but of this we have no scientific evidence. It may seem odd that life should occur by accident, but in such a large universe accidents will happen.

And even if we accept the rather curious view that the cosmic purpose is specially concerned with our little planet, we still find that there is reason to doubt whether it intends quite what the theologians say it does. The earth is likely to remain habitable for some time, but not for ever. Perhaps our atmosphere will gradually fly off into space; perhaps the tides will cause the earth to turn always the same face to the sun, so that one hemisphere will be too hot and the other too cold; prhaps the moon will tumble into the earth. If none of these things happen first, we shall in any case be all destroyed when the sun explodes and becomes a cold white dwarf, which, we are told by Jeans, is to happen in about a million million years though the exact date is still somewhat uncertain.

A million million years gives us some time to prepare for the end, and we may hope that in the meantime both astronomy and gunnery will have made considerable progress. The astronomers may have discovered another star with habitable planets, and the gunners may be able to fire us off to it with a speed approaching that of light, in which case, if the passengers were all young to begin with, some might arrive before dying of old age. It is perhaps a slender hope, but let us make the best of it.

Coursing round the universe, however, even if it is done with the most perfect scientific skill, cannot prolong life for ever. The second law of thermodynamics tells us that, on the whole, energy is always passing from more concentrated to less concentrated forms and that, in the end, it will have all passed into a form in which further change is impossible. When that has happened if not before, life must cease. To quote Jeans once more "with Universe as with mortals the only possible life is progress to the grave". This leads him to certain reflections which are very relevant to our theme.

The three centuries which have elapsed since G. Bruno suffered martyrdom for believing in the plurality of worlds have changed our conception of the universe almost beyond description, but they have not brought us appreciably nearer to understanding the relation of life to the universe. We can still only guess as to the meaning of this life which, to all appearance, is so rare. Is it the final climax towards which the whole of creation moves, for which the millions of millions of yeara of the transformation of matter in uninhabited stars and nebulae, and of the waste of tradition in desert space have been only an incredibly extravagant preparation? Or is it a mere accidental and possibly quite unimportant by-product of natural processes, which have some other and more stupendous end in view? Or, to glance at a still more modest line of thought, must we regard it as something of the nature of a disease, which affects matter in its old age when it has lost the high temperature and the capacity for generating high-frequency radiation with which younger and more vigorous matter would at once destroy life? Or, throwing humility aside shall we venture to imagine that it is the only reality which is created by the colossal masses of the stars and nebulae and the almost inconceivably long vistas of astronomical time?

The last possibility that mind is the only reality and that the spaces and times of astronomy are created by it is one for which logically, there is much to be said. But those who adopt it, in the hope of escaping from depressing conclusions, do not quite realise what it entails. Everything that I know directly is part of my 'mind' and the inferences by which I arrive at the existence of other things are by no means conclusive. It may be, therefore that nothing exists except my mind. In that case, when I die the universe will go out. But if I am going to admit minds other than my own, I must admit the whole astronomical universe, since the evidence is exactly equally strong in both cases. Jeans's last alternative, therefore, is not the comfortable theory that other people's minds exist, though not their bodies; it is the theory that I am alone in an empty universe, inventing the human race, the geological ages of the earth, the sun and stars and nebulae, out of my own fertile imagination. Against this theory there is, so far as I know, no valid logical argument; but against any other form of the doctrine that mind is the only reality there is the fact that our evidence for other people's minds is derived by inference from our evidence for their bodies. Other people, therefore, if they have minds, have bodies, mind but only if oneself alone exists.

Modern men of science, if they are not hostile or indifferent to religion, cling to one belief which, they think, can survive amid the wreck of former dogmas — the belief, namely, in cosmic purpose. Liberal theologians equally, make this the central article of their creed. The doctrine has several forms, but all have in common the conception of evolution as having a direction towards something ethically valuable, which in some sense, gives the reason for the whole long process. J.A. Thomson, says that "science is incomplete because it cannot answer the question why? Religion, he thought, can answer it". Why are stars formed? Why did the sun give birth to planets? Why did the earth cool, and at last give rise to life? Because, in the end, something admirable was going to result — I am not quite sure what, but I believe it was scientific theologians and religiously minded scientists.

The doctrine has three forms — theistic, pantheistic and what may called 'emergent'. The first, which is the simplest and most orthodox, holds that God created the world and decreed the laws of nature because He foresaw that in time some good evolve. In this view the purpose exists consciously in the mind of the creator who remains external to His creation. In the Pantheistic form, God is not external to the universe, but is merely the universe considered as a whole. There cannot therefore be an act of creation, but there is a kind of creative force in the universe, which causes it to develop according to a plan which this creative force may be said to have had in mind throughout the process. In the emergent form, the purpose is more blind. At an earlier stage, nothing in the universe foresees a later stage, but a kind of blind impulsion leads to those changes which bring more developed forms into existence, so that in some rather obscure sense, the end is implicit in the beginning.

Within this narrow framework science was expected to confine itself, and those who thought 6,000 years too short a time for the existence of the visible universe were held up obliquely. They could no longer be burned or imprisoned, but theologians did everything possible to make their lives unhappy and to prevent the spread of their doctrines. Newton's work — the Copernican system having been accepted — did nothing to shake religious orthodoxy. He was himself a deeply religious man, and a believer in the verbal inspiration of the Bible. His universe was not one in which there was development, and might well, for aught that appeared in his teaching, have been created all of a piece. To account for the tangential velocities of the planets, which prevent them from falling into the sun, he supposed that initially they had been hurled by the hand of God; what had happened since was accounted for by the law of gravitation. It is true that, in a private letter to Bentley, Newton suggested a way in which the solar system could have developed from a primitive system, which is nearly uniform distribution of matter; but so far as his public and official utterances were concerned he assumed to favour a sudden creation of the sun and planets as we know them, and to leave no room for cosmic evolution.

From Newton, the eighteenth century acquired its peculiar brand of piety, in which God appeared essentially as the law-giver, who first created the world, and then made rules which determined all further events without any need of His special intervention. The orthodox allowed exceptions; there were the miracles connected with religion. But for the theists everything without exception, was regulated by natural law. Both views are to be found in Pope's *Essay on Man*. Thus in one passage he says:

> The first Almighty cause
> Acts not by partial, but by gen'ral laws;
> The exceptions few

But when the demands of orthodoxy are forgotten, the exceptions disappear:

> From Nature's chain whatever link you strike,
> Tenth, or ten thousandth, breaks the chain alike.
> And if each system in gradation roll
> Alike essential to the amazing whole,
> The least confusion not in one, but all
> That system only, but the whole must fall.
> The earth unbalanced from her orbit fly,
> Planets and suns run rawless through the sky;
> Let ruling angels from their spheres be hurl'd
> Being on being wreck'd, and world on world;
> Heav'n's whole foundation to their centre nod,
> And Nature tremble, to the throne of God.

The Reign of Law, as conceived in the time of queen Anne, is associated with political stability and the belief that the era of revolutions is past. When men again began to desire change, their conception of the workings of natural law became less static. The first serious attempt to construct a scientific theory of the growth of the sun, the planets, and the stars, was made by Kant in 1755, in a book called *General Natural History and Theory of the Heavens* or *Investigation of the Constitution and Mechanical Origin of the whole structure of the Universe*, treated according to Newtonian principles. This is a very remarkable work, which in certain respects, anticipates by setting the results of modern astronomy. It begins by setting forth that all the stars visible to the naked eye belong to one system, that of the Milky way. All these stars lie nearly in one plane, and Kant suggests that they have a unity not unlike that of the solar system. With remarkable imaginative insight, he regards the nebulae as other similar but immensely remote groups of stars — a view which is now generally held. He has a theory in part mathematically untenable, but broadly on the lines of stars which was subsequently investigated. That the nebulae, the galaxy, the stars, planets, and satellites, all resulted from condensation of an originally diffuse matter about regions in which it happened to have somewhat more density than elsewhere. He believes that the material universe is infinite, which, he says, is the only view worthy of the infinity of the Creator. He thinks that there is a gradual transition from chaos to organisation, beginning at the centre of gravity of the universe, and slowly spreading outwards from this point towards the remotest regions — a process involving infnite space and requiring infinite time.

What makes this work remarkable is, on the one hand, the conception of the material universe as a whole, in which galaxy and the nebulae are constituent units, and on the other hand, the notion of gradual development from an almost undifferentiated primal distribution of matter throughout space. This is the first serious attempt to substitute evolution for sudden creation, and it is interesting to observe that this new outlook appeared first in a theory of the heavens, not in connection with life on the earth. From this work of Kant evolved Laplace's famous nebular hypothesis which was published in 1796 in his *Exposition du systeme du Monde*, apparently in complete ignorance of the fact that it had been in a considerable degree anticipated by Kant. He held that what is now the system of the sun and the planets was originally a single diffuse nebula that gradually contracted, and in consequence rotated faster; that centrifugal force caused lumps to fly off, which became planets; and that the same process, repeated, gave rise to the satellites of the planets. Living, as he did, in the epoch of the French Revolution, he was a complete free thinker, and rejected the creation altogether. Laplace's great work on *Celestial Mechanics* contained no mention of God, the astronomer replied; "Sire, I have no need of that hyothesis." While the great geologist Woodward in 1695, explained the sedimentary rocks by supposing "the whole terrestrial globe to have been taken to pieces and dissolved at the flood, and the strata to have settled down from this promiscuous mass as any earthy sediment from a fluid." He taught, as Lyell says, that "the entire mass of fossiliferous strata contained in the earth's crust had been deposited in a few months." Thomas Burnet, who had published his *Sacred Theory of the Earth: Containing an Account of the Original of the Earth*, and of all the general changes which it hath already undergone, or is to undergo, till the consummation of all things." He believed that the Equator had been in the plane of the ecliptic until the flood, but had been pushed into its present oblique position. He thought that the sun's heat had cracked the earth and allowed the waters to emerge from a subterranean reservoir, thereby causing the flood. A second period of chaos, he maintained, was to usher in the millennium. His views, should however, be received with caution, as he did not believe in eternal punishment. When his error on the equator, and his other errors as well were avoided by Whiston whose book were published in 1696, it was called *A New Theory of the Earth*; wherein the creation of the world in six days, the Universal Deluge, and the General Conflagration, as laid down in the holy scriptures, are shown to be perfectly agreeable to reason and philosophy. This book was partly inspired by the comet of 1680, which led him to think that a comet might have caused the flood. In one point his orthodoxy was open to question; he thought the six days of creation were longer than ordinary days.

Mythological Evolution

We now turn to the lines of mythological evolution within the *Ṛgveda*. In the hymns to the Dawn, the sun and the Fire, among others, we are face to face with the corresponding physical phenomena exercising directly their beneficent powers. The process of personification next thus emerges the concrete figures of Uṣas, Sūrya and Agani with whom the poet holds, as it were, direct communion. We are not so fortunate in the case of the greatest figures of the Ṛgvedic pantheon, namely Varuṇa and Indra, regarding whose physical basis no certain conscious have yet been arrived at. But in the case of a large number of Ṛgvedic gods, we are able to trace the original forces or events in nature. Where the personification does not dominate the conception, the name of the deity is identical with that of the natural phenomenon, as in the case of Uṣas and Sūrya. Where the names differ, the personification has evidently advanced to the stage of anthropomorphism and apotheosis. The number of gods is now on the increase, the increase being due either to some striking attribute abstracted from the concrete personality of a deity and founding the conception of a new deity which develops independently, as in the case of Sāvitrī, taking up a concrete form later through association with some cosmic function or natural power.

Although the divine rank thus got swollen, there is no fixed order of seniority among the gods, as in a pantheon, in the strict sense of the term. Far too many functions, powers and offices are held in common by two or more deities. There is a sort of communism among them, though it is not thoroughgoing and for this "the belief in individual Gods alternatively regarded as the highest" (i.e., Henotheism as Max-Muller has named it) is responsible. The particular deity that the poet happens to be invoking monopolises, for the time being all attributes. The god is addressed for the moment as if he were the greatest and the only god. In the same breath, however, this mighty god is described as dependent on others.

In fact, the joint exercise of various powers, functions, and notable deeds by two or more or all the Gods is almost a favourite theme in the *Ṛgveda* hymnology. In a thoroughly impartial spirit, the mutual cooperation, interdependence, and subordination of the various deities in pairs or larger groups is often described. There is hardly a God in the *Ṛgveda* so insignificant as not to receive homage from others, not excluding the highest. 'Henotheism' in the strict sense of the term is not to be thought of because the divine host of the *Ṛgveda* is not a pantheon with an acknowledged overlord. Various explanations have been offered to account for this apparently inconsistent evaluation of divine ranks and dignities in the *Ṛgveda*. It has been urged, for example, that the inconsistency may be due to the partiality of a particular *ṛṣi* to a particular god. But the force of this repetition and their even distribution throughout the text. As Bloomfield observes, "no theory as to the character and origin literature is in a sense epigonal and they forbid pungent theories about profound differences between the family books, their authors, and their geographical provenance."

It has also been contended, as Macdonell points out that, "in the frequent hymns addressed to the Viśvedevas, all the deities, even the lesser ones, are praised in succession, and that as the great mass of the Vedic hymns was composed for the rituals of the *soma* offering, which included the worship of almost the entire pantheon, the technical priest could not but know the exact relative position of each god in that ritual." This explanation rests on the unwarranted assumption that the ritualists of a later age, when sacrificial technique was enormously developed, had to, and could, preserve very scrupulously the mythological values of Ṛgvedic poetry.

Another approach to the problem of introducing order and system into this apparent chaos has been through classification. There is, first of all, the traditional classification hinted at *Ṛgveda* and followed by *Yakṣa*, giving us triple divisions of the Vedic gods corresponding to the three orders, namely terrestrial, intermediate and celestial. *Pṛthivī*, Agni, Soma, Bṛhaṣpati and the rivers belong to the first order; to the second order Indra, *apam-napāt*, Rudra, *Vāyu-vāta*, Parjanya, *āpaḥ* and Mātariśvan; while the last order is Dyaus, Varuṇa, Mitra, Sūrya, Sāvitrī, Pūṣan, Viṣṇu, the Ādityas, Uṣas and the Aśvins. This classification is found on the natural basis which the deities represent, and is thus the most practical and least open to objection, which invokes Sūrya, Vāta and Agni for protection from the predecessors of *Yaṣka* whose views are quoted in the *Nirukta*, and who hold that there are only three representative deities — Sūrya in heaven, Vāyu in air and Agni on earth, each of these having various appellations according to differences of function. We now turn to the individual deities and give a brief survey of their noteworthy characteristics in the order of the spheres to which they belong. The oldest among the gods of heaven, going back to the Indo-European period, and identical with the Greek Zeus, is Dyaus, and a personification of the sky, a personification which, however did not advance beyond the idea of paternity. He is called ruddy bull bellowing downwards, a poetic description, probably of the colour of lightning, the fertilising power of rain and the thunder of heaven. The image of the beautiful star-studded sky of the night is obviously called up when Dyaus is once compared with a black steed bedecked with pearls. Dyaus is generally paired with *pṛthivī*, the earth, in the compound Dyāvāpṛthivī, the Universal Parents, who are celebrated in six hymns.

Varuṇa is addressed in the Ṛgvedic hymns as small in number. Varuṇa is the upholder of the physical and moral order symbolised by the *ṛta* with which he is more intimately connected than any other god. The Varuṇa hymns which are predominately ethical and devout in tone give us the most exalted poetry in the *Ṛgveda*. He supports heaven, earth and air. He, with Mitra, is most frequently invoked as a bestower of rain. He regulate the seasons. Neither god not mortal may violate his ordinances. Varuṇa's special connection with the waters is unmistakable. He is the regulator of the waters and causes the rivers constantly to pour into the sea. If the ocean does not overflow, although the rivers constantly pour into it, it is because of *māyā* of Varuṇa. He is, above all, the *dhṛtavrata,* the upholder of ordinances, such as the fixed paths of the luminaries across the sky. He stands out pre-eminently as the moral governor among all the deities. The fetters with which he binds sinners are characteristic of him in his capacity. Varuṇa in the *Ṛgveda* is pre-eminently the All-Pervader, the All-Encompasser, the All-Enveloper — an aspect fully agreeing with his name which appears to be derived from the root *vṛ*. This all-encompassing character is in keeping with his lordship over the twin spheres of light and darkness, of night as well as day, and with his position as supreme ruler of the physical and moral world and as the custodian of *ṛta*. This *ṛta*, which like a wheel circumscribes the universe, regulates it, and keeps it in place, is Varuṇa's *pāśa* and has for its physical basis, the belt of the Zodiac from which no luminary may deviate and the penalty for transgression whereof is ensnarement by the hackles of non-*ṛta* or darkness and death. This is one side of the all-ancompassing character of Varuṇa. Another and a more important side of Varuṇa's overlordship of the waters which is far more intimately connected with him in the *Ṛgveda*.

The waters are both terrestrial and celestial. The attributes to the latter in the *Ṛgveda* cannot all be satisfactorily accounted for on the hypothesis that they are rain-waters. (2) The release of the water and the breaking forth of the dawn or the emergence of light are described as simultaneous events. (3) In fact the movement of the waters and the spreading forth of the rays of light originate from the same source and follow the same path simultaneously. (4) These waters are described as moving upwards by Indra, simultaneously with the luminaries, after the killing of *Vṛtra*. Their downward movement is, of course, described in the *Ṛgveda* as when the seven rivers are said to flow into the jaws of Varuṇa as into a surging abyss. (5) The universe is said to have consisted of nothing but undifferentiated waters in the beginning. These waters are coeval with the universe. (6) The cosmic evolution of the celestial waters and the simultaneity of the free flow of waters and the rising of the Dawn are stated unambiguously in the Avestā. (7) This theory of the cosmic circulation of the waters is not peculiar only to the

Indo-Iranian mythology, but is found in Greek and Egyptians mythologies also. In other words, the celestial waters or watery vapours which pervaded the regions above, below, and around the earth were supposed by the *Ṛgvedic* poets to be stuff out of which the universe was created, and were, like the ether of modern scientists, the medium of the transmission of the light of the luminaries.

Ṛgvedic literature is no less colourful. The earliest attempt to classify Vedic hymns systematically according to contents is to be found in Yāska's *Nirukta*. Yāska proceeds to specify the characteristics and cite instances of the various types of hymns. There are, to begin with, hymns in pure praise of the deity without any prayers, as, for instance, the Indra-hymn being unmistakable characteristics of a popular ballad.

> The heroic deeds of Indra shall I proclaim, the deeds
> that the thunder-wielder performed first
> He slew the dragon, freed the waters, slit the bowels
> of the Hills.
>
> He slew the dragon resting on the hill
> Tvashta had forced for him the shining thunder,
> And the waters springing forth rushed towards the ocean,
> like cows lowing (at the sight of their calves)
>
> Like a broken reed there he lay.
> Over him flowed the waters gladdening hearts;
> These whom Vritra held beleaguered by his body —
> at their feet now he lay,
>
> As Dasa-wives stayed with waters guarded by the dragon, like the cows restrained by the panis the watery pit which was sealed — that he opened by slaying Vritra, and released the waters.
>
> Indra is the monarch of all that move and rest,
> the thunder-wielder is monarch of tame and horned animals;
> He indeed is ruler of all the peoples;
> like a felly round the spokes of a wheel he protects all.

Mitra is so closely associated with Varuṇa, that only one hymn is addressed to him alone separately and his individual character cannot be definitely established. His distinctly peculiar epithet is Yataya-jana the 'bestirrer of the people', because he marshals people into activity as the great Āditya. Mithra is a sun-god, the guardian of faithfulness in the Avestā, and Ṛgvedic evidence points to Mitra as a solar deity in the aspect of the benevolent power of nature as suggested by the name Mitra which originally meant 'an ally'.

Sūrya is the most concrete of the solar deities, the name (which designates the orb of the sun as well as the god) showing that this character seeing god, he is often called the eye of Mitra, Varuna. Agni and other gods. The dawns produce Sūrya and he is said to be the son of the goddess Aditi and Dyaus. He is a bird that flies through space. He is the eye cognate with the Avestic are, 'sun' who has swift horses and who is the eye of Ahura Mazda. Pūṣana is a god who acts as envoy of Sūrya with his golden aerial ships, and as a charioteer drives downward the golden wheel of the sun. He is the guardian of the roads, the deliverer *par excellence* from danger, and takes care of cattle. Aghrini is an exclusive epithet of his. Very probably, he was originally a solar deity standing for the beneficent power of the sun manifested chiefly in its pastoral aspect.

The word *aditi* is primarily a noun meaning 'non-binding'. Hence as a goddess, Aditi is naturally invoked to release her worshipper from bondage. This original meaning of unpersonified 'freedom' seems to survive in a few passage of the *Ṛgveda*. Now the Ādityas are several times described as the sons of Aditi, and this expression may have meant in the pre-Vedic age simply 'sons of freedom' and probably described a prominent quality of Varuṇa and the other Ādityas. Macdonell wonders, "But how are we to account for so early a personification of such an abstract idea, and in particular for Aditi becoming the mother of the Ādityas?." The explanation probably is as follows: "Aditi becoming the mother which is unmistakably connected with light in the *Ṛgveda*. Varuṇa — the Aditya — is connected prominently and almost exclusively with *ṛta*; so is Aditi. This *ṛta* has for its physical basis the belt of the Zodiac. Now the *devas*, the heaven, seem to be ancients to recover their freedom from clutches of darkness and to restart on their bright career from a fixed point in the east, lying on the belt of the zodiac or the *ṛta*. This point is thus into freedom and light from this fixed point received the epithet "sons of Aditi." Diti was the exactly opposite point on the path of the Zodiac in the west, where the light went out.

It will not be necessary on this theory to suppose that the name of Diti as goddess was merely an antithesis to that of the Aditi, formed from the latter to express a positive sense, as *sura*, 'god' was later evolved from *asura* 'demon'. It is to be noted in this connection that none of the wind or storm gods are called Ādityas. The latter are all gods of light. Six Ādityas are enumerated once the number being stated as seven and even eight in the last books of the *Ṛgveda*. In the case of Uṣas, the goddess of Dawn, the personification is slight, the poet never losing sight of the beautiful physical phenomena behind the deity. Yāska's brief and purely formal classification of the contents of the *Mantra*-texts, is however, anything but satisfactory. It is true that the main body of the hymns contain praises or prayers or both. But from the literary point of view they should best be regarded as lyrical poems adapted to the purpose of ritual. Of these the hymns addressed to Heaven's daughter Aurora (Uṣas) and perhaps the oldest and certainly the most beautiful have something of the lyrical beauty and love of nature of Shelley and Wordsworth, and one cannot help feeling that they were inspired by the sight of the sunrise over the snowclad peaks of the Himālayas. A few stanzas of the first hymn to Uṣas will suffice to reveal the spirit of simple adoration in which the goddess was invokved by the *ṛsis*.

Light us up with happiness, O Ushas, daughter of heaven,
with great lustre, O radiant one, with wealth, O bountiful
goddess.
Like a fair maiden comes Ushas, gladdening (all),
She comes awakening four-footed beasts, and makes the birds
rise into the air
O Ushas, shine with shimmering radiance, O daughter of
heaven bringing us ample happiness, as you new
light upon the daily sacrifices.

The breath and life of the whole world is in you
O noble one, as you shine forth;

as such, O resplendent one with towering chariot, give ear to our cry O bestower of various gifts.

O Ushas, win then (for us) the prize that is admired among the human folk.

With that, hasten to the sacrifices of your worshippers, the sacrificers who are chanting your praises.

Whenever were the Rishis of old that invoked you for protection and support, O noble one,

Yet accept our hymns and bestow on us a gift in token of your satisfaction, O Ushas, with brilliant lustre.

Here it is simplicity and not greed that is begging gifts of the goddess. Her association with the sun is naturally very close. He is her lover, but she precedes him, she is also said to be the his mother. She is the sister of the night. She is also associated with Agni.

The Aśvins, who are sons of Dyaus, who ride through the sky with their steeds, and have a sister, greatly resemble the two Lettic God's sons, who come riding on their steeds, to woo the daughter of the sun, either for themselves or for the moon, and the Twin Horsemen of Greek mythology, the sons of Zeus and the brothers of Helen. Another plausible theory is that which considers the Aśvins as the morning and evening stars. The astronomical fact that the latter are not two but one is no serious objection, as the identity of the two stars was recognised long after the physical basis of the Aśvins was forgotten. The invariable separation of the two stars, whereas the Aśvins appear both together in the morning, is an objection that can be explained, if we remember that the Aśvins are spoken of separately in a passage or two, and that the Aśvins are invoked sometimes in the morning and evening, though sunset plays but little part in Vedic worship. Weber's opinion that the twin constellation of the Gemini receives striking support from the theories of Tilak advanced in his Orion and The Arctic Home in the *Vedas*. If as, Tilak says, the sacrifice or the year once commenced with Aditi at the vernal quinox in or near Punarvasu, i.e., in the twin constellation of the Gemini, and if there are reminiscences in the *Ṛgveda* of the year-long day and night of the Arctic regions, then the twin stars, Castor and Pollux, represented by the Aśvins, would herald the Arctic Dawn, appearing after the long Arctic night or at the beginning of the year. But as the Arctic theory is far from being accepted by scholars, the morning and evening star theory remains the most plausible theory advanced so far.

4

The Role of the Gods

Indra, the favourite national god of the *Ṛgveda,* has the largest number of hymns, nearly 250, i.e., about one-fourth of the total number of hymns in the *Ṛgveda*, addressed to him. He is more addicted to *soma*, which stimulates him to battle than any other god, the epithet *somapa* 'Soma-drinker', being characteristic of him. His father is Dyaus according to some passages, Tvaṣṭṛ according to others. Agni is his twin brother, most often conjoined with him as dual divinity. The Maruts are his principal and constant allies, the epithet *marutvant* being peculiar to him. The essential myth forming the basis of his nature and repeated frequently and with variations, is the basis of his nature in the Vṛtra myth. Accompanied by the Maruts and exhilarated by Soma, he attacks Vṛtra, often called the Ahi. He smashes Vṛtra who encompasses the waters, and so deserves the exclusive epithet *apsu-jit* 'conquering in the waters'. In this struggle, which is constantly renewed he also pierces the mountains and releases the pent-up waters, like imprisoned cows. The demons, whom Indra throws down, dwell on the *parvata* or *giri* (mountain or cloud?) and an *adri* (rock) is said to encompass the waters. The clouds containing the waters are figured as fortresses of the aerial demons, described either as autumnal or as made of iron or stone, and as 90, 99 or 100 in number. He is, therefore, characteristically called the fort-destroyer, but his exclusive and chief epithet is 'Vṛtra-slayer'.

The release of the waters is simultaneous with the winning of light, sun, and dawn. Independent of the Vṛtra fight also, he is said to have found the light, the dawn or the sun, and made a path for the latter. The cows mentioned with the sun and dawn must be understood to be the morning beams. The gaining of Soma is also associated with the winning of the cows and the sun and with the Vṛtra fight. His connection with the thunderstorm is indicated when he is said to have created the lighting of heaven and directed the flow of the waters downwards. The cosmic actions usually attributed to all the gods are attributed to him also. His particular achievement is that he settled the quaking mountains and plain.

The true character of Indra can be understood by ascertaining that of Vṛtra, his opponent. A more reasonable view is that, he was originally a frost and winter demon from whose grasp the waters have to be wrenched free every year, that thunderstorm and rain are not the only natural basis of the Vṛtra myth, and that the geographical and climatic environments in the later home of the Vedic Indians only helped to revise the original myth and to render very plausible the interpretation of the mythological figure of Indra as the god of the thunderstorm. In support of this view the following facts may be stated.

(1) Thunderstorms or rains are hardly mentioned in the Indra-Vṛtra myth and the clouds play quite a minor part in it. (2) As the waters released by Indra are described as running like horses, in a race, rain water could not be meant, as it does not flow horizontally nor could races be imagined as run vertically. The Maruts — the storm gods — form an important group of deities numbering thrice sixty. They are the sons of Rudra and Pṛśnī, the cow (representing the mottled storm-cloud) also of *vāyu*, and are sometimes described as self-born. They are all brothers of equal age, having the same birthplace. They are golden, ruddy and self-luminous and are associated with *vidyut* particularly having the epithet lightning-speared; the cars on which they ride gleam with lightning. Among their personal decorations, such as helmets, garlands, etc., armlets and anklets are peculiar. They make a loud noise, represented by thunder and the roaring of the winds, and as such are pre-eminently the singers of heaven, their songs inspiring Indra. Their chief function is to shed rain which is figuratively called either milk, honey or *ghī*, and which is connected with the thunderstorm. At the same time they produce light and make a path for the sun. They are constant allies of Indra, in whose company they are addressed as

'priests' their songs representating Rudra. They are invoked to avert lightning, the arrow and the bolt from the worshippers, and also to bring healing remedies. Vāyu and Vāta are almost interchangeable terms; when distinguished, the former is chiefly the god, the latter the element. The name Parjanya means literally 'rain-cloud' which, when personified becomes an udder, a water-skin or a pail. Parjanya is also described as a bull that quickens the plants and the earth. As regards *āpaḥ* (the water) the personification is only incipient. They are celestial as well as terrestrial, and the view has been mentioned above that the celestial waters were probably looked upon as an ether-like medium on which the luminaries made their fixed journeys along the zodiac, and that the blocking of them by Vṛtra was supposed to prevent the rise and movements of these luminaries thus causing long darkness. As the waters are invoked as *apo* in the Avestā, their deification is pre-Vedic.

The hymns of Varuṇa by *Kūrma Gārtsamada*, for example, opens in the usual flattering tone:

> May this (hymn) addressed to Aditi's son who is wise and
> self-supreme excell all the existing (hymns) in greatness;
> The god whom it is exceedingly pleasant to worship —
> of what affluent Varuna do I beg glorious fame.

But the tone soon changes, and adulation turns into admiration for god created cosmic harmony:

> Aditi's son unleashed them (i.e. the rivers) and
> started them on various paths,
> the rivers course along in obedience to Varuna's ordinance;
> Never released are they, nor ever tired,
> like birds they swiftly fly in never-ending course
> Loosen the bond of sin like a girdle, O Varuna;
> we shall fully conform the rule of equity you have ordained
> May not the thread snap while I am still weaving my prayer song
> may not the measuring rod breed out of season.
> Avert terror from me, as a righteous ruler
> Release me from anguish, as a claf from the rope;
> not even for a moment can I live away from you,
> Do not strike us, Varuna, with the weapons which, in your search

O Asura, destroy those who commit sin
May we not have to bid adieu to light;
loosen the hold of the envious on us, so that we may live

That virtue is its reward, and , as a spiritual quality, is incommensurable in terms of material advantage, does not seem to have been realized by the Ṛgvedic poets. The spirit of the people that peeps through the thick veil of ritual pedantry is one of gladness, aspiring ever for more, pray and never knowing rest or contentment. Absence of evil is not what they pray for most. Their supreme desire is to triumph over poverty and resistance. Their chief god is Indra who does not possess a single spiritual trait. But their minds are fresh, and, therefore deeply impressed by the trait. Atri's hymn to Parjanya is perhaps the most striking example;

He strikes down the trees, he strikes also the Rākṣasas
the whole world is afraid of carrying mighty arms.
Even the sinless quake before the bull-like god,
when Parjanya, thundering, strikes the evil-doers.

Like the charioteer lashing forward his horses by the whip
does he announce the messengers of rain
Lion's roars from a distance are heard
When Parjanya renders rainy the sky.
Winds blow fast and lightnings flash,
plants shoot up and heaven swells
Quickening showers fall for all
when Parjanya gladdens the earth with his seed.

Roar and thunder, sow the seed,
come flying hither in squelching car;
Turn downward the skin unbound,
so that be levelled high lands and low.

Hymns of this type are unique in world literature, for nowhere else can the deification of natural phenomena be so clearly perceived.

The martial spirit is well reflected in the hymn, though evidently it is not a real war-song, but rather a magical incantation supposed to secure victory in battle:

Like a thunder-cloud becomes his face
When the mailed warrior plunges into the thick of battle
Be victorious without being injured in body,
May the strength of the armour protect you.

By the bow well win the cattle, by the bow the battle,
by the bow shall we win the mighty struggles
The bow destroys the enemy,
by the bow shall we conquer the regions.

As if to whisper the string near the ear,
holding in embrace its dear friend
Stretched on the bow it lisps like a girl,
this string, that helps on to victory

While in the *Atharvaveda*, which speaks about the Varuṇa as

The mighty lord on high our deeds, as if at hand, espies;
The gods know all men do, though men would fain their acts
disguise

Whoever stands, whoever moves or steals from place to place
or hides him in his secret cell — the gods his movements trace
wherever two to ether plot, and deem they are alone,
King Varuṇa is there, a third, and all their schemes are known.
The earth is his, to him belong these vast and boundless skies
Both seas within him rest, and yet in that small pool he lies

Whoever far beyond the sky should think his way towing,
He could not there elude the grasp of Varuṇa the king
His spies, descending from the skies, glide all this world around;
Their thousand eyes all-scanning sweep to earth's remotest bound;

Whate'er exists in heaven and earth, whate'er beyond the skies
Before the eyes of Varuṇa, the king, unfolded lies
The ceaseless winkerings all he counts of every mortal's eyes;
He wields this universal frame as a gamester throws his dice

Terrestial God

Agni, a personification of the sacrifical fire, presents in its conception the household life of the Vedic Āryans, and is second in importance only to Indra, whose conception presents their external life of struggle and conquest. The anthropomorphism of the physical appearance of Agni is naturally very slight. He is butter-backed, and flame-haired and eats and oblations with his tongue. Wood or *ghī* is his food and melted butter his beverage, though he drinks *soma* with other gods. He is nourished three times a day. Although he is invoked to partake of the sacrificial offerings himself, he is more prominently the mouth by which the gods eat the sacrifice. His splendour is naturally his most prominent quality. He shines by day and night. He is called 'smoke-bannered' and is said to be supporting the sky with his smoke as with a post. He is a charioteer of the sacrifice and brings the gods in his golden lightning car. He is said to be a son of heaven and also of heaven and earth. Indra, with whom he is more closely associated than with any other god, is called his twin brother.

There are various myths about his birth, form and abodes. He is daily produced from the two kindling-sticks which are called his parents or mothers, and therefore he is ever young, though ancient. He is called the 'son of strength' probably because of the strength required to kindle the fire, the ten fingers being exercised in the process. Agni's origin in the aerial waters is often referred to. As the son of waters he has become a separate deity. He is also said to be born in the highest heaven and was brought down from heaven by Mātariśvan. This is his third origin — the celestial one. The threefold nature of Agni is a favourite topic with Ṛgvedic poets; his heads, bodies, stations, splendours and births are each threefold. He is the earliest representative of the famous Indian trinity and yet sometimes he is called *dvī-janman* from the point of view of a twofold division of the universe into heaven and earth.

As the central figure of the sacrifice, he is called variously *ritvij*, *vipra*, *purohita*, *adhvaryu* and brāhmaṇa and is thus the divine counterpart of earthly priesthood. He is pre-eminently omniscient or one who knows all created beings. The funeral hymn distinguishes all created beings by means of the hymns in favour of Agni, in the conveyor of offerings and the *krayvad* form of Agni, that burns the dead body on the funeral pyre. Even in the Indo-European period, the sacrificial fire was a well-known institution, as offering gifts to the gods by casting them into the fire was customary among the Italians and Greeks. In the Indo-Iranian period, a vast ritual has already developed around the sacrificial fire which is personified and worshipped as a beneficent god.

Ṛgvedic mythology is dominated by two all-pervading figures, the sun and the fire. There are but few deities in the Ṛgvedic pantheon that cannot be explained, as manifestations of either the one or the other. Now the sun is regarded as a form of Agni, and Agni is said to be born as the rising sun in the morning. This ultimate unity underlying the divine diversity may provide the solution to many a puzzle in Ṛgvedic mythology. The dismal hymn ends with two more verses notable only for their extreme obscenity. It is in these *dānastutis* that the Brāhmaṇical god appears in the *Ṛgveda*. Every priestly family has its own *Apri*-hymn, and all of them are constructed in the same pattern which is designed in man form meant for animal sacrifice. Eleven deities and deity groups in as many different verses have been invoked in each *Apri*-hymns in the same order. Only in regard to the second deity both Tanuapat and Narasamasa, each has a verse for himself. Moreover at the end of the second *Apri*-hymn, there is a special verse invoking Indra. Thus the first *Apri*-hymn consists of twelve, the second of thirteen and each of the rest of eleven verses. The *Apri*-hymns, though of no literary value, are of immense importance for the history of Vedic religion. They prove conclusively that also in the oldest period, as at later epochs, ritual had never been fully standardised. There is no reason to doubt the these hymns were actually used at animal sacrifice as tradition maintains. But there is nothing in the *Apri*-hymns to suggest that in the Ṛgvedic period the animals sacrificed were regarded as substitutes for the sacrifices themselves, as was the case in the ritual.

The funeral hymns too seem to have been composed for ritual purposes, but they contain truly noble sentiments. As cremation and burial were both in vogue, we have both burial and cremation hymn. But the character of the respective hymns leaves scarcely any doubt that burial was the earlier custom. It is significant that the deceased, if a man, still holds a bow in his hand, which the priest takes away from him at the time of burial with these words.

> The bow I take from the hand of the deceased
> for our power and glory and strength;
> Even there where you lie may we as good heroes
> repulse all the attacks of the foes.

The martial spirit of the Vedic Āryans finds truest expression in this verse. Even at the moment of death the thought supreme in the minds is that of war. Twice in the *Ṛgveda* man has been called *mṛtyubandhu* "regarding death as a relation". The Ṛgvedic Indians were passionately fond of life, but they were not afraid of death. A gentler but more sophisticated spirit is revealed by the cremation-hymn

1. Do not burn him, Agni, do not scorch him either,
   do not tear asunder his skin or body;
   When you have devoured him, O, Jātavedas
   then do you send him on to the fathers.
2. When you have devoured him, O Jātavedas,
   then do you give over to the Fathers;
   When he reaches the other world of the dead
   then may he obey the will of the gods.
3. Let the eye go to the sun, let the breath go to the wind;
   to heaven or to earth according to their desert;
   or to waters go, if that is your lot,
   or set you up in the plants with your limbs.

The last verse is of special interest for various reasons. Pantheism of the primitive variety is discernible in the first line. The second line suggests the idea of retribution though as yet far short of the philosophical doctrine of *karma*. Belief in a life after death is also revealed in these verses, but there is no suggestion as yet of rebirth or hell. The first occurs only in the *Atharvaveda*, and the second clearly appears for the first time in the *Upaniṣads*.

Quite a number of philosophical hymns are contained in the *Ṛgveda*, and they have been often discussed and translated. An important point on which hinges the whole of later *Vedānta* philosophy has been discussed in terms of *māyā* and *rūpa*. *Rūpa* in the *Ṛgveda* never signifies real form, but only transient and deceptive appearance;

and *māyā* in most passages has been used to signify only that occult power by means of which the deceptive appearance can be assumed or discarded. If the doctrine of *māyā* and *rūpa* is the essence of *Vedānta* then it may as well be called *Vedādi*.

Nowhere in ancient literature have the gods been more concretely conceived as in the *Ṛgveda*, but the same *Ṛgveda* also reveals the fact that already there were some who would not believe in the existence even of Indras, the most concrete of the Vedic pantheon. Quite in the strain of "O God, if there be a God", a poet in the *Ṛgveda* makes this astonishing remark.

> Chant the hymn, striving for strength
> unto Indra, the truthful, if indeed he exists.
>
> One says to ether, Indra does not exist,
> Who has him seen? whom shall I praise?

Next to Indra, Soma god plays the intoxicating role. Other gods like Pṛthivī, Dyāus, and Uṣas play a minor role in the *Veda*s. The doctrine of *Śaiva-Siddhānta* has many things in common with the other schools of Indian theism. It has also certain unique features. In this system, God is the only efficient cause of the world; the material cause is *māyā*. Even on *māyā*, God does not act directly, but through his Ś*akti* which is the instrumental cause. The *Siddhānta* believes that God is revealed through Scripture, as do all the orthodox systems which are theistic. Reasoning, however, is not without its use. Especially in refuting the doctrines that do not accept the authority of Scripture, there is no point in quoting scriptural texts. So, the *Siddhāntin* formulates arguments for the existence of God. In fact, the very first *sūtra* of the *Śiva-jñāna-bodham* contains the cosmological argument. The cosmological argument seeks to show that there must be an efficient cause for the universe as a whole. This cause is God. The universe is a pluralistic whole. The particular constituting it may be classified in different ways. The most convenient perhaps, is the classification on the principle of gender. On this principle, we speak of the particular reality as 'he', 'she' or 'it'. This itself shows that there is regularity or order in the universe. There must be a reason why a 'he' must be a 'he', a 'she' a 'she', and an 'it' an 'it'. If there is regularity or order, as there is, a whole undergoes regulated changes. It comes into being, stays for sometimes and disappears and this process is repeated. Since the universe is subject to regulated changes, it cannot be self-caused and self-established. It is evidently a product; a product requires to be produced, which implies a producer. Who is this producer? That cannot be anything that is inert for efficient causality cannot belong to anything that is devoid of intelligence. Nor can that be the soul possessing finite universe intelligence, for that is unequal to the task of producing the universe with its regulated men, women and things. So there must be postulated an infinite, omniscient and omnipotent being as the efficient cause of the universe. That is God. *Hara* is God as the destroyer of the universe. It is only out of him that the universe can come. A thing can emerge only from that into which it has earlier resolved. At the time of *pralaya* when everything is destroyed, *Hara* alone stands without a second. So, it is from him that creation must proceed.

After setting forth this argument as found in the *Bodham*, the *Siddhiyar* proceeds to establish it through a progressive criticism of the *prima facie* views.

The first to be examined is the *Lokāyata* view. The Materialist may say that the universe is neither created nor destroyed, that, in fact it is permanent. Obviously, he cannot justify this view even on the evidence of perception, which is the only evidence he recognises. Perceptual experience reveals nothing in the world that is permanent. The component parts of the universe have, each of them a beginning and an end. The *Lokāyata* may shift his position to suit his purpose and say that, while admitting creation, he maintains the view of natural creation. But what does this phrase 'natural creation mean'? If it means nature becomes natures, it carries no sense at all. If it be said that nature changes because its nature is so, then there will be nothing called nature. What the *Lokāyata* means by nature is the four elements — water, earth, fire and air. He does not accept the fifth element, ether because it cannot be sense-perceived. If the four elements constitute nature according to the *Lokāyata*, and they undergo change, there must be admitted an efficient cause which makes them change; for, what is inert cannot change of its own accord. To avoid the need for an efficient cause, the origin, etc., of the four elements may be explained thus. Air produces the other three elements; fire destroys the other elements; water contains them all; and so on. As the elements themselves cause these changes through a system of distributed labour as it were, no efficient cause is necessary. In reply to this, it is has to be pointed out that the *Lokāyata* has not counted the cost. He imagines that one element leads to another or is resolved into another. But what happened is that all the elements merge together and are destroyed together. In other to account for this fact we must postulate an efficient cause which has neither a beginning nor an end.

The Sautrāntika-Buddha believes that there is no need for a first cause, as he regards the world process as a successive chain of events. Each event is the product of its immediately succeeding event. Nothing stays even for two consecutive moments. There is a constant coming into being and ceasing to be. Just as seed and sprout are perpetual, so are all events that are related as cause and effect. So, why then postulate a God who is superfluous? This is refuted even by another school of Buddhism viz., the *Mādhyamika*. The question to be asked of the *Sautrāntika* is; what is it that appears? Does it exist prior to its appearance. If it does not exist, it cannot appear. What exists need not be produced; what does not exist cannot be produced. So, the *Mādhyamika* would say that what appears is indeterminable.

Is the *Mādhyamika* position intelligible? What is this category which neither 'is' nor 'is not' nor 'both is and is not' nor 'neither is nor is not'? Such a category defies all attempts at understanding. That a thing is — we can understand. That a thing is not-yes. But the other alternatives do not seem to have any meaning, and violate the laws of logic. The *Mādhyamika* teaches *śūnyavāda*. He seems to believe that the world comes out of nothing, that nothing is ultimate. But such a view is untenable. Even to speak or think of nothing is to deny the ultimacy of nothing.

The Jainas believe in the multiple-nature of things. A thing that is produced cannot be characterised simply as existing or non-existing. It has the nature of existing and non-existing, and the various combinations of these. The doctrine which is known as *anekāntavāda* and *syādvāda* gives formulation to the view of identity and difference.

The *Siddhāntin*'s criticism of the Jaina doctrine is that by no trick can the logical law of non-contradiction be set aside. How can one and the same thing be identical and different, existent and non-existent? The Jaina may say that a thing exists as cause and does not exist as effect. This statement too is unintelligible, because there is no difference in substance between cause and effect. The *siddhāntin* who advocates *satkāryavāda*, maintains that the effect is pre-existent in the cause. For him the view that the effect is non-existent in the cause is not acceptable.

The *Mīmāṁsaka* holds the view that the universe is eternal, and therefore does not find any need for postulating a creator. While parts of the world may come and go, the world as a whole persists and remains always the same. There is a saying to the effect: "Never the world otherwise than what it is". There is neither *sṛṣṭi* nor *pralaya*, the world is a going concern. There is no need for an agent either for its inception or for its destruction. The *Siddhāntin*'s reply is based on the evidence of scripture, perceptual experience and reasoning. There are scriptural texts which declare the origin of the universe and its destruction; and the *Mīmāṁsaka* accepts scripture as the highest authority. Even if the texts be set aside or interpreted otherwise, there is the evidence of perceptual experience as well as that of reasoning by parity. It is not true to say that only individuals come into being and go out of existence. There are seasonal fruits, for instance, which appear in the appointed season and disappear all together at the end of that season. Similarly, it is intelligible that the world as a whole appears and disappears at fixed times. There must be an efficient cause which produces and destroys the world periodically.

The *Kālavādin* admits that the world is produced and destroyed periodically, but he urges that what affects production and destruction is Time, and not God. If the expression 'God' is to be used at all, let us call Time God. The *Siddhāntin* has no difficulty in showing that the *Kālavādin*'s thesis is untenable. Time is inert and unintelligent. It cannot, therefore, be the efficient cause of the universe. It is true that time produces changes. But it does so only as impelled by God. Time is the instrumental cause. God alone is the efficient cause.

The *Naiyāyika* traces the origin of the universe, to the atoms and their coming together in various ways. Destruction of things means their reduction to atoms. When the world of things has been destroyed, again after a time the atoms come together, and the world is formed. God is only one of the causes like *karma* and time. It is the collocation of the atoms that is the distinctive cause of creation. The criticism advanced by the *Siddhāntin* against the *Kālavādin* holds good here also. The atoms are inert, and do not possess a sense of direction. Moreover, at the time of *pralaya* the atoms themselves are destroyed and resolved in their causes, *māyā*. The *Naiyāyika* may argue that, if the atoms are destroyed, it is not possible for the world to emerge again. But that argument does not take into account the existence of *māyā* even in the absence of the atoms. It is from *māyā* which is eternal that the world re-emerges. *Māyā* is the material cause of the universe. As energised by *cit-śakti*, it produces the world. The atoms cannot be the ultimate causes of creation — they are effects. That they are effects is evident from the fact that they are many and have parts. The atoms are not without parts. If they had no parts, how is it that they combine and give rise to things that have parts? *Māyā* has no parts, and is indestructible. It is *Māya* that is the primal material cause of the universe.

According to scripture, *māyā* is the prior to creation and god is the wielder of *māyā*. Even if we analyses common usage, it will be clear that there is the widespread belief in *satkāryavāda*. It is said, for instance, that the tree with branches of, etc. is contained in the seed in a subtle form and that if it were not so, the tree would not come out of the seed. The world in the seed-form we call *māyā*. If it be urged that the leaves, etc. that fall from a tree are not seen to go back to their source, the reply is that when the leaves, etc. are reduced to their primal condition, they will, again shoot into a tree, given the time and the other auxiliary causes. Similarly, when the world is retracted into its primal source at *pralaya*, again after some time it is reproduced, and we call that *sṛṣṭi*.

Although God is the efficient cause of the universe, he does not undergo any change on account of this process. He is like the sun in whose presence the lotus blooms sway. In the presence of the sun various processes take places — some of them even diametrically opposed to one another. The lotus blooms, burning-glass emits fire and water in the earth evaporates. So also, the reality of God makes possible the divergent cosmic processes such as creation and destruction, and the varied activities of phenomena.

Why does God create the universe and retract it after time in order to create it again? He could have nothing to accomplish for himself through creation. What has he to gain from the world-process? We can only say that creation is his play or from our standpoint, the standpoint of the *paśu*, we may say that the grand drama he enacts is for effecting the release of souls. The world is a vale of soul-making. God creates the universe in order that the soul may eat the fruit of its past *karma* and acquire the necessary means for release. He destroys the universe in order to give rest to the souls. Just as sleep refreshes the individual, *pralaya* affords rest to all the souls. Again, at *sṛṣṭi* the process of purgation starts. By trial and error, and by the grace of God, the souls get rid of their impurities and attain release. God has five functions — creation, maintenance and destruction of the world, veiling the truth and bestowing grace on the soul. The first four have for their end the last one which is redeeming the soul through grace. The world process serves to discipline the soul and make it mature. Obstruction has the same purpose. As the *tāntrikas* say, through *māyā*, *māyā* has to be transcended. And, this is accomplished through divine grace.

"Give me matter and motion" said Descartes, "and I will construct the universe". The mind reverses this — "Give me a world — a world in which there are relations — and I will construct matter and motion". Are there then no genuine laws in the external world? Laws inherent in the substratum of events, which breakthrough into the phenomena otherwise regulated by the despotism of the mind? We cannot foretell what the final answer will be; but, at present, we have to admit that there are laws which appear to have their seat in external nature. The most important of these, if not the only law, is a law of atomicity. Why does that quality of the world which distinguishes matter from emptiness exist only in certain lumps called atoms or electrons, all of comparable mass? Whence arises this discontinuity? That is a law due to the mind; indeed the mind seems rather to take pains to smooth the discontinuities of nature into continuous perception. We can only suppose that there is something in the nature of things that causes this aggregation into atoms. Probably our analysis into point — events is not final; and if it could be pushed further to reach something still more fundamental, then atomicity and the remaining laws of physics would be seen as identities. This indeed is the only kind of explanation that a physicist could accept as ultimate. But this more ultimate analysis stands on a different plane from that by which the point is reached. The world may be so constituted that the laws of atomicity must necessarily hold; but, so far as the mind is concerned, there seems no reason why it should have been constituted in that way. We can conceive a world constituted otherwise. But our argument hitherto has been that, however the world is constituted, the necessary combinations of things can be found which obey the laws of mechanics, gravitation and electrodynamics, and these combinations are ready to play the part of the world of perception for any mind that appreciates them; and further, any world of perception of a different character would be rejected by the mind as unsubstantial.

If atomicity depends on laws inherent in nature it seems at first difficult to understand why it should relate to matter especially since matter is not of any great account in the analytical scheme, and owes its importance to irrelevant considerations introduced by the mind. It has appeared, however, that atomicity is by no means confined to matter and electricity and the quantum mechanics, which plays so great a part in recent physics apparently an atom of action. So nature cannot be accused of connivance with the mind in singling out matter for special distinction. Action is generally regarded as the most fundamental thing in the real world of physics, although the mind passes it over because of its lack of permanence; and it is vaguely believed that the atomicity of action is the general law, and the appearance of electrons is in some way dependent on this. But the precise formulation of the theory of quantum mechanics and the action has hitherto baffled physicists.

There is a striking contrast between the triumph of the scientific mind in formulating the great general scheme of natural laws, nowadays summed up in the principle of least action, and its present defeat by the newly discovered but equally general phenomena depending on the laws of atomicity of quanta. It is too early to cry failure in the latter case;

but possibly the contrast is significant. It is one thing for the human mind to extract from the phenomena of nature, the laws of atomicity over which it has had no control. It is even possible that laws which do not have their origin in the mind may be irrational, and we can never succeed in formulating them. This is however, only a remote possibility; probably if they were really irrational it would not have been possible to make the limited progress that has been achieved. But if the laws of quanta do indeed differentiate the actual world from other worlds possible to the mind, we may expect the task of formulating them to be far harder than anything yet accomplished by physics.

There are in the human soul what are called intuitions, self-evident truths, *ātmapratyaya*, say the *ṛṣis*, which arise in it spontaneously and which we cannot put to proof in a logical form. No process of logical reasoning is a prerequisite to their recognition. They spring right from the centre of our nature and are deeper and firmer than logical methods. For instance, there is our reliance on the permanence and uniformity of the laws of nature by which we mean that certain phenomena always happen.

5

Science, Modern and Ancient

All are mad, some after money some after enjoyment some after name and fame, and so on. But not mad after the unreal, the transitory, but after the Real and the Eternal.

Śrī Rāmākriṣṇa

Modern science starts with two hypotheses or as it wants to have them called, two primary facts. Man is the one and the universe around is the other one. What does it understand by 'man'? An embodied being, a Mr. so and so having a certain nationality, a faith and a creed. In short it understands by the word 'man' an ordinary man of the world with sound common sense. Man is he who sees, hears, smells, tastes and touches by means of his senses, and thinks, feels and wills by means of his mind; and whatever he can observe and experiment upon by means of these senses, he regards that to be a fact, a reality. Everything has to come down to the level of his senses in order to be regarded as a reality, as they alone have the power of establishing the existence of an object by observation and experiment.

He also finds himself to be full of various wants, nay he finds his whole life to be a series of almost, incalculable wants, and to his great relief he finds out at the same time that the world around him has the power to remove them. But although he finds the world to be perfectly capable of removing them, he has to force it to do so. He has to fight with his environment in order to get from it all that he wants. By mere coaxing words he can get nothing out of it. He has to wage an incessant war with it to get all he desires. That is why Charles Darwin, the father of modern evolution, has described life as a 'struggle for existence' and has pointed out that only the fittest survive amidst such a struggle. The post also has described the world to be a battlefield in the following simple and forcible language:

In the world's broad field of battle,
In the bivouac of life,
Be not like dumb, driven cattle,
Be a hero in the strife.

Whether he wills or not, constituted as he is, he cannot keep quiet here, as that means death to him. He wants to gather power, and he finds out that knowledge brings that much needed power to him. Formerly electricity used to be regarded as only a destructive force. But now that men have been able to know something about it, they have been able to make it very useful, as a carrier of their messages, as motor power for their carriages, as illuminer of their cities and towns. The knowledge of steam power has facilitated communication from one place to another with incredible rapidity; and thus they are very hopeful of getting almost all things necessary from the knowledge of the universe in the near future. That is why there is an incessant struggle going on between man and nature; and as a result of such struggle man has been able to evolve science or right knowledge about persons and things. In wanting to know about the heavenly bodies, he has evolved astronomy; in wanting to know about the animal kingdom, he has evolved zoology; in wanting to know about the vegetable kingdom, he has evolved botany in wanting to know the elements out of which the world has come into existence, the laws which govern everything around him, the constitution of his physical organism and the method of its working, the constitution of the world in which he lives and so on, he has found out evolved chemistry, physics, anatomy, physiology, geology and so on.

By studying matter he has found out its indestructible nature. Although the candle has been burnt out, by weighing the gaseous product of the burnt candle he has found out that not a particle has been lost. Thus matter, being indestructible is real, and all material bodies are, on that account, real as well; and as the universe is composed of material bodies, only it must also be real. By the study of this material universe we get whatever we want. Hence its study is absolutely necessary. Speculation about the eternal nature of souls is useless, as, being about the immaterial souls cannot be brought within the scope of observation and experiment. Now what sort of a universe has been given to us by modern science? Assuredly a soulless one. It is a universe that does not respond to our call; by sheer exertion, we ourselves are required to get out of it all that we want — both physical and mental. Again the universe is so very infinitely vast, and our capacities are so very deplorably limited, that it is absurd on our part to entertain any hope of knowing it as a whole and hence our knowledge about it will always remain undesirably partial.

The indestructibility of matter was not unknown to our ancient sages, Kapila, Gautama, Kanāda, Patañjali, Jaimini, and many others. However you may try to destroy matter, it will baffle all your attempts to do so. Some years ago, the scientists believed that they had arrived at a final division of matter, which could not be divided any more, and which, on that account, they named 'atom'; but after the discovery of electrons which are finer than atoms, that theory has fallen to the ground. Again ethereal particles are regarded as even finer than electrons, and the future, which will make even ether appear as coarse. Thus, however, you may go on analysing matter, you can never reduce it to nothing. It will always remain something, and baffle all our attempts to destroy it. Thus modern material science has not been able to arrive at a final division of matter and so it has no firm ground to stand upon, and as such it is unreliable and empirical. We have learned from science it the indestructible nature of matter, and also its ever-shifting, ever-changing nature. Every material form is liable to change. Heat expands and cold contracts it. It admits of any number of divisions. The big ones become smaller, the smaller still smaller, and so on. So it is constantly changing. Now let us analyse the phenomena of change. Whenever any form changes into another, the old form exists no more or dies, and a new form comes to exist or is born. So the words 'birth' and 'death' may be substituted for the word 'change'. Thus we see that every material form has to change or die unceasingly on a background which is changless or is without birth and death. On account of this birthlessdeathless and eternal background, the ever dying material form is saved from destruction, as it is inseparably united with it amidst all its vicissitudes.

Now let us see what sort of a thing this eternal background is. Is it formful? No, as in that case it would also have to die like that which rests upon it. Hence it must be formless; and as every form is limited, that which is formless must be limitless or infinite. The finite form exists on this infinite background, but where does this latter exist? Does it exist in space and time? It cannot, since space whose existence depends upon the co-existence of things, and time whose existence depends upon a succession of events are not independent, and have therefore beginning and end or are, in other words, finite. How can the infinite one live in the finite? Space begins to exists after the co-existence of things, and it ceases to exist when that co-existence ceases. Time begins to exist when two events occur one after another, and ceases to exist when no such concession, and succession is takes place. Again, when two things co-exist they must be known to exist together, which means that one of them must be the knower and the other the known. There must also be the mind, and for this, knowledge to arise. So space conception must be in the mind. Succession of events bringing along with it two or more different ideas, also presupposes the existence of mind; for how can there be an idea without a mind to give birth to it? Hence also time and conception exists in the mind. Therefore, both space and time exists in the mind. But is mind limited or limitless? That it is limited, requires no proof, and as such you cannot localise the limitless one in it. Now what else is there that exists besides mind, space, time and the universe that has its basis in them? Only the self; that alone remains. Is this self limited or limitless? It is beyond the three *guṇas* — *sattva*, *rajas* and *tamas* or the five *kośa*s comprising the three bodies, gross, subtle and causal. Having nothing to limit it. It is limitless. Here, therefore, we can localise the limitless background of limited material forms. But you may say that two infinites may clash against each other. Hence the infinites may not live together as one and the same, but must live separately. Let us take your affirmation for granted and let us then examine its validity. According to you, there are two infinites — one is conscious and forms the background of all individual selves; the other is unconsciousness, and forms the background of all material forms.

The old Vedic sages are looked upon with pity by western scholars, as according to the latter, these people had no idea of God and therefore had to personify the inanimate powers of nature as living gods. After what we have learned just now, this commiseration on the part of western scholars is absolutely groundless and if any man is to be pitied, it is he who has allowed his ignorance to drive the soul out of the entire universe, and place himself inside a dead body, making himself as soulless and dead as the body itself. The Vedic sage never personified natural forces. Personification is mere imagination. It is imagining life where there is really none. But if one sees a living being as living, there is personification. The Vedic sage actually saw, a living sun, a living moon, nay a living universe. Did Prahlāda imagine a living God in the stone pillar? If it were mere imagination, then none could see the living God inside the pillar and so the living God had to come out of it to save His loving devotee.

Thus we have seen God to be eternal and infinite. Is He one with our souls? In that case, everyone of us would be all-knowing like him and there would not be any variety of souls. But that is not a fact. No man as man, is all-knowing. When he frees himself from the limitations of body and mind even in this life, by means of one-pointed concentration, he is then not a man; he is one with the infinite. One and hence become all-knowing. But an ordinary man who identifies himself with his body and mind, both of which are limited, can have only limited knowledge, and that alone he has. Is he also limited in this life? So long as he identifies himself with his body, he has his birth and death. But he is not only an embodied being but also a thinker, i.e., he not only identified himself with his body, but also with his mind. Moreover in his health or natural condition, he seldom identified himself with his body; for the idea that he has got a body only comes to him when he is reminded of it by some local pain such as headache, colic, etc., or when the whole of it is burning, as it were under a very high fever; or, in other words the idea of his having a body only comes to him in his unhealthy or unnatural condition. In his healthy or natural condition, he feels as if he has no body. So the natural man is more a mind than a body.

With the help of this mind he is able to discriminate the permanent from the impermanent, the real from the unreal and when he goes on examining and analysing himself with the help of it, he finds out that he is made up of three factors — he himself, his mind and his body. He again finds out that his body is very changeful. It is incessantly changing ever since its embryonic condition, throughout babyhood, boyhood, youth, manhood, etc. and he finds out also that his mind is changing along with it as well. But though his body and mind may be changing, he knows himself to be the same man — the one man who was once a baby, then a boy, then a young man and now has become a grown-up man. He knows he has not changed along with the changes of his body and mind; and so he finds out that he is the one changeless-factor amidst the two. This intuitive faith enables us to determine the nature of everything, and makes the existence of science possible. Therefore, when I see that I remain changeless though my body and mind are incessantly changing all through my lifetime, I cannot help accept my nature to be changeless and eternal or without birth and death. Mathematics, mathematical concepts like addition, substraction, multiplication and division are known to Ṛgvedic people. A number bigger than thousand is a *yuga* whose exact value is not clear. The biggest number which occurs in *Ṛgveda* is 60099. The lowest number mentioned is *eka*, i.e., one. Though zero is not specifically mentioned, it is indirectly mentioned in number ten.

(a) *Addition*: In *Ṛgveda*, the number is divided into 3 and 1 by implication saying that 3 +1 = 4. The particle 'CA' is used to indicate addition.

(b) *Subtraction*: The same passage in the *Ṛgveda* (1.164-45) illustrates that the Vedic people knew, when 3 is taken out from 4, number 1 is the balance.

(c) *Multiplication*: The idea of multiplication is built-in the idea of addition, such as "there groups of eleven or twice the number five." That means in modern terminology, the multiplication of 3 and 11 or 2 and 5.

(d) *Division*: The word *tridha* and *tredha*, *caturadha* pointed out the derivation of the division of a unit into different parts.

(e) *Idea of parts*: The *Ṛgveda* people seem to know the idea of parts of fractions, e.g., the passages 10.27-16 in which the 1/10th part is mentioned. Again in the passage 10.114-9, 1/8th part is suggested.

(f) *Idea of correspondence*: *Ṛgveda* describes the seven deities with seven arms in their hands, each having one sword. This is presented in the words *saptanam sapta ṛṣṭayaḥ* which reveals the basic concept of correspondence with seven, each on both the sides.

(g) *Idea of groups*: The concepts of groups of ten hundreds, or thousands is denoted in the passage like *dasa-śate*, *dasa-sahasra*, or *vimśatim-śata*. This idea of grouping some numbers in one group of groups thus formed is used for further counting big numbers. Thus instead, of saying *dva sahasra* (two thousand), the *Ṛgveda* people said *vimśatim śata* (20 groups of one hundred, i.e., 2000).

From the aforesaid we can infer that *Ṛgveda* people had sound knowledge of basic mathematical concepts and operations. The idea of roots or square roots of higher mathematics is not in evidence in *Ṛgveda* except in later literature.

Vedic mathematics is far superior to our present mathematics. Our highest number is one crore. But their highest number soars up to one lakh crore. Their number were *dasa*, *śata*, *sahasra*, *ayuta*, *niyuta*, *prayuta*, *abduda*, *nyabduda*, *samudra*, *madhya*, *antardham* and *parardham*. Hence *niyatam* for a lakh, *abdudham* for a crore.

Modern Science and Vedānta

The *Upaniṣads* assert that the senses cannot reach the ultimate reality, the (unenlightened) mind cannot grasp it, words cannot describe it. The ultimate reality, declares the scriptures, can, however, be known when a pure mind meditates on it. It is in this way that man can touch the immortal core of life. The new findings in the field of modern physics corroborate the relationship between mind and matter.

VEDĀNTA AND THE NEW PHYSICS

Since the beginning of this century the sure foundations of a materialistic concept of science have begun to crack. By 1914 Einsteinian relativity established matter as a form of energy. It also established the relative and limited knowledge of the world of matter that experimental science can grasp. By 1925 Heisenberg's uncertainty principle demolished once for all, to the unbelief of Einstein himself, "two pillars of the old-science, causality and determinism". He established the irrefutable fact that an electron can never be known in its entirety. "Quantum Theory", Heisenberg asserted, "does not allow a completely objective description of nature." (*Physics and Philosophy,* W. Heisenberg, p. 96).

He finally rejected the classical notion that the reality round us is actual. The reality that we claim to perceive with our senses is just an 'illusion' and this truth one realises when one looks inside the sub-atomic world of electrons. The ontology of materialism rested upon the illusion that the kind of existence, the direct actuality of the world around us, can be extrapolated into the atomic range. The extrapolation is, however, impossible (*Physics and Philosophy,* W. Heisenberg, p. 126). The old deterministic idea that a reality can actually be cognised had to be finally abandoned in quantum physics. Robert Oppenheimer brilliantly puts this new indeterminism about our knowledge of matter in the following lines (quoted in *The Eye of Shiva*, Amnary De Reincourt, p. 64):

> If we, ask, for instance whether the position of the electron remains the same, we must say "No"; if we ask whether the electron position changes with time, we must say "No"; if we ask whether the electron is at rest, we must say "No"; if we ask whether it is in motion, we must say "No".

The *Vedānta* philosophy of the *Upaniṣads* had already conceived the phenomenal reality with its multitudinous spatio-temporal nature as *māyā* or something that "is" and, at the same time, "is not". *Māyā* in Vedānta philosophy is therefore indescribable and unpredictable (*anirvacanīya*). Erwin Schroedinger later illustrated the unpredictability of the electron existence through his well-known analogy of Schroedinger's cat. The movement and behaviour of an individual electron can only be predicated by a statistical probability, since the electron behaviour betrays a free-willing, voluntaristic movement. In fact, Quantum Physics discovers with surprise that an individual electron emitted at a particular time may or (at the same time) may not move in that direction at all. The uncertainty principle, therefore, showed once for all that a sure cause and effect relation, as found in our normal experience, does not exist in the electron world.

Scientific search for a sure cause behind every effect seemed futile. In April 1973 Heisenberg declared in his presidential speech in the Congress of Scientists, convened by the Smithsonian Institute and National Academy of Sciences at Washington D.C.: "What is really needed is a change in fundamental concepts. We are probably forced in our concepts to abandon the atomic materialism of Democritus and to turn to the ideas of symmetry in the philosophy of Plato". He also said, "We cannot exclude the possibility that after sometime the current themes of science and technology will be exhausted, and a younger generation will turn for rationalistic and pragmatic attitudes towards an entirely different approach". By 1970s the nucleus that was still considered as the basic building block of matter was sub-divided into as many as 216 sub-nuclear particles. The smallest one found is called "resonance" which lives only 2 to 3 particles seconds (a particle second is 0.0000000000000000024 second) and charges into another kind of extremely small and short lived particles known as hadrons. "A resonance" writes Fritzof Capra," is a particle, but not an object. It is much better described as an event or happening". Heisenberg echoes the same feeling when he says that in modern physics, the "world appears as a complicated tissue of events". The new findings, especially the withering of the idea of a purely objective world of matter, emergence of the "subjective element" and the consciousness of the experimentor having direct connection with the objects have brought out profound admissions from scientists like Heisenberg who says, "Our Judeo-Christian and Greco Roman heritage, our Hellenic tradition has compelled us to think in exclusive categories. But our experience challenges us to recognise a totality richer and far more complex than the averge observer could have suspected, a totality which compels him to think in ways which logic of dichotomies denies".

This Cartesian partition, this ontological dualism, this dichotomy of mind-matter, soul-body, man-god is fundamental in the western way of thinking in general, and is typical of the analytical mind of the West. The fundamental schism between mind and matter started in the West right from the time of Greek Democritus, and was handed down through Pascal, Descartes, Newton and even so great an intuitive mind as Einstein. And this dualism is responsible, to put it in the words of Amuary De Reincourt (*The Eye of Shiva* by Reincourt, p. 158), for the "Schizophrenic culture of the Western civilization" which repeatedly failed to correlate the mystical feelings of "One all-pervading consciousness" expected from time to time by Western mystics with the rigid theological framework of religion that upheld an extra-cosmic god, a ruling monarch dispensing judgement eternally separate and distinct from puny mortals called Man.

Even Einstein who believed in a Jewish God or the God of Spinoza had to admit intellectually that "the root of the modern conflict between science and religion lies in the concept of a personal God; and that contemporary theologians should have the courage to reject it" (*The Eye of Shiva*, A. Reincourt, p. 170).

Vivekananda struck at the root of this dogmatic and theological belief in a personal god in heaven, when he spoke to the Western audience in San Francisco in 1890.

> What is the idea of God in heaven? Materialism. The Vedāntic idea is the infinite principle of God embodied in everyone of us.God sitting up on a cloud, Think of the utter blasphemy of it. It is materialism, downright materialism. We have seemingly been divided, limited, because of our ignorance. But all nature is given this delusion in every moment. I am not that little man or little woman out of from all else; I am the universal existence. This Vedānta is everywhere, only you must become conscious of it. These masses of foolish beliefs and superstitions hinder our progress. Throw away all matter. The conception of God must be truly spiritual". (Is Vedanta the Future Religion? Complete Works, Vol. VIII. pp. 126-39)

Heisenberg's startling discoveries of "uncertainty principle" and the demolition of causality and determinism was closely followed by another equally great Nobel physicist Erwin Schroedinger. In the middle of the 20th century, nearly 60 years after Vivekananda's first prophetic utterance in London, 1895 that *Advaita Vedānta* (the monastic *Vedānta*) is the only religion that can have any hold on intellectual people, Schroedinger gave a powerful defence of Monistic *Vedānta* as the only solution to the questions raised by Quantum Physics.

"In all world," writes Schroedinger in his book *My View of the World* (Chapter IV), "there is no kind of framework within which we can find consciousness in the plural; this is simply something we construct because of the temporal plurality of individuals, but it is a false construction . . . The only solution to this conflict insofar as any is available to us at all lies in the ancient wisdom of the *Upaniṣad*". "Consciousness is numerically one," he concluded. The vision of plurality is *māyā,* he asserted, in the line of non-dualistic *Vedānta.* Such a startling metaphysical conclusion, Schroedinger anticipated, might be termed as "transcendence or Mysticism" which has got little to do with experimental science, but any attempt to reject this metaphysical and the mystical view of matter would result in, Schroedinger asserted (*My View of the World*, p. 7), "infinitely more Native and petty ones".

The attempt to resolve the dualism of mind and matter was also attempted in the West in the past but the attempt was always on the material plane and therefore, it failed. Schroedinger offers his comments on this attempt. "It is odd that it has usually been done on material basis... But this is no good. If we decided to have only one sphere, it has got to be the psychic one, since that exists anyway." (*My View of the World*, pp. 62-63) Did Einstein fail to finalise his unified field theory primarily because he failed to rise above the monotheistic concept of Judaism?

In the last years of the nineteenth century Vivekananda upheld this impersonal *Vedānta* and interpreted Christ's words according to *Vedānta* to the Western man. The essence of *Vedānta*, says Vivekānanda, is that there is but one being and that every soul is that Being in full, not a part of that Being. All the sun is reflected in each drop. Appearing in time, space and causality, this Being is man, as we know him, but behind all appearance is one Reality. We are not drops to fall into the ocean and be lost each one in the whole, in the fetters of illusion. Infinity cannot be divided; the "one without a second" cannot have second, all is that one . . ."

The greatest teacher of the *Vedānta* philosophy was Śaṅkarācārya. He unified all the conflicting descriptions of *Brahman*, and showed that there is only one infinite reality. We see something akin to this in the teaching of Jesus; Jesus spoke to a different people of a Father in heaven and the need to pray to Him. Next he rose a step higher and told them, "I am vine, you are the branches" and lastly he gave them the highest truth, "I and my father are one" and "the kingdom of heaven is within you".

Schroedinger's bold assertion of the Vedantic monism has broken, for the first time, the old barrier of Cartesian dualism between mind and matter, and has in a sense made a big dent in the schizophrenic culture of the West. *Vedānta* philosophy, obviously, interprets Christ's word in acceptably rational terms. Western rationalists who tried to cling dogmatically to the old theological Christianity or agnostic materialism were plunged in a deep metaphysical abyss. The noted astrophysicist Fred Hoyle said that what dogmatic Christianity gave him was an "eternity of frustration" (*The Nature of the Universe* — Tred Hoyle, p. 124). Bertrand Russell poignantly expressed this predicament that came in his life. "As regards metaphysics, I experience the delight of believing that the sensible world is real. Bit by bit, chiefly under the influence of physics, the delight has faded, I find myself in a vast mist of solitude both emotional and metaphysical from which I can find no issue (*The Autobiography of Bertrand Russell*, Vol. 2, pp. 160). It is precisely because Einstein, a devoted Zionist, failed to rise above the idea of the Jewish God that he could not accept wholeheartedly, till the end, the quantum principle of uncertainty. Physicist Max Born who saw this failure in Einstein remarked that he died with a sense of tragedy.

The meeting of modern physics and eastern mysticism triggered off far-reaching changes in the Western scientist's way of thinking. Intuition slowly emerged as the most powerful element in scientific discoveries. To Heisenberg, Einstein categorically said, "It is the theory which decided what can be observed", and put away the traditional way of experiment-observation-inference as "nonsense". In his Herbert Spencer lectures, Einstein admitted, "I hold that pure thought can grasp the reality as dreamed" (*Essays in Science,* A. Einstein, p. 17). Closely following Einstein, Nobel Physicist Hideki Yukawa wrote (*Creativity an Intuition*, H. Yukawa, pp. 57-58) ". . . but the fact remains that in order to survey the whole with intuition . . . for us, the scientist's imagination is an important ingredient . . it would seem that Indians are amply endowed with imagination".

British astronomer James Jeans anticipated the Vedāntic approach to modern science long ago when he said "the stream of knowledge is heading towards a non-mechanical reality. Mind no longer appears as an accidental intruder into the realm of matters; we are beginning to suspect that we ought rather to hail it as the creator and governor of the realm of matter". (*Mysticism and the New Physics,* Michael Talbot, p. 16). The concept of inter-connectedness between the observer and the observed reality was further developed by John F. Wheeler.

"Nothing is more important about quantum principles than this that it destroys the concept of the world as 'sitting out there' with the observer safely separated by a 20 cm slab of glass . . . The measurement changes the state of electron. The universe will never afterwards be the same. To describe what has happened one has to cross the word 'observer' and put in its place the new word 'participator'." (*The Physicists, Concept of Nature*, John F. Wheeler, p. 224) Biophysicist Lyall Watson writes humorously in his latest book *Lifetide* (p. 314, Bantam Image Book, first published 1979, New York), "Experiments about electrons coil down in the end to experiments on professors".

Quantum Physics had already entered (by the 1960s) the realms of *Vedānta*. One must know the knower, says *Vedānta*. Only the whole universe is known. How to know the knower, how to dive into the consciousness of man himself in the depth of which alone the mysteries of this universe has been resolved — this is the theme that the *Upaniṣads* deal with.

The *Upaniṣads*, again and again, assert that the senses cannot reach the ultimate Reality, the (unenlightened) mind cannot grasp it, words fail to describe it. The mystic author of the cloud of Unknowing says that a cloud of unknowing always persists when man goes to comprehend God by ordinary mind." The letter killeth," says St. Paul. This negative approach so far described is also accepted by agnostics. But *Vedānta* goes further. The ultimate Reality can be known, says the *Upaniṣad,* when a pure mind (freed from all other desires) guided by an enlightened will meditates on it. It is in this way that man can touch the immortal core of life, the immutable bedrock of eternal existence. Therefore, the constant refrain of the *Upaniṣads* is meditate (*anupaśyati*) and know thy real self which is *ātman* or the Reality which is hidden inside one's consciousness. And without this supreme realisation, says the *Upaniṣad*, man is condemned to live a suicidal existence.

Reality, in Quantum Physics, therefore, is no more purely objective, but connected with the subjective in Man. Michael Talbot coins the word "omnijective" to express the new conception of reality. And the acceptance of this omnijective Reality, he believes, is going to have a far reaching influence in the West. Mr. Talbot says, "How the omnijective nature of reality will change Western civilisation remains to be seen. The only certainly is that the changes will be stupendous." (*Mysticism and the New Physics*, M. Talbot, p. 17). Talbot also admits that mystic Vivekānanda spoke in a language which is indistinguishable and interchangeable with the language of mathematician Hermon Minkowski who first theorised that space and time are continuum. Talbot quotes Vivekānanda's exposition on Vedāntic concept of causality (i.e., causality in the ultimate analysis is a misnomer) and says (*Mysticism and New Physics,* pp. 114-15), "Vivekānanda further exposes a view that has become the backbone of quantum theory; there is no such thing as strict causality". In *Jñāna Yoga* Vivekānanda analyses the futility of search for cause when man realises the reality as the One all-pervading existence and consciousness. "What you call motion and causation can be done with the help of reality, when there is no more."

"Therefore, *Vedānta* formulates," says Vivekānanda, "not universal brotherhood, but universal oneness. It is one body, one mind, one soul throughout Spirit never dies."

Astronomy

Prof. David R. Frawley says that there are astronomical evidences pertaining to about 12,500 BC in the *Ṛgveda*. He says that a lunar calendar of twelve months with an intercalary month is mentioned in the *Ṛgveda*. A sun-wheel with 12 fellies and 360 spokes is mentioned in *Ṛgveda* indicating a knowledge of the twelve signs of the Zodiac and its 360 degrees circuit.

General Mathematics

Rāśi vidyā is described in the *Chāndogya Upaniṣad* when Varada (the master of that *vidyā*) came to Sanatkumāra for higher learning. Later on, this science became popular as *gaṇita*. *Vedāṅga Jyotiṣa* says "As are the crests on the heads of peacocks, as are the gems on the hoods of the snakes so is the *gaṇita* at the top of the sciences known as *Vedāṅga*. In this period, *gaṇita* is a comprehensive term which includes arithmetic, algebra and astronomy. Geometry was also investigated, but it was placed in a different general science known as *kalpa*. Indians were the first to use the decimal either to increase or decrease the value of the figure which was presided by Laplace, the great French mathematician. We are the first to use 'zero' as a symbol in mathematics. Our Indians invented the present numerical system. Indian teachers taught arithmetic and algebra, Vedic *Śulva Sūtra*s were earlier than the Alexandrian geometry of Hero. The earliest available work was *Bakshali Manuscript*. *Gaṇita-Sāra-Sangraham* of Mahaveera *ācārya* who lived between Brahmagupta and Bhāskarācārya.

Śrīdhara's (11th century) *Triśati* which deals with quadratic equations in algebra are important works. Jain authors' works deal with permutations and combinations. Nārāyaṇa Paṇḍita's *Bajīgaṇitavatamsa* and *Gaṇita Kaumudī* are also important. The 'Pythagoras theorem' which is stated in *Śulva Sūtra*s by Baudhāyana's: "The diagonal of a rectangle produces both areas, which its length and breadth produce separately." Ārya Bhaṭṭa discovered the method of finding out the areas of a triangle, a trapezium and a circle.

The approximate value of an 'irrational number', i.e., 2 (*dvī-karaṇī*) (1.4143256) and 3 (*tri-karaṇī*) (1.7320513) can be obtained,

Baudhāyana and Āpastamba.

In the geometry of the circle, 'Āryabhaṭa I' gave a value for pi (*tyajya*) which is correct to the four decimal places in a *śloka* (Śaṅkara Varman's treatise on astronomy, *Sadratnamālā*) theorems and their deductions:

> Lemma of Brahmagupta for integral solution or the indeterminate equation of second degree. John Pell discovered this in the seventeenth century. Our people discovered it a thousand years earlier.

Theory of Numbers

Bhāskara II's '*Cakravāla* or cyclic method' is described by Hankel as the finest thing in the theory of numbers in modern mathematics.

Āryabhaṭa I's 'sidereal period of earth's rotation about its axis is astonishingly close to the modern one.

Bhāskara I's 'word numeral system' is noteworthy, for example:

20 = *Nakhaḥ* (nails)

30 = *Dantī* (teath)

2 = *Nayan* (eyes)

It was also proved that infinity, however divided, remains infinite represented by the equation. Numbers seemed to have attracted the Indians of the Vedic and post-Vedic periods.

Algebra: Simultaneous equations with four unknown quantities, general solution of the degree, "Rules of involution and evolution". Arithmetic progression, both of numbers and of squares and cubes in Āryabhaṭṭīyam, in the bionomial theorem for positive integral exponents known in India as *meru prastara,* a pyramidial expansion of the numbers of combinations of 1, 2, etc. — syllables formed by short (*laghu*) and long (*guru*) sounds in Piṅgala's *Chandas-sūtra* using letters to denote unknown quantities in algebraic operation and indeterminate equations, of the first and second degree ($NY^2 + 1 = X^2$) in Bhāskara II's '*Siddhānta Śiromaṇi* — Śrīdhara's mehtod of solving 9 quadratic equation in his

Gaṇita-tilaka are some commendable achievements.

The Residual Pulveriser : Devarāja, son of Varadarāja, wrote a separate book *Kutta Kara Śiromaṇi* dealing with a rule for indeterminate equation of the first degree.

Geometry : The important properties of the circle, the projective geometry of the thread or measuring line — a part of *Kalpa Sūtras* which deal with rules of alter construction, specification of the measuring chord, gnomon of Managa and Varāha — construction of squares, rectangles, relation of the diagonal to the sides equivalent, rectangles and squares, equivalent circles and squares of Mānava and Kātyāyana — a square to the sum of two different squares like

$$3^2 + 4^2 = 5^2$$

$$5^2 + 12^2 = 13^2$$

$$12^2 + 35^2 = 37^2$$

$$15^2 + 36^2 = 39^2$$

of Āpastamba and Baudhāyana — Kātyāyana's theory 'If the sides of a right angle — triangle are a and $a = 2$ then the hypotenus is $a = 3$, Brahmagupta's formulae for the value of a prism, are a cyclic the length of two diagonals of cyclic quadrilateral indeterminate equation of the second degree $NY + 1 = X$ (what modern call Euler's remarkable theorem) and not insignificant.

Trigonometry: The 'sign functions' were used for solving the astronomical problems. Āryabhaṭṭa called it *bhujya*. His equation of spherical trigonometry is highly relevant even in the modern times.

Calculus: Bhāskara almost hit upon the root idea of the differential calculus.

Statistics: The present statistical theories are recent in origin. Some crude statistical methodologies were in vogue in ancient India, as seen from the *Mahābhārata* and the *Arthaśāstra*.

Physics

In the realm of physics, remarkable contributions have been made by our Indian scientist. Kaṇāda, the founder of the *Vaiśeṣika* system of philosophy, expounded that the entire matter in this world consists of atoms as many in kind as the various elements. Kaṇāda's atom would then correspond to the modern atom. Some Jain thinkers went a step further. They thought that all atoms are of the same kind and variety emerged because they entered into different combinations. The Jain atom may correspond to the particles of which all atoms are composed. Probably these particles can be called molecules. Kaṇāda taught that light and heat are variations of the same reality. Then this phenomenon forecasts Maxwell's Electromagnetic theory, which unified all forms of radiant energy, including heat and energy and light. Vācaspati interpreted light as composed of minute particles emitted by substances and striking the eye. This is a clear anticipation of the corpuscular theory of light, which was proposed by Newton but rejected till the discovery of the proton.

Modern physicists confirmed that the sun's rays travel in a curved way, but not in a straight line. Our ancestors told that the sun's chariot was drawn by seven horses tied by snakes. As the movements of the snakes are crooked and curved, so also the sun's rays. This phenomenon is described in a metaphysical poetic line *bhujagana mita sapta turaga*. The chapter on light says that there are seven colours in the white ray of the sun. *Atharvaveda* says that there are seven types of sun's rays, *sapta sūryasya raśmayaḥ*.

The law of gravitation discovered by Brahmagupta anticipated Newton by declaring that "all things fall to the earth by a law of nature; for it is the nature of the earth to attract and keep things". Due to the correct recitation requirements of *Veda*s, the sciences of acoustics made good progress. Very early the octave was divided into 22 *śruti*s.

Electricity: Its generation is described in the *Yajurveda*. In about five *mantra*s, electricity is described as the form of Agni, with two-heads, through which it will be coming and going in the shape of sparks and some details are furnished.

Sound: How a word travels from one place to another place is mentioned in ancient works like *Śābarabhāṣya*, *Vātsāyanabhāṣya* and also in *Praśastapādabhāṣya*. In *Praśastapādabhāṣya* it has been clearly mentioned that the word propagates in accordance with the wave theory.

Virūpākṣa and the Gravitation Power : The Purāṇic story shows that there are eight elephants, which are holding the earth tightly, from the eight corners of the earth, so that it cannot move here and there, from their folds. They are called *diggaja*.

Virūpākṣa is the name given to the elephant which holds the earth from the east. The word *virūpākṣa* means the gravitation power that has no shape and size. *Vi* means Not, *Rūpa* means shape and size and *akṣa* means gravitation power. In fact, it is the gravitation power of the sun that is holding the earth from the east. Because, wherever the sun moves, there the east is. Therefore *virūpākṣa* is nothing but the gravitation power of the sun.

The gravitation power is commonly known by the name of *virūpākṣa* and *ādhāra śakti* and it features in the Vedic *mantras* of daily use. Bhāskarācārya also revealed that the earth has got gravitational forces.

Aero-dynamics: The principle of parachute jumping was utilised in discovering a method of coming down from a great height, when no other ways are available. It consists in jumping down with an open parasol made of skin which descends slowly to the ground on account of the resistance of the air. Udayana in his *Kiraṇāvalī* tried to prove that air has no weight and that a gas/smoke-filled balloon floats in the air, whereas an air-filled ballon descends. Whatever may be the validity of his conclusion, we can at least see the scientific process at work.

The theory of velocity was discovered by the western scientists in the fourteenth century whereas that theory was explained in a book called *Vyomavati*. So also the *Rules of Impetus*.

Meteorology: Devala, a great authority on astrology, predecessor of Varāhamihira described more than 108 comets of nine types appearing in the triad of asterisms beginning from *Kṛttikā* and ending with *Bharaṇī*, forecasting good and evil effects.

Mechanics: In the *Ṛgveda*, it is mentioned that a three-wheeler*

---

* No source is available. There are only a few words about the three-wheeler aeroplane. So it is difficult to give a detailed explanation.

aeroplane of rurush was capable of travelling both in air and on land. King Bhoja's *Samarāṅgaṇa-sūtradhāra* mentions about the aerial cars. *Yantras* are mentioned in *Ṛgveda, Vājasaneya Saṁhitā, Rāmāyaṇa* and *Mahābhārata*.

Mechanical Engineering: The chapter on *Yantra vidhāna* in King Bhoja's *Samarāṅgaṇa-sūtradhāra* deals with machines, their basic elements, their qualities, various types of machines, the design and art of making a few machines. Some of their concepts and technical terms are relevant even today. Kauṭilya's *Arthaśāstra* mentions two types of *yantras* — static and moveable, automatic door leaves and *vivasa ghaṭe* which sinks when the enemy placed his full weight on it, to storm the fort.

Mineralogy and Metallurgy: Patañjali, the learned commentator on Pāṇini's grammar, was also a metallurgist. The iron pillar of Delhi, created about 4000 BC is rust-proof till today, though exposed to the sun and rain for the past 1500 years. Mining operations were extensively carried on as early as the third century BC. The use of gold, silver, copper, lead and tin was made even in the third millennium BC as revealed by the Mohenjo-Daro excavations.

Astronomy: One of the subsidiary studies of Vedic lore was *Jyotiṣa*, as a primitive astronomy designed mainly for fixing the dates and times for the performance of sacrifices, right from the Vedic period. They determined that the shape of the earth was spherical. The *Śatapatha Brāhmaṇa* clearly states that the earth is a globe or sphere. The *Ṛgveda* states that the earth is suspended freely in the air and adds that the axial rotation and the orbital motion of days, night, months, years and seasons are caused by the sun, which is known by the axial rotation of the sun. The earth is held by the sun and other heavenly bodies, by his mysterious power. Here the gravitational principle is anticipated. The moon shines from the borrowed light of the sun. Varāhmihira epitomised all these astronomical systems in his *Pañca Siddhāntika*. A summary of *Sūrya Siddhānta* was also incorporated in his work. He also summarise Āryabhaṭṭa's* views about eclipses and equinoxed. "The sphere of the

* Āryabhaṭṭa was born in AD 476 and he lived in Eastern India at Kusumpura (Palibothra). He composed his works at the young age of 23. According to Al-birunī, he was a native of Kusumapura, i.e., Pāṭaliputra and belonged →

stars is stationary and the earth by its revolution, produces the daily rising and setting of planets and stars." Brahmagupta was the illustrious successor to Āryabhaṭṭa and Varāhamihira.* They accurately calculated the diameter of the moon, eclipses of the moon and sun, the position of the poles and the position and motion of the major stars. Bhāskarācārya's** *Siddhāntaśiromaṇi* contains mathematics and

→

consequently to the east of India. Aryabhaṭṭa and the authors of the following five *siddhānta*s are looked upon as ancient astronomers: namely, the unknown author of the *Brahna-Siddhānta,* or *Pitāmaha-Siddhānta*; next, the author of the *Śaura-Siddhānta*, who is called Lāṭ by Al-birunī, and may possibly be identical with the Lagaṭa, Lagadha mentioned as author of the *Vedāṅga* treatise *Jyotiṣa* as well as with Ladha, a writer occasionally quoted by Brahmagupta; further Puliṣa, author of the *Pauliṣa-Siddhānta*; and lastly, Śrīśena and Viṣṇucandra, to whom the *Romaka-Siddhānta* and the *Vasiṣṭha-Siddhānta* — works said to be based upon Āryabhaṭṭa's system — are respectively attributed.

* The Arabs do not mention Varāhamihira although he was prior to Brahmagupta (the latter repeatedly alludes to him) and he gathered the teaching of these five *siddhānta*s in a work styled by the commentators *Pañcasiddhāntikā* but which he himself calls by the name *Karaṇa*. This work seems to have perished and only the astrological works of Varāhamihira have come down to us, namely, the *Saṁhitā* and the *Horā-śāstra*. The latter, however, is incomplete, only one-third of it being extant. Varāhamihira mentions a great number of predecessors, whose names are in part only known to us through him, for instance, Māyā and the Yavanas (frequently), Pārāśara, Manittha, Śaktipūrva, Viṣṇugupta, Devasvāmin, Siddhasena, Vajra, Jīvaśarman, Satya. Of Āryabhaṭṭa, no direct mention is made, possibly for the reason that he did nothing for astrology in the *Karaṇa*. While Āryabhaṭṭa still computes by the era of Yudhiṣṭhira, Varāhamihira employs the Śaka-kāla, Śaka-bhūpa-kāla, the era of the Śaka king which is referred by his scholiast to Vikrama's era.

** After Varāhamihira and Brahmagupta, various other astronomers distinguished themselves. Of these, the most eminent is Bhāskara. The identification of the period to which he belonged, however, poses a peculiar difficulty. According to his own account he was born *Śaka* 1036 (AD 1114) and completed the *Siddhānta-Śiromaṇi* in *Saka* 1072 (AD 1150) and the *Karaṇa-kutuhala* in *Saka* 1105 (AD 1183). The modern astronomers agree with this and assign to him the date *Śaka* 1072 (AD 1150). But Al-birunī who wrote in AD 1031 (that is 83 years before Bhāskara's birth) not merely mentions him but places his work — here called *Karaṇasāra* —132 years earlier, namely, in AD 899 so that there is a discrepancy of 284 years between the two accounts.

astronomy. Lalla and Bhoja were the other writers in the field. Āryabhaṭṭa revealed that the shadows of the earth and the moon are the causes for the eclipses. He also added that the moon has no self-illumination and the moonlight is due to the reflected days of the sun. The correct length of the year 365.2586805, the explanation of the eclipse, the correct expression of the angular diameter of the earth's shadow at the moon orbit longitude of the sun's apogee and the sidereal period of the moon's nodes of Āryabhaṭṭa are some of the landmarks in the faculty.

We have already seen that astronomy was cultivated to a considerable extent even in Vedic times. It was expressly specified by Strabo as a favourite pursuit of the brāhmaṇas. It was at the same time remarked, however, that this astronomy was still at a very elementary stage, the observations of the heavens being still wholly confined to a few fixed stars, more especially to the 27 or 28 lunar asterisms and to the various phases of the moon itself. The circumstance that Vedic year is a solar year of 360 days and not a lunar year does indeed presuppose a tolerably accurate observation and computation vis-a-vis the phenomena of the nocturnal heavens, and we must rather assume it to have been based upon the phenomena of the length or shortness of the day. To the elaboration of a quinquennial cycle with an intercalary month, a pretty early date must be assigned; although its origin from observation of the moon's phase may possibly be of extreme antiquity, it can only have attained its complete development towards the close of the Vedic period. Megasthenes, as we know, found the *yuga* system flourishing in full perfection. That the Hindu division of the moon's path into 27 lunar mansions is of Chinese origin, as asserted by Biot (*Journal des Savants*, 1840, 1845), can hardly be admitted. Notwithstanding the accounts of Chinese writers, the contrary might equally well be the case and the system might possibly have been introduced into China through the medium of Buddhism, especially as Buddhist writings adhere to the ancient order of the asterism — commencing with Kṛttikā (star) — precisely as we find it among the Chinese. To me, however, the most probable view is that these lunar mansions are of Chaldean origin, and that from the Chaldeans they passed to the Hindus as well as to the Chinese. The Indians may either have brought the knowledge of these lunar mansions with them into India or else have obtained it at a later time through commercial relations of the Phoenicians with the Punjab. At all events, they were known to the Indians from a very early period and as communication with China is altogether inconceivable at a time when the Hindus were perhaps not even acquainted with the mouths of the Ganges, Chinese influence here is quite out of the question. The names of some of these asterisms occur even in the *Ṛgveda-Saṁhitā*, for e.g. the Aghas (i.e.) Maghas and the Arjunyau, i.e. Phālgunyau — a name also applied to them in the *Śatapatha-Brāhmaṇa* — in the nuptial hymn, *maṇḍala* X. 85.12; further *Tiṣya* in *maṇḍala* V. 54-12 which, however, is used by Sāyaṇa for the sun. The earliest complete enumeration of them with their respective regents is found in the *Taittirīya Saṁhitā*. A second exhibits variants of the names, betokening a later date, and it occurs in the *Atharvaveda Saṁhitā* and the *Taittirīya Brāhmaṇa*. The majority of the names are also given in Pāṇini. This latter list contains names employed by the later astronomers; and it is precisely these later ones that are enumerated in the so-called *Jyotiṣa* or Vedic calendar (along with the zodiacal signs too). To this latter treatise an importance has hitherto been attached which its contents do not justify. Should my conjecture be confirmed that the Lagadha, Lagaṭa, whose system it embodies, is identical with the Lāṭ who is mentioned by Al-birunī as the author of the ancient *Sūrya-Siddhānta*, then it would fall in the fourth or fifth century or other era; and even this might almost be too early a date for this somewhat insignificant tract, which has only had a certain significance — that, too, on account of relating it to the *Veda*.*

A decided advance in astronomical science was made through the discovery of the planets. The earliest mention of these occurs, perhaps, in the *Taittirīya-Āraṇyaka* though this is still uncertain. They are not noticed in any other work of the Vedic period. Manu's book is unacquainted with them; Yājñavalkya's code book inculcates their worship; in the works of Kālidāsa, in the *Mṛcchakaṭikam* and the *Mahābhārata*, as well as the *Rāmāyaṇa*, they are repeatedly referred

* This is why it adheres to the old order of the lunar asterism, as is done even in the present day when writing upon the *Veda*.

to.* Their names are peculiar and of purely Indian origin; three of them are thereby designated as sons respectively of the sun (Saturn), of the Earth (Mars) and the Moon (Mercury) and the remaining two as representatives of the two oldest families of *ṛṣis* — Aṅgiras (Jupiter) and Bhṛgu (Venus). The last two names are probably connected with the fact that the adherents of the *Atharvaveda* — which was likewise specially associated with the *ṛṣis*, Aṅgiras and Bhṛigu — took the lead at this time in the cultivation of interest in astronomy and astrology. Besides these names others are also common: Mars, for e.g., is termed "the red"; Venus, "the white" or beaming; Saturn, "the slow-travelling" — this last being the only one of the names that testifies to any real astronomical observation. To these seven planets (sun and moon being included) the Indians added two others, Rāhu and Ketu, the head and tail respectively of the monster who is conceived to be the cause of the solar and lunar eclipses. But this number nine is not the original number — if indeed it be planets that the passage from the *Taittirīya-Āraṇyaka* cited above refers to. Only seven are mentioned in this text. The term for plant *graha*, the seizer, is evidently of astrological origin; indeed, astrology was the focus in which astronomical inquiries generally converged and from which they drew light and animation after the practical exigencies of worship had been once for all satisfied. Whether the Hindus discovered the plants independently or whether the knowledge came to them from without, cannot as yet be determined; but the systematic peculiarity of the nomenclature points to the former view.

Astronomers and Mathematicians: Vedic sage Dīrghatamas was said to be the first astonomer. He was the first person who realised the importance of having an era. There is no record of the life of this great *sāvant*. He pioneered the foundation for the Vedic astronomy. He worked indefatigably for ten full *yugas*. According to the tradition, the sage Dīrghatamas was the son of Mammaṭa. He was the disciple of Sage Ucathya. With a dedication, he observed the days, nights, the movements of the moon and the sun. He also noticed discrepancies existing between the lunar and solar years.

---

* In Pāṇini, IV 2.26, śukra might refer to the planet Śukra, but it is preferable to take it in the sense of *soma*-juice.

Dīrghatamas means long-drawn nights. Tilak presumes that this first astronomer was a native of the north pole region where there are long drawn nights of 6 months and equally long-drawn days. According to him, the ancient sages described the astronomical scenes and conditions as were actually seen by them in their region of the North pole. They evolved time units, which were determined by the astronomical considerations and which were not arbitrary. Since they had no other means of keeping records, they evolved a system of sacrifices to measure the time units. As the Vedic sages came down to the plains, the astronomical data changed. Due to these changes they were obliged to make suitable adjustments in the current time systems and the *yajñas* pertaining to them. One of the disciples of Dīrghatamas was Kāksivan and another Aświja. In the *Ṛgveda,* 242 *mantras* are attributed to Dīrghatamas, which are in the first book, Hymns 140 to 164. This sage Dīrghatamas with his disciples, laid the solid foundation of one of the most important sciences during an age when writing and recording were in an embryonic stage. The credit for the established 'era' concept squarely belongs to this sage Dīrghatamas. *Ṛgveda* says: "Dīrghatamas, the son of Mammaṭa, has grown old after the tenth *yuga*. He is the Brahma of those who seek to obtain the object of their works; he is their charioteer".

Lagadha is the first Indian astronomer to systematise and codify the available knowledge and to promote its scope. He is the famous author of the *Vedāṅga Jyotiṣa*. There are two recensions — the *Ṛgveda Jyotiṣa* and the *Yajurveda Jyotiṣa*. Though the cogents are almost the same they slightly differ in the number of verses. The *Vedāṅga Jyotiṣa* is very important for fixing auspicious *muhūrtas* for various religious rituals and for the correct interpretation of the *Vedas*. "Thus spoke Lagadha of his exposition of months, years, *muhūrtas*, *lagnas*, *parvas*, days, seasons, *ayanas* and months. The learned man who knows the movements of the moon, the sun, and the *nakṣastras*, will be blessed with progeny in this world, and (after death) get into the world of the moon, the sun and the *nakṣatras*. Lagadha was the systematiser of astronomy, the first book writer of astronomy, the first to work out simple formulae to derive unknowns from the known quantities."

The Science of Warfare

The science of warfare described in the book *Narapati-Haya-carya* and Bhoja is *Yukti-kalpataru*. Bhoja quotes from Vatya's works on swords and Śārṅgadhara's books *Lohārṇva Lohapradīpa*. *Ahirbudhnya Saṁhitā* is a text of *Tantra* devoted mainly to the worship of *Sudarśana* in *yantra* form. This is a missile *par excellence*. It appears that this *Sudarśana cakra* is responsible for the creation of all destructive weapons and missiles to be used against evil powers trying to turn the cosmos into chaos. There are also offensive and defensive weapons. Śrī Kṛṣṇa's *Sudarśana cakra*, represented a type of ancient Indian *Muktāstra*. It was specially designed as a flinging weapon and could cut and behead the enemies and return to Kṛṣṇa, after finishing its job. On the basis of the features of this weapon as mentioned in the sources, it may be compared to modern fire-arms, like missiles or with some fire-emitting machine. The only difference is that the present machine will not return to its sources of origin. The achievements of the Purāṇic and the epic age in the field of fire-arms and the science of warfare were in no way less advanced than modern scientific discoveries.

Archery

This science is narrated in *Dhanurveda* and Vasiṣṭha's *Dhanurveda Saṁhitā*.

Civil Engineering

Roads and road planning were mentioned in Kauṭilya's *Arthaśāstra* and King Bhoja's *Samarāṅganasūtradhāra*. King Bāsavarāja who ruled the Keladi kingdom of Karnataka wrote an encyclopaedic work *Śiva Tattvaratnākara* in Sanskrit. This work contains chapters on history, geography, religion, philosophy, science, arts, architecture, royal entertainments, sports, etc. In this work Hindu architecture is divided into three groups — town planning, palace construction and temple construction. The author had discussed the qualities of the suitable land, types of towns, and habitation like *grāma*, *khetaka*, *droṇa*, *madamba*, *aṭṭāna* and *nagara*, allotment of different professions under town planning. Under palace construction Bāsavarāja had dealt with soil test, selection of suitable wood and timber, inauspicious trees, auspicious days and time for wood-cutting, types of palaces having one, two, three or four *sata*s the necessity of building *catuska* and *alinda*, *muktakoṇa*, *sarvatobhadra*, *śrīvatsa*, *nadyavarta*, *vardhamāna*, *svastiaka*, etc. sixteen types of palaces with one *śālā*, *aṭaka śālā*, etc. Under temple construction, the author dealt with the following subjects: worthy sites, soil test, four types of land according to colour, site-allocation to men of the four castes, stone collection, suitable places, and timings for the same, different types of stones, position and orientation of temples, types of temple, *garbhagṛha*, *vāhanālaya*, *prakāra*s, etc.

Chemistry

Ancient masters of chemistry are Patañjali, Bhūyadattadeva, Vyādi, Swaccanda, Dāmodara, Vāsudeva, Caraka, Suśruta, Hārīta, Vāgbhaṭa, Somadeva's *Rasendracūḍāmaṇi*, Yaśodhara's *Rasaprakāśa Sudhākara*, Govindācārya's *Rasasāra*, Viṣṇudeva's and others *Ratnaghoṣa*, *Gahanānanda-nadha*, *Carpatinadha* are the Buddhist chemistry. About the distillation of liquor, Mallinātha's commentary on Kālidāsa's *Meghadūta* makes a mention. Alberuni says that 'alchemy' was mentioned in Nāgārjuna's *Ras-Ratnākara* and in *Kākacaṇḍeśvarī matatantra* and *Suvarṇatantra*.

The characteristics of mercury were the roughly researched in India, centuries before it was studied in Europe. By 1200 itself, a large number of apparatus and instruments in chemical technology were in vogue. The invaluable research conducted by P.C. Ray has bequeathed to us concrete evidence of our unique Indian achievement in pure and industrial chemistry.

Botany

In the *Atharvaveda* there is reference to 150 herbs of which only a few are known to us. They are Odina pinnata (Ajātaśṛṅge), Colavsauthus Indica (Arathu) Ficus Religiousa (Aswattha), Ficus glomarata (Udumba), Castus specius (kustha), Acacea catechu (*khadir*), Solsmum nigrun (Nitatuni), Achayrcuthus aspera (*Apamarg*). It is obvious that these seers had some idea regarding economical division of plants and were aware of different categories of plants such as acquatic amphibrus, terrestrial, etc.

Parāśara's *Vṛkṣāyurveda* (the science of the life of the plants) was very well developed even in those days. This *śāstra* and its practitioners were referred to in the *Agni Purāṇa*, *Bṛhat Saṁhitā* and the *Arthaśāstra*. The student was asked to study the art of the collection and selection of seeds, the fruitful germination of the seeds, various methods of propagation such as grafting, and cutting, planting, manuring, rotation of crops, cultivation, under different weather conditions, treatment of plants in health and disease, location of plants for improving the aesthetic and hygienic surroundings of the homestead, etc. Rigorous tests were conducted for the students in the collection and identification of plant specimens.

Symbiosis

The ascent and circulation of sap is discussed by Kaṇāda, Śaṅkaramiśra, and in the *Śāntiparva* of the *Mahābhārata*. The *Śāntiparva* 'vividly' states that plants prepare their nutrients from the sap with the help of the solar energy and a component of air. With the help of Agni and air, this sap is digested, prepared into proper food and it is due to the assimilation of this food, that the plants grow. Kaśyapa, and Bhaṭṭotpala studied the etiology, diagnosis and treatment of plant diseases. Regular classification of plants with its sub-divisions, various aspects of plant life and origin of the first organic body in Parāśara's *Vṛkṣāyurveda* — selection of the soil, plant classification, plant propagation, recipes for the nourishment and treatment of their disease, in *Upavana-vinoda* — in the plan of sowing trees, their diseases and cure, manuring, improving, fruits and flowers, even altering their colour, scent as explained by Varāhamihira — life in plants, death, sleep, waking, disease, drugging, transmission of specific characters by means of ova and movements towards favourable and away from unfavourable conditions, their dormant consciousness, the capacity to feel pain and pleasure, sensitivity to cold and heat, the sound of the thunder, odours, etc. as described by Udayana — are no small steps in progress.

The sun's rays are responsible for the generation of chlorophyl in the green leaves and also for the ripening of fruits by the process of 'Photo-synthesis'.

> *arkambhito vivsre brahaddha tta stau*
> *bhuvana shvantah.*

Plants have not only life but also react to pain and pleasure as the *Mahābhārata* says:

> *vallī vestayate vṛuṣam sarvataścāpi gacchati glayate*
> *sūryate cāpi sparaśtenatra vidyate*

Atharvaveda as Monuments of Indian Medicine

Compared to other *Veda*s, *Atharvaveda* contains more specialised knowledge on worldly affairs and *Āyurveda* — meaning, the science of life, which describes particular herbs, medicines, diseases and organic disorder. In several of its hymns, some of which will be cited here, different types of bacilli and bacteria have been deacribed along with their pathological effects. If one reads this *Veda*, one would not fail to notice that this pertains to theosophy, spiritualism, state-craft society, family, sciences like botany, chemistry, physics, veterinary science, agriculture, geography and natural elements. These have been described in great detail extending to several hymns. These may be applied to any country and nation, without any distinction. Hence, it is but natural that some scholars term it as *Rāṣṭraveda* or *Rājyaveda* and Western scholars like Macdonell call it "the oldest literary monument of Indian Medicine". One of its epithets *Brahmaveda* testifies to the abundance of spiritual and theosophic material in it.

First *kāṇḍa* is devoted solely to topics like medicines, herbs, diseases, bacteria, pathological condition, treatments, human psysiology and its normal functioning. The very first hymn deals with the prime importance of *medha* (intellect) symbolised by strong and purified speech and cites the means to sharpen it through prayer and application of herbs like Vācaspati and Vāsapati. (***Vide*** *Atharvaveda* I.1, IV.30 and VI.108 and VI.61). These hymns provide the basis for *Kauśitakī-sūtra* and *Gṛhyasūtra* for prescribing practices for Medhajanan. The two medicinal plants referred to, viz., Vācaspati and Vāsaspati, are Acarus Calamuse Linn and Agati grand flora. The practical usage of these medicines is also given. The second and third hymn of this *kāṇḍa* deal with urinary ailments and their treatment including the surgical one. Hymns 4, 5 and 6 deal with the medicinal properties and natural varieties of water. Hymns 7 and 8 deal with different types of intestinal and other worms along with viral germs. The 11th hymn deals with midwifery and gynaecological, embryonic and associated deformities together with their surgical and medicinal treatment. The 12th hymn deals with different kinds of ailments as well as prayers for their removal. The 13th hymn stresses the medicinal aspect of electricity, the 16th one describes the medicinal properties of lead, the 17th deals with arteritis, the 18th one deals with curative application of sunrays, 19-21 hymns contain the prayers for curing diseases. The 22nd hymn refers to the diseases of liver and heart, the next two to the medical application of certain herbs, the 25th indicates the curative aspect of bodily heat, etc. Up to the 12th *kāṇḍa* different types of ailments, and their treatments — be they physical (*vyādhis*) mental or spiritual (*adhi*) — have been dealt with without any interruption. In the remaining *kāṇḍa*s also, we come across such hymns occasionally. The *Atharvaveda* covers a large amount of medical and scientific know-how providing basis for eight branches of later *Āyurveda*. Hence, it is clearly the "the oldest literary monument of Indian Medicine". Thus the concept of *Āyurveda* or Indian medicine is not restricted to physical derangement in life and treatment to human beings but, by its very etymological definition, it is concerned with the knowledge of life and its longevity, etc. *Atharvaveda* deities are primarily concerned with the physical well-being of human beings through removal of diseases as well as mental and spiritual uplift of all beings.

Occultism and Prayers for Material Welfare

Positive sciences refuse to accept anything which is not openly verifiable but there are many things in life which are not verifiable from the material point of view. Such phenomena come within the indefinite extensible domain of occultism. Occultism believes not only in the law of causation but supercausation as well — that all calamities are caused by displeasure of Gods and spirits who are the controlling powers of this universe. The *Atharvaveda* which has rites to appease

Gods and secure earthly benefits is considered by many as the parent-source of Indian occultism. To cite a few examples:

1. *Mantra* for prosperity — *AV*, III.11.4.
2. For victory in War — *AV*, III.1.
3. For evil purposes, to kill an enemy — *AV*, II.19.
4. To drive away demons — *AV*, IV.16.
5. *Mantra* for healing — *AV*, I.4.1.

There are hymns to cure fever (*takman*), leprosy, jaundice, dropsy, scrofula, cough, ophthalmia, baldness, lack of vital power, fractures and wounds, the bites of snakes and injurious insects, poison in general, mania and other ailments. The use of appropriate herbs is mentioned:

A few hymns/*mantra*s are given below as examples.

Mantra against cough:

> Just as the soul with soul desires
> Swift to a distance flies away
> So even though, O cough, fly forth
> Along the soul's quick darling course (McDonell)

Mantra for cure of leprosy by means of a dark-coloured plant:

> Born in the night art thou, O Herb
> Dark coloured, sable, black of hue
> Red tinted tinge this leprosy
> And stain away its spots of grey (McDonell)

Mantra to destroy demons and enemies:

> Bend sound and pass us by, O Curse
> Even as a burning fire a lake
> Here strike him down that curses us
> As heavens lightning smites the tree (McDonell)

Threat held out against evil-doers and oppressors:

> Water with which they bathe, the dead, And
> that with which they wet his beard.
> The Gods assigned thee as thy share

Oppressor of Brahman Priest.

Auspicious hymns to secure long life and health:

> If life in him declines or has departed
> If life in him declines or has departed
> If on the very brink of death, he totters
> If snap him from the lap of Desolation
> I free him now to live a hundred autumns

Hymns to secure prosperity in the house or field, in cattle, in trade and good luck at play, etc.:

> As at all times the lightning stroke
> Smites irresistibly the tree
> so gathesters with dice would I
> beat irresistibly today

To secure harmony, to allay anger, strike and disease and procure ascendency in the assembly:

> O assembly we know thy name; Frolic truly
> by name thou art
> May all who meet and sit in thee
> Be in their speech at one with me

Hymns for Royal consecration in conferment of lustre and glory and victory for him for striking terror into the enemy:

> Arise and arm ye spectral forms
> Followed by meteoric flames
> Ye serpents, spirits of the deep
> Demon of night, pursue of the foe (McDonell)

Medical Science

When we speak of the beginnings of the healing art in Vedic times it is the *Atharvaveda* that occupies a special position : in this literature, its oldest fragments are to be found — fragments, however, of a rather sorry description, and limited mostly to spells and incantations. The Indians themselves consider medicine as an *Upaveda*, and expressely entitle it *Āyurveda* by which term, however, they do not understand any special work, as has been supposed. They derive it, as they do the *Veda* itself, immediately from the gods; and as the oldest of human writers upon it they mention, first Ātreya, then Agniveśas, Caraka*, Dhanvantari, and, lastly, his disciple Śuśruta. The first three names belong specially to the two divisions of the *Yajus*, but only to the period of the *Sūtras* and the school development of this *Veda*. The medical works bearing these titles can, in no case, therefore, be of an earlier date than this. How much later they ought to be placed is a point for which we have at present only the limit of the eighth century AD — at the close of which, according to Ibn Beitar and Al-birunī, the work of Caraka and, according to Ibn Abi Usaibiah, the work of Śuśruta also were translated into Arabic. That Indian medicine had in Pāṇini's time itself attained a certain degree of advancement appears from the names of various disease specified by him though nothing definite results from this. In the *gaṇa* "Kartakaujapa" we find the "Śauśrutaparthavas" instanced among the last members; but it is uncertain what is meant by this expression. The *gaṇas*, moreover, prove nothing in regard to Pānini's time. In the *Pañcatantra,* two physicians, Sālihotra and Vātsyāyan whose names are cited even today are repeatedly mention; but although this work was translated into Pahlavī in the sixth century, it does not at all follow that everything now contained in it formed part of it then. I am not aware of any other references to medical teachers or works. I may only add that the chapter of the *Amarakośa* on the human body and its diseases certainly presupposes an advanced knowledge of medical science.

An approximate determination of the date of the existing works will only be possible when they have been subjected to a critical examination both in respect of their contents and language. But we may even now dismiss, as belonging to the realm of dreams, the naive views that have quite recently been advanced as to the age of some works. One example is the work bearing Śuśruta's name. In language and style,

* In the *Caraka Saṁhitā* itself Bharadvāja, Kapiṣthala leads the list as the disciple of Indra. Of his six disciples — Agniveśa, Bhela, Jātukarana, Parāśara, Hārīta, Kṣarapāṇi — Agniveśa first composed his *tantra*, and then the others composed theirs severally, which they thereupon recited to Atreya.

this work and the works resembling it with which I am acquainted manifestly exhibit a certain affinity to the writings of Varāhamihira. "If then" — here I make use of Stenzler's words* "internal grounds should' render it probable that the system of medicine expounded in Śuśruta has borrowed largely from the Greeks, there would be nothing at all surprising in such a circumstance so far as chronology is affected by it. But in the meantime, no such internal grounds whatever appear to exist; on the contrary there is much that seems to tell against the idea of any such Greek influence. In the first place the Yavaṇas are never referred to as authorities; and amongst the individuals enumerated in the introduction as contemporaries of Śuśruta, there is not one whose name has a foreign sound. Again, the cultivation of medicine is by Śuśruta himself as well as by other writers, expressely assigned to the city of Kāśī — in the period, to be sure, of the mythical king Divodāsa Dhanvantari, and incarnation of Dhanvantari, the physician of the gods. And lastly, the weights and measures to be used by the physician are expressely enjoined to be either those employed in Magadha or those current in Kaliṅga; whence we may fairly presume that it was in these eastern provinces which never came into close contact with the Greeks, the medicine received its special cultivation."

Geo-Botany

Varāhamihira's *Bṛhatsaṁhitā* reveals that the bioindicators are the same in the exploration for both ground water and metalli-ferous deposits in tropical regions. Modern science has to realise the truth about the geo-botanical knowledge of our ancient personalities.

Horticulture

The systematic and scientific knowledge of horticulture was available and cultivated in India even from times immemorial. This fact is seen in *Mānasollāsa* of the twelfth century AD. It is called *Abhilāṣitārtha-*

* From his examination of Vuller's view in the following number of *Jamus* II.453, I may remark here that Wilson's words, also quoted in the Preface to his system of *Hindu Medicine,* p. xvii, have been utterly misunderstood by Vullers. Wilson fixes "as the most modern limit of our conjecture" the ninth or tenth century AD but Vullers takes it to be BC.

Cintāmaṇi published by the Gaekwar oriental studies. It is a Sanskrit work composed by Someśvara II, the Cālukya king of the twelfth century AD. This *Mānasollasa* has two chapters called *Bhūdhara krīḍā* and *Vana krīḍā*, which contain much material about horticulture and botany. There are 160 verses, which shed light on the plan of a beautiful garden, the preparation of the soil, the treatment of the seeds, the process of sowing the seeds, the plantation of saplings, the various methods of grafting, the process of watering, the plants, their nourishment and protection, their diseases, and treatments and some botanical marvels. It also describes the various artificial plants and trees, maintained in royal orchards and prescribes certain amusements which a king should enjoy in such a garden.

Spies

In the Vedic period there seems to have been a large staff of spies. "From the sky," says the *Atharvaveda*, "his (Varuṇa's) spies go forth hither; thousand-eyed they look over the earth."* From the curious allusion in the *Ṛgveda*, one is inclined to infer that spies detected or caught criminals. Afraid of spies, Yama rejects the love of his sister.** It is interesting that the *Taittirīya Saṁhitā* mentions *dūta*s as well as *prahita*s.*** Many centuries later Sāyaṇācārya, the great Vedic commentator, explained that the *dūta* was a regular representative of the king while the *prahita* was a mere spy.

Prognostication

Prognostication is the science which indicates the future events, Varāhmihara's *Bṛhat Saṁhitā* deals with this.

Physiognomy and Palmistry

Physiognomy tells us about the character and fate of men and women according to their physique. This science is mentioned in

---

* *Atharvaveda,* IV.16.4.

** *Ṛgveda,* X.10.1-6.

*** *Taittrīya Saṁhitā,* IV.7.1.

Viṣṇudharmottara. Nārada was the poineer for astrology.

Relativity

> The views of time and space, which I have to set forth, have their foundation in experimental physics. Therein is their strength. Their tendency is revolutionary. From henceforth space itself and time in itself sink to mere shadows, and only a kind of union of the two preserves an independent existence.
>
> — H. Minkowshi (1908)

There are two parties to every observation — the observed and the observer.

What we see depends not only on the object looked at, but on our own circumstances — position, motion or more personal idiosyncracies. Sometimes by instinctive habit, sometimes by design, we attempt to eliminate our own share in the observation, and so from a general picture of the world outside us which shall be common to all observers. A small speck on the horizon of the sea is interpreted as a giant steamer. From the window of our railway carriage we see a cow glide past at fifty miles an hour, and remark that the creature is enjoying a rest. We see the starry heavens revolve round the earth, but decide that it is really the earth that is revolving, and so picture the state of the universe in a way which would be acceptable to an astronomer on any other planet.

The first step in throwing our knowledge into a common stock must be the elimination of the various individual standpoints and the reduction to some specified standard observer. The picture of the world so obtained is nonetheless relative. We have not eliminated the observer's share; we have only fixed it definitely.

To obtain a conception of the world from the point of view of no one in particular is a much more difficult task. The position of the observer can be eliminated; we are able to grasp the conception of a chair as an object in nature looked at the all round, and not from any particular angle. We can think of it without mentally assigning ourselves some position with respect to it. This is a remarkable faculty, which has evidently been greatly assisted by the perception of solid relief with our two eyes. But the motion of the observer is not eliminated so simply. We had thought that it was accomplished; but the discovery in the last chapter that observers with different motion use different space and time-reckoning shows that the matter is more complicated than was supposed, as specified by Einstein in his book *Theory of Relativity*.

Whether we are able to go still further and obtain a knowledge of the world which not merely does not particularise the observer, but does not postulate an observer at all; whether if such knowledge could be obtained it, would convey any intelligible meaning; and whether it could be understood — these questions need not detain us now. The answers are not necessarily negative, but they lie outside the normal scope of physics.

The circumstances of an observer which affect his position are his position, motion and gauge of magnitude. More personal idiosyncracies disappear, if instead of relying on his crude senses, he employs scientific measuring apparatus. But scientific apparatus has position, motion and size, so that these are still involved in the results of any observation. There is no essential distinction between scientific measures and the measures of the senses. In either case our acquaintance with the external world comes to us through material channels; the observer's body can be regarded as part of his laboratory equipment, and so, far as we know, it obeys the same laws. We therefore group together perceptions and scientific measures, and in speaking of 'a particular observer', we include all his measuring appliances.

Position, motion, magnitude, scale — these factors have a profound influence on the aspect of the world to us. Can we form a picture of the world which shall be a synthesis of what is seen by observers in all sorts of positions, having all sorts of velocities, and all sorts of sizes. As already stated we have accomplished the synthesis of positions. We have two eyes, and it has been dinned into our minds from infancy that the world has to be looked at from more than one position. Our brains have so far responded as to give us the idea of solid relief, which enables us to appreciate the three-dimensional world in a vivid way that the world would be scarcely possible if we were only acquainted with strictly two-dimensional pictures. We do not merely deduce the three-dimensional world; we see it. But we have no such aid in synthesising different motions. Perhaps if we had been endowed with two eyes moving with different velocities, our brains would have developed the necessary faculty; we should have perceived a kind of relief in a fourth dimension so as to combine into one picture, the respect of things seen with different motions. Finally if we had two eyes of different sizes, we might have evolved a faculty for combining the points of view of the mammoth and the microbe.

It will be seen that we are not fully equipped by our senses for forming an impersonal picture of the world. And it is because the deficiency is manifest that we do not hesitate to advocate a conception of the world which transcends the images familiar to the senses. Such a world can perhaps be grasped but not pictured by the brain. It would be unreasonable to limit our thought of nature to what can be comprised in a sense picture. As Lodge has said "our senses were developed by the struggle for existence, not for the purposes of philosophising on the world".

In the theory of the Michelson-Morley experiment, according to current physical views, our standard of size — the rigid measuring rod — must change according to the circumstances of its motion; and the aviator's adventures illustrate a similar change in the standard of duration of time. Certain rather puzzling irregularities have been discovered in the apparent motions of the Sun, Mercury, Venus and the Moon; but there is a strong family resemblance between these, which leads us to believe that the real phenomenon is a failure of the time-keeping of our standard clock, the Earth. Instances could be multiplied where a change of the observer or his standards produces or conceals changes in the world around him.

The object of the relativity theory, however is not to attempt the hopeless task of apportioning responsibility between the observer and the external world, but to emphasise that in our ordinary description and in our scientific description of natural phenomena, the two factors ar indissolubly united. All the familiar terms of physics — length, duration of time, motion, force, mass, energy and so on — refer primarily to this relative knowledge of this world; and it remains to be seen whether any of them can be retained in a description of the world which is not relative to a particular observer.

Hinduism was able to explain relativity with the help of Arutprakāśa Vallalar who practised the doctrine of invisibility. On 30.1.1874 at '0' hour Vallalar became invisible. Rather he became one with Divine Light. He himself became luminous and when he merged with the Divine light, he became invisible. Is this scientifically possible. Yes. When the body moves faster than light it becomes invisible. It is the ultimate *yoga* which mankind seeks.

Yoga, in principle is the reasonant energy available in the universe. Our *ṛṣis* were one step ahead of the modern concept of Relativity and their concept is the final step before the attainment of oneness. Basically the difference between the two concepts is that Relativity assumes conversion of one form of energy into another form, matter into energy, energy into matter, whereas *yoga* is to become one with the so-called form of energy or matter.

The ancients of Bharat were aware of the existence of atoms and subtler constituents, which we are not aware of today. They are the final particles of the constituents, having direct relation to *Brahman*. *Brahman* is the absolute form of zero and infinity. So, one can attain or merge in *Brahman* when he can assume zeroness or infiniteness. This is possible only when we know the next immediate cause and then mastering that cause, we can get back to the subtlest form.

To achieve the omnipotent or the omnipresent, to choose a constituent in the universe which can be zero, infinity both in space and time — that which can satisfy these two requirements in the physical world is the first reason or a reason next to *Brahman*. Such a super physical constituent is mind.

Mind in the relative sense expresses itself through brain. But, Mind as an independent factor is absolute, having no define shape, matter, time, energy, etc. which means it is the constituent which can be resonant with anything in the physical world without undergoing any change in its own form or energy.

By knowing the sequence from Brahmā to the physical world, they tried the reverse process, the process to go from body through *prāṇa*, mind. They succeeded in it. The reversal of the creation is to make the grossest body to merge in the subtlest *Brahman*. Patañjali gave a final touch to the techniques of achieving the effects of *yoga* and *yoga* itself. The concept of relativity is at the gross level, whereas the *yoga* is oneness at the subtlest level. For example, add salt to water and mix thoroughly. The salt does not reach but occupies the intermolecular space in water. This is because there is a perfect state of resonance in the consciousness of the *paramāṇu*s of both, and the after effect is the solution of co-existence. This is the case of natural *yoga*.

Instead, add sodium to water. There will be a vigorous reaction. The atoms of sodium cannot get into intermolecular space but can react with water to produce heat. After this another molecule is formed called compound at the gross level. This is a natural state of non-coexistence or *viyoga*. It is here that our ancients turned inwards into the subtler level of matter. They wanted to know the relative reactions and bring about a change in such a way as to effect a natural coexistence. This was possible only by knowing the inner particles of matter. To do this, a technique was necessary. The technique was to condition the mind and make it flow into the matter and energy to bring about a *yoga*. To achieve *yoga,* our *ṛṣi*s have found different techniques which were recodified and condensed by Patañjali as *Yoga Sūtra*s.

Mental flux should be made to stabilise within one's own body. When our brain senses the presence of mental flux in our body, that shows the state of steadiness of the brain with the Mind. Mental flux which has no physical attributes when it flows into the body occupies the complete inter-*paramāṇu* space. When such a flux gets established in the physical body, a mental impression is created about the physical characteristics of the body. The impression helps in controlling *paramāṇu*s and hence the gross body. This impression is the right knowledge about the body.

To achieve the mental impression the manifested form of mind in the brain should be controlled and the agitation should be stopped. This is possible only when the sense-organs stop learning about external objects. This can be done by negating the mental impression created by the sense-organs or by de-sentising the sensors. Both require the conditioning of the brain. Even if we close the sense-organs, the earlier mental impressions in the brain will try to open out of the sense-organs because of the continuous mental agitation/mental waves.

If we have to stop the agitation of the brain, *prāṇa* should be clear and steady to have a steady potential *prāṇa* then the steady mental flux in the body. For the *prāṇa* to be steady, the life holding *paramāṇus* of the body must be pure and stable. Which tells us that controlling of breath, food intake, waste output and energy level in the physical body is a must. This clearly proves that creation is from the *paramāṇu* level to the Gross level.

The *paramāṇu* level can be recognised by looking inwards from the gross level of activity. All these things are happening with respect to another subject factor — the time flux. These are the reasons why *Vedāṅga Jyotiṣa* and *Āyurveda* form the two most important subjects of studying the time and mind at the gross level. Having known the levels of mind and the physical body, the techniques of *sādhanā* have to be found out.

Let us now study the mathematical approach to the physical body and mental flux

F = Ma

F = mv/t

M = Mass

a = Acceleration

F = Force

Let us now resubstitute in this formula as below:

v = Velocity

t = time of change of mass at a velocity v

When a = 0 then $F = 0$ body can still have velocity with respect to mind. If the *paramāṇus* reach weightlessness because of the mental flux, then even if the mind travels at infinite speed, force created is zero. This results in many effects.

1. Disappearance of a physical body.

2. Appearance of a physical body.
3. Movement of physical body in another physical body.
4. Movement of physical body at the speed of mind without effecting a conversion of energy.

This shows that the mind is capable of making the gravitational field zero, increasing the speed of light of any amount and bringing down the static field on the *paramāṇus* to zero. It is the technique of achieving this principle of physics which is very difficult. Because of the incapability of providing the technology, the moderns call it a heap of myth or a fiction. The right technique of achieving the fruits of body and mind from the gross level to the subtlest level is greatly and precisely dealt by Patañjali in his *Yoga Sūtras*. A re-orientation of this text is required to correct the tilt of brain of modern people. This calls for some formulae, physical significance, etc. Reaching the state of weightlessness is possible by going out of the gravitational field of the mass, which means that we should go out of the solar system. In the same way when the *paramāṇus* can reach the state of weightlessness by being in the fields of gravity, magnetism and electricity through the action of the negative mass of mind, a state of zero force is achieved having a resonance with mind. At resonance, the physical body acquires all the characteristics of the mental flux causing it to lose weight and acquire any velocity the mind can acquire:

$$F = \frac{m\,(v_1 - v_2)}{t} = m\,\frac{dv}{dt}$$

If $m = 0$ then $F = 0$, so that $dv/dt = 0$. Therefore v is a constant from 0 to n. This shows that velocity can be beyond 3×10^{10} m/second. Only mind can achieve these speeds. So, a technique is required to convert the mass to zero so that body can acquire any speed comparable to that of mind without disturbing the forces, i.e., without effecting a change in energy.

The Philadelphia experiment performed by Einstein in 1943 proved that invisibility is scientifically possible. What Einstein did to the Cruizer Eldrige was done by Vallalar to the human body. What is the

Philadelphia project? One day, in 1943 the U.S.A. Eldrige a fully manned destroyed — escort, vanished into a green fog, and within seconds appeared in Norfolk, Virginia and then reappeared in Philadelphia. The U.S. Navy continues to reject this experiment; however the following questions remain unanswered:

1. Why were all the men abroad the ship who survived discharged as mentally unfit?
2. Why did a scientific enquirer on the project meet with a mysterious death?
3. Why were the identities hidden, documents lost?
4. Why did Einstein destroy the relevant papers? Nobody has so far answered these questions.

In the Three Field Theory, Einstein did succeed in this by reducing the gravitational, nuclear and electro-magnetic fields to a common unified field. It is a development of the $E = MC^2$. The question is whether matter can become invisible. Yes, when its speed is faster than that of light. What is it that has a speed faster than light? Mind.

The Philadelphia experiment had been accomplished by using naval type magnetic generators, known as degaussers which were 'pulsed' at resonant frequencies so as to create a tremendous magnetic field in and around a docked vessel. This use of magnetic reasonance, says Dr. Jessupis tantamount to temporary obliteration in our dimension but it tends to get out of control. Actually it is equivalent to transference of matter into another level or dimension, and could represent a dimensional breakthrough if it were possible to control it.

Reverting to Arutprakāśa Vallalar, what he did was an experiment on unified light theory which was an improvement of the UFT of Einstein. Vallalar had channelised mental energy and he could play with it. Here he followed sage Patañjali who in *vibhuti yoga* verse 21 says:

> *kāya-rūpa-samyamatt tadgrāhya śakti-stambhey eakśeṣa*
> *prakāśam-prayougey antardhānam*

By performing *saṁyama* on the form of the body, on suspension of the receptive power, the contact between the eye of the obscurer and light from the body is broken, and the body becomes invisible. The invisibility is effected by preventing the light from his body reaching or effecting the eyes of the perceiver. What is *saṁyama*. It is the process of *dhāraṇā*, *dhyāna* and *samādhi* when applied to any object. These three are different levels of the mind — rather they are three layers of mind. By unifying them, it is possible to prevent the light from a person's body reaching or affecting the eyes of the perceiver. The result is invisibility. The USSR has done a lot of research in mental energy.

The string theory explains the science behind invisibility. The theory, as it is commonly known, (some scientists call it superstring theory) does away with the familiar image of the universe composed of billiard-ball-like particles pushed and pulled by familiar forces like gravity and electricity.

The quantum theory had already revealed in the 1920s that billiard-balls have curious wave-like properties; they are more like vibrations than well-defined points in space. Now the string theory is proposing that these points, in fact, are tiny loops or closed strings. The strings vibrate invisibly in subtle resonance and these vibrations, so the theory goes, make up everything in the universe — from light to lightning bugs, from gravity to gold.

Imagine a closed string — a loop — of some kind of fundamental stuff. Now imagine that the loop rotates, twists and vibrates not only in the three dimensions (plus one dimension of time) but also in six other dimensions we can't perceive. As the loop wriggles, it resonates in many different modes, like a ten-dimensional violin string sending out a cosmic versions of A or C flat. These vibrations, if the string theory is correct, determine all the possible particles and forces of the universe. These extra dimensions aren't stranger than a lot of other things physicists think about. Still the notion of a ten-dimensional universe and the absence of any experimental data that could prove it have made many physicists highly skeptical. It is not obvious how the string theory explains certain striking facts about the universe, says Frank A. Wilzeck of the Institute of Theoretical Physics at the University of California, Santa Barbara.

This string theory is called 'The Theory of Everything' in modern physics. An eminent physicist, Erwin Schroedinger whose name is associated with the wave equation of quantum mechanics is reported to have delved deep into our *Upaniṣads* like his mentor Schopenhauer, and did not deviate from a religious understanding of our mysterious universe till his old age. Scientists who are objective and impartial can never deny the existence of a cosmic being ruling the universe.

Albert Einstein while indicating his abiding interest in equations is reported to have said "an equation is something for eternity". The spiritual laws evolved by our Upaniṣadic sages thousands of years ago have also been found to be eternal and in the Einstein's equation $E = Mc^2$ in the light of Upaniṣadic thoughts.

In terms of the equation, mátter and energy are interchangeable and the total quantum of energy and matter in the universe will always remain constant. By the term 'energy' is meant anything that activates and that which moves matter. Energy could be of diverse kinds ranging from physical and psychical in the animates to kinetic, electrical, thermal, fossil and nuclear energy in the field outside animates.

From the original equation, we can derive another equation $Mc^2 - E = 0$. When the potential energy latent in the animate beings and the supply of energy to inanimate things like planes, vehicles, etc. stops, the inert remains dormant, inactive or lifeless. Both planes and birds fly, fishes and submarines move in water, and vehicles and animate beings move on land. What is the basic difference in the energy that moves animate and inanimate things. In the animate being, the food which is basically matter is converted into energy while in the case of inanimate things like planes, ships, vehicles, machineries, etc. energy is derived out of coal, oil, electricty. For comprehending the basic forms of energy that activate the inanimates, we can use another derived equation. In simple words this may means that when matter is converted into energy or *vice versa*, only one will remain and the form of the other will be obliterated.

From time immemorial man has been trying to find an answer to the basic question, "What is it by knowing which everything can be known". Right at the beginning of *Muṇḍaka Upaniṣad* the same question is being asked by a disciple. Science is a quest for finding an answer to this question through energy, matter, atoms, etc. and religion is also a quest in the same direction for finding out the truth about the eternality of the soul, cosmic soul, etc. Interestingly, the cosmos is known as the universe signifying unity, harmony, patterns and the integrated wholeness of the cosmos. To find an answer to the basic question raised above let us see what the *Upaniṣads* say. The Upaniṣadic seers boldly say without any fear of contradiction: *sarvam khalvidam brahman* — All these are verily *Brahman.* In the *Kaṭhopaniṣad*, the *Brhahman* has been described Anoraniam Mahatomahian — infinitesimal as an atom and infinite. According to science all tangible mass is made up of atoms of elements and the atoms are stated to be made up of nuclei around which electrons circle and the nuclei in turn are made up of protons and neutrons. In terms of *Sāṃkhya* philosophy, existence is on account of disequilibrium between three *guṇa*s or qualities called *sattva, rajas* and *tamas.* The three *guṇa*s seem almost to correspond with the three ingredients of the atom. The protons are stated to the positively charged corresponding to *rajas*, while the electrons are negatively charged corresponding to *tamas.* It s said that the neutrons have no charge and may perhaps be equivalent to *sattva.*

According to *Sāṃkhya*, the three *guṇa*s exist in a latent form in inert matter. Once the *puruṣa* principle enters into contact with *prakṛti*, the inert primordial nature, the *guṇa*s are activated. According to Indian evolutionary thought, the living principle passes through 84 lakh different forms of life depending on its action. Action emanates from energy in the animate beings and the struggle through life is to restore the equilibrium of *guṇa*s. The living principle familiarly known as energy of science and spirit in religion animates and activates matter.

Inanimate seeds planted on the soil sprout with the aid of water and sunshine and grow into a plant and tree. From where does life or the energy to grow comes? This has been the basic question agitating the minds of scientists. According to the equation $E=Mc^2$, energy should come out of matter, but can life energy arise out of inert matter? The mystery of the origin of life is too difficult to solve on a scientific basis. According to Upaniṣadic thought, life energy has no origin as it is eternal, imperishable and unborn, and evolves to other state of beings through nature. There will, therefore, be no point in trying to discover the origin of life as it does not have any origin at all and it will be humanly impossible to discover the origin of life. The Upaniṣadic seers intensively experimented in their intellectual laboratory and finding the inadequacies of matter, they gave up the chase on the external world and delved deep within to know the truth of the life energy and ultimately discovered that there is an eternal energy in the ephimeral body and they called it *ātman*.

The conclusion of science in terms of the equation, $E = Mc^2$ seems to be that energy could neither be created nor destroyed and is eternal. As the total quantum of energy and matter in the universe remains constant, if energy leaves the human body it should either continue to remain as energy or it should revert back to matter as total quantum energy and matter. What is the type of energy that leaves the human body at the time of death. It could only be psychic energy as physical energy could remain dormant in a lifeless body. Psychic energy could reappear in matter only in another body. The survival instinct in preserved in all animate beings and a mammal starts sucking after birth. A new-born sweeps or smiles of its own accord in deep-sleep indirectly signifying a previous state of existence. All these seem to support the Indian view of the transmigration of eternal psychic energy which may be called spirit, soul, *ātman*, mind, and by any other name, as a name is only a description for identification.

Human beings live on two levels viz. the physical and the psychical. Psychologists say that the frontiers of human mind know no barriers. The Upaniṣadic sages considered the human psyche most precious and equated it with the cosmic mind saying *tat tvam asi* — "You are that". The psychic power in human beings can be cultivated and developed to attain extraordinary and even miraculous results.

According to the equation, matter at the speed of light will become energy. The question is, "Will the human body which is made of matter also become energy at the speed of light?" What will be the reaction of the human body, if it were to travel at the speed of light?" What will happen if the body can stand within speed of light?" It is said that if human beings were to travel at the speed of light, the body will attain agelessness. The synonymn for agelessness could be immortality or eternality. Death is energy leaving the body and immortality is attaining the speed of light.

The firm conclusion of the Vedāntists, is that immortality is not on the physical plane but on the psychic plane. With the present or even future level of scientific progress it looks impossible in the light of the Upaniṣadic statements for the human beings to achieve agelessness by making the body travel at the speed of light. In terms of the derived equation if the cosmic energy is penetrated by the psychic in the human body, the psychic energy should attain oneness and union with cosmic energy and join its source. Agelessness does not therefore appear to refer to the human body but to the reunion of psychic energy in the human body in its purest state of enlightenment with the cosmic energy and this probably may be the ultimate of Einstein's equation $E = Mc^2$ and also the basic purpose of human life.

Once this state is attained we can also probably claim like Vedic seers "All this is really *Brahman*". It is on account of this energy that the earth rotates and also the moon and stars shine in outer space. Einstein's equation seem to be totally in agreement with the eternal spiritual laws, discovered by the Vedic seers and so it will not be improper to call Einstein a Vedāntist.

WEATHER SCIENCE IN ANCIENT INDIA

The post-Vedic scholars evolved several techniques of long-range forecasting of rainfall based on observation of the winds, clouds, sky conditions, etc. on selected days characterised by the relative position of the sun and the moon with respect to the stars as well as the position of planets with respect to the sun, moon and stars. A survey of these techniques is made in A.S. Rāmānāthan's paper.*

Introduction

The year-to-year variations of the weather occurrences as well as

* Thanks to A.S. Rāmānāthan, for his article published in the *Veda the Word Eternal*.

extremes of weather like floods and droughts did affect the post-Vedic scholars and they were naturally compelled to study more deeply the causes of such variations. After careful observation of the day-to-day weather over a prolonged period, their natural tendency was to correlate certain weather disturbances during the western disturbance period as well as the period immediatly following it with the quantity of rainfall, its intensity and time of occurrence during the rainy or monsoon season. These constituted the first steps in the formulation of the rules of forecasting rainfall on the long range in ancient India. Careful observation of the conditions of the sky, wind temperature, halos round the sun and the moon and even the behaviour of animals, birds, etc., as well as plants and trees, some hours or even more days prior to the occurrence of heavy or moderate rainfall in a place also enabled them to formulate rules for forecasting rainfall in short and medium range.

Long Range Forecasting

There were three broad approaches possible for the post-Vedic scholars in this field. They were the following:

(1) To work within the framework of the concepts handed over to them by the Vedic scholars and improved by them.

(2) Rainfall is essentially a *yajña* process in which both Sun and Soma play important roles.

(3) By virtue of being a *pratikṛt* of Soma of the upper regions, the moon has an influence on the rainfall process.

(4) The period that elapses between formation of the rain foetuses and rainfall delivery is 195 days. In other words, the formulation of rainfall forecasts on the long range can be based in the observation of winds, clouds, rain, sky conditions, etc. on selected days characterised by the relative positions of the moon and the sun with respect to the stars in all the months prior to the commencement of monsoon rainfall.

(5) To assume that the eclipses of the sun and the moon, comets, the relative position of various planets with respect to the sun and the moon do influence rainfall and formulate the

forecasting rules accordingly. The idea of rainfall cycles perhaps has its origin here.

(6) To interpret certain shapes of clouds, state and colour of the sky, fall of meteors, unseasonal winds, abnormal weather conditions, etc. as indicative of oncoming extremes of weather and forecast the same accordingly.

Before we proceed further, it is pertinent to point out at this stage that we are dealing with an extremely difficult subject from the scientific point of view, while the natural tendency of any scientisit will be to dismiss these concepts as not conforming to any scientific standards and, therefore, not worth going into, a scientist tracing the historical development has necessarily to probe deeply into them and see on what framework or on what basic concepts such a large number of detailed thumb rules of forecasting rainfall were developed. To understand these we have to go into some basic principles of astronomy as known to our ancients.

From very ancient times man has wondered at the complexity of the objects he observed in the sky, night after night and day after day, and their motions. Their varied nature, brightness, and colour enabled him to identify certain principal stars in addition to the sun, the moon and the planets. Then gradually the regular motion of the sun and the moon and their daily shift in the background of the stars was understood and could also be mapped. The following facts known to our ancients are relevant to us.

(1) The sun slides back with respect to the stars and completes one round in a year. (The annual motion of the earth round the sun was most probably not known to them clearly.)

(2) The sun moves through the 27 asterisms of the Indian system during the above period and stays in each for a period of a little over 13 days.

(3) The moon stay in each asterism for one day, and completes one round of the heavens in 27.3 days.

(4) The apparent north-south motion of the moon during a lunar month is as much as the north-south motion of the sun during

a year. The annual path of the sun in the celestial sphere is more or less followed by the moon also with a deviation of 5 degrees north and south.

(5) The apparent path of the moon in the sky is zig-zag.

(6) In the winter period Kārttika to Māgha, the moon moves from south to north in *śukla pakṣa* and from north to south in *kṛṣṇa pakṣa*.

(7) In the summer months of Caitra to Āsāḍha, the moon moves from north to south in the *śukla pakṣa* and south to north in the *kṛṣṇa pakṣa*. Phālguna and Bhādrapada are transition months.

(8) The asterism, according to our ancients, are distributed in the zodiac in a belt of 48 with a speed of 24 on either side of the celestial equator. The planets also move within this belt.

Initially they had 28 asterisms. Later Abhijit, which was assumed to be located partly in Uttarāsādhā and partly in Śrāvaṇā was dropped, leaving 27 asterisms covering the zodiac. In order to identify the *nakṣatras*, the ancients first developed the idea of a group of stars, having shapes of animals, birds, men, etc. In each group they identified one bright star which was called *yogatārā*. The asterisms Aśvini, Bharaṇī, etc. were located with the help of these *yogatārā*s which were referred to be the same names. In order to facilitate the location of these stars, the separate paths in the celestial sphere in which these stars are distributed. They imagined three broad belts parallel to the celestial equator and these were named Irāvat, Jaradgava and Vaiśvānara. Vaiśvānara is on the southern side of the equator, Irāvat on the northern side and Jaradgava in the middle. Each of these three broad belts was further subdivided into three secondary belts, so that there were a total of nine *vīthī*s, three on the northern side, three on the southern side and three in the middle. These nine *vīthī*s from north to south have the following names:

(1) Naga, (2) Gaja, (3) Irāvata on the northern side, (4) Vṛṣa, (5) Go, (6) Jaradgava in the middle, (7) Mṛga, (8) Aja, (9) Vaiśvānara on the northern side.

It is interesting to note that for a man located outside these belts in the northern hemisphere, the span of these belts above the horizon would appear smaller and smaller as one proceeds southwards and the names of the belts are quite suggestive of this diminution. In fact, the seven horses which the sun rides, three on the southern side, three on the northern side and one in the middle (alone the celestial equator). They are incorporated in the *Veda*s as seven metres being associated with the southernmost track and *jagatī* being associated with the northernmost track. Bṛhatī is the track along the celestial equator.

The movement of the moon across the sky is not only associated with one *yogatārā* everyday but also with each of these belts. In other words the *nakṣatra*s are distributed in the nine *vīthī*s, three in each:

Bharaṇī, Kṛttikā, Svātī	Naga *vīthī* (northernmost)
Punarvasu, Puṣyā, Aśleṣā,	Vṛṣa *vīthī*
Maghā, Pūrvaphālgunī, Uttarā-phālgunī	
Rohiṇi, Mṛgaśīrṣā, Ārdrā	Gaja *vīthī*
Pūrva Bhādrapadā, Uttarabhādrapadā, Revatī	Go *vīthi*
Pada, Revatī, Aśvini	Irāvata *vīthī*
Śrāvaṇā, Dhaniṣṭhā and Śatabhīṣaj	Jaradgava *vīthi*
Anurādhā, Jyeṣṭhā, Mūlā	Mṛga *vīthī*
Hastā, Citrā, Viśākhā	Aja *vīthī*
Pūrvāṣāḍhā and Uttarāṣāḍhā	Vaiśvānara *vīthī*

There will be some differences from author to author in the above distribution but we shall not bother about the reasons for these just now.

With the above information, we shall now revert back to our subject.

We have already seen the importance of Soma for rainfall as understood by the Vedic seers and endorsed by the post-Vedic scholars. Soma is the fertilising agent which mixes with water and comes down as rain. The post-Vedic scholars used this idea to formulae their improved model of rainfall. The formation of rain foetuses takes places as a result of the injection of *soma* from the north in a process of fertilisation. That is why during this period a soft wind from the north is considered a favourable symptom. The northern region is the abode of Soma and the south the seat of Agni, so that the southward movement of Soma and the northward movement of Agni are essential for the functioning of the cycle of *ṛtu*s or seasons which are caused by the interaction of Soma and Agni. To put it in a more direct way, the western disturbances push Agni in the south or its restoration to the south are most conductive for the orderly functioning of the seasons and more particularly the rainfall cycle which is the principal cause of origin and maintenance of life on earth.

Keeping in mind the above ideas, the post-Vedic scholars believed that whenever the moon moves in a northerly track or is restored to a northerly track, condition are favourable for the formation of healthy rain foetuses and whenever he moves in a southerly track, with sun on its northern side or whenever a condition of Soma being overpowered by Agni is created, it favours abortion of rain foetuses if the foetuses are not fully developed, and a healthy delivery of rainfall if the foetuses have gone through their full period of growth. With this basic hypothesis, they made careful observations of sky and weather conditions as well as the positions of the sun and the moon with respect to the stars and related the nature and distribution of rainfall during the delivery period to certain favourable and unfavourable sky conditions and the corresponding position of the sun and the moon during periods of formation and growth. When once a star is made in this direction, the natural tendency will be to go into elaboration and bring in the influence of *nakṣatra*s and planets on the rainfall process after attributing the quality of Soma or Agni or related qualities to them, especially when they have been taught by the Vedic seers that Agni and Soma are the two basic things which have given rise to everything that we witness in this universe. Thus a new talent was developed for which the Vedic seers had shown the way. Though initially this art of rainfall forecasting was practised by a few experts like Garga, Parāśara, Nārada, Devala, Vasiṣṭha, Bhṛgu, Druhina, Ṛṣiputra, Kāśyapa, Varāhamihira, etc., later in the light of careful observations covering more regions, the number of experts increased and naturally the thumb rules also increased in number. In some recent books on this subject many hundreds of such rules have been collected from ancient literature and presented. Many of these have been handed down the generations and they have been incorporated in local proverbs or sayings.

The examination of the scientific validity of the above thumb rules is a time-consuming investigation, the result of which may be most disappointing. But in the opinion of the author, in this process one gets greater insights into the ramifications of the mind of our ancients. However, the very magnitude of the work involved repels anyone from attempting the same. We, therefore, propose to present a selected number of these thumb rules. In a subsequent period of discovery it was introduced to the readers.

It will not be out of place here to point out that in the opinion of the author, most probably the subject of Astrology which aims at the prediction of the future of a person's life history, had its origin in the basic principles which according to our ancients govern the prediction of the nature and distribution of rainfall especially since, rainfall also has to go through the three stages of conception, growth and the influence of the sun, moon stars and planets. It is quite interesting to note also that the science of weather was always dealt with by them in texts which deal with Astrology though in separate section.

Before we state the thumb rules, some general remarks on Indian weather may be of help for a correct appreciation of their implications. The Vedic seers as well as the post-Vedic scholars should have been well aware of the striking difference in the nature and rainfall potential of the western disturbances and the monsoon. Especially, the bang characterised by dark clouds, lightning, thunder, wind and torrential rain which ushers in the monsoon over north-west India, sustaining all forms of life, and its prolonged presence with breaks, was compared by them with the fleeting type of western activity with occasional light rain from thinly overcast sky, occasional lightning, thunder, mist, fog and winds, which are sometimes pleasant when they are from the north or north-east behind a moving disturbance on a clear sunny day, and then the concepts of the formation of rain foetuses, their growth and delivery were developed. Naturally when once western disturbance was considered as the beginning of the rainfall cycle, its nature and feature should be indicative of the nature and features of the end-product viz., the monsoon rainfall.

By carefully observing the weather and sky conditions day after day for a prolonged period, it should have been easy for the post-Vedic scholars to recognise the following features of the weather patterns during the various months.

The monsoon completely withdraws from north-west India in the begainning of the month of Kārttika. The days are characterised by clear skies in the region and temperatures show a falling trend especially in the nights.

In the month of Mārgaśīrṣa, the western disturbance slowly picks up and we get one or two disturbances, which normally are mild to moderate. The anticyclone at the lower levels over north-west Pakistan and adjoining Iran begins to build up. Because of the prolonged absence of rain, haze in the sky increases. The temperatures have not yet fallen appreciably. In the month of Pauṣa, the frequency of western disturbances increases and temperatures fall sharply. The plains sometimes get appreciable rain and behind the disturbances the sky clears and the haze decreases.

In the month of Māgha the western disturbances reach a peak, sometimes giving rise to thick fog or frost, especially whenever the skies are clear in the night after the passage of a western disturbance. The foggy conditions during the day keeps the maximum day temperatures the lowest of the year. In the month of Phālguna, westerlies assert themselves in the region. Haze which cleared during peak western disturbances actvity again increases. In the month of Chaitra westerlies continue, temperatures slowly build up and the first thunderstorm occurs and decreases the haze. In the month of Vaiśākha, the temperature increases, skies are clear except when there are thunderstorms which gain in strength as summer advances. One of the interesting observations of the ancients was that too much rain during the period of initial growth of the rain foetuses results in poor rainfall at the time of delivery. They imagined that rain foetuses are destroyed if there is too much rain during the time of their early growth period.

It was till very recently believed that too much western disturbance affects the monsoon rainfall of the subsequent season. In fact the very first forecast of monsoon rain issued by Blanford, the first chief of the Indian Meteorological Department, after the successive famines of 1876 and 1877 was based on the negative correlation between winter snow fall and the subsequent monsoon rainfall and it proved to be correct at that time though we know now that it is very rare that the monsoon will fall successively for three seasons.

It was also believed by our ancients that the hotter the conditions are in the months of Vaiśākha and Jyeṣṭha, the better will be the performance of the monsoon. This was also the view of the meteorologists in the early stages of development of forecasting techniques.

Thumb Rules for Long Range Forecasting

We shall now proceed to state the thumb rules which we have selected for presentations:

1. Rain foetuses that develop when the moon is in any of the asterism Pūrvabhādrapadā, Uttarabhādrapadā, Pūrvāṣāḍhā, Uttarāṣāḍhā and Rohiṇi in any season will yield plenty of rain. Those that are formed in Śatabhīṣaj, Āśleṣā, Ārdrā, Svāti or Maghā, prove fertile and rains for many days. If they go through their full period of growth without any impediments, they will give rain as given below, according to the month in which they form:

Month of formation of foetus	*Duration of rainfall (at the time of delivery)*
Mārgaśīrṣā	8 days
Pauṣa	6 days
Māgha	16 days
Phālguna	24 days
Caitra	3 days
Vaiśākha	3 days

2. The following symptoms favour healthy growth of the rain foetuses in the various months as shown below:

(a) Absence of severe cold condition in Mārgaśīrṣa.

(b) Heavy snow fall in Pauṣa.

(c) Sky reddish near horizon during mornings and evenings, both in Mārgaśīrṣa and Pauṣa.

(d) Sun and moon appearing dim because of thick fog or mist and severe cold conditions in Māgha. Sunrise and sunset hidden by fog or low cloud in the same month.

(e) Rough and strong winds, appearance of clouds, incomplete halo round the sun, coppery colour of the sun in the month of Phālguna.

(f) Winds, clouds, rain and halos in the month of Caitra.

(g) Wind, rain, white clouds, lightning and thunder in the month of Vaiśākha.

In all the above conditions are present in the respective months and if there are no adverse symptoms in any of the months the monsoon rains will be very good.

3. If the formation of rain embryo in any month is accompanied by all the five *lakṣaṇa*s viz. wind clouds, light rain, lightning, and thunder, it will rain over a span of 100 *yojana*s, and it will rain over a span of 50 *yojana*s if three are present, and over a span of 25 *yojana*s, if one or two only are present. The quality of rainfall will be 3 *adhaka*s, and of the wind alone is present 6 *adhaka*s, for lightning alone, 9 *adhaka*s for clouds, 12 *adhaka*s for thunder. If all are present it will yield 5 *droṇa*s.

4. If at the time of the formation of rain foetuses, the sun and moon are in conjunction with the *saumya* planets, like Jupiter of Venus, the monsoon rainfall will be very good. If, on the other hand, it in conjunction with *āgneya* like Mārs and Saturn, it results in the occurrence of hailstorms. Hailstorms will also occur if at the same time of delivery, the moon or sun is associated with the above condition of planets and rainfall

occurrence is delayed.

5. If, at the time of formation of rain foetuses, the moon entering the asterisms Kṛttikā, Rohiṇi, Mṛgaśīrṣā, Maghā, Caitrā, Viśākhā, Anurādhā, Jyeṣṭhā, Mūlā, Pūrvāṣāḍhā makes her exit, on the northern side, then it is very auspicious and portends good rainfall and prosperity. If she makes her exit on the opposite side, it portends bad times.

6. If there is rain on 2nd, 3rd, 9th, 11th, 12th and 13th days of the bright half of the month of Kārttika, there will be very good rainfall during the subsequent monsoon season. The 11th and 12th days mentioned above are named *abhradhruva* and are usually characterised by sun in Svāti or Viśākhā and moon in Aśvini or Revatī. If these days are cloudy then there will be plenty of rain in the month of Āṣāḍha. If these days are clear, the monsoon rains will be poor.

7. If on the *pūrṇimā* day of the month of Kārttika, the moon stays in the asterism Kṛttikā for the whole period of 24 hours commencing from sunrise, there will be good rainfall in the subsequent monsoon season. If the asterism is Rohini on that day, the rainfall will be poor in some other places.

8. The eleven days commencing from the 2nd day of the bright half of Mārgaśīrṣa are extremely favourable for the formation of rain foetuses. If on any of these days there is rain or cloudiness, there will be good monsoon rainfall during the subsequent rainy season.

9. If on the 10th day of the bright half of Mārgaśīrṣa there is a northerly wind throughout the day, it may be taken that conception has taken place.

10. If on the 12th day of the bright half, and on the new moon day in Mārgaśīrṣa there is rain, the subsequent monsoon rainfall will be good.

11. The 9 days commencing from the 4th day of the dark half of Mārgaśīrṣa are most favourable for conception. If the symptoms are present in these days, there will be surely rain in the bright

half of Āṣāḍha.

12. If there is wind from the east on the 8th day of the dark half of Mārgaśīrṣa, there will be prosperity in the region. Wind from other directions of this day brings distress conditions.

13. If there is wind from all directions on the 12th and 13th, 14th and 15th days of the dark half of the month of Mārgaśīrṣa, there will be good rain in the month of Āṣāḍha.

14. If the asterism on the *amāvasyā* day of the dark half of Mārgaśīrṣa is Mūlā, the prices of foodgrains will come down, and if it is Jyeṣṭha, foodgrains will become clear.

15. If the formation of rain foetuses takes place in the first 10 days of the bright half of Pauṣa, there will be good monsoon rainfall in the region if no miscarriage of the rain foetuses takes place in the month of Caitra.

16. If there is cloudiness during the sun's stay in the asterism Pūrvāṣāḍhā in the month of Pauṣa, then there will be rain almost daily during the period when the sun moves through the asterism Ārdrā to Mūlā.

17. If in the month of Pauṣa, there are no indications of conception, in all probability the monsoon will be failure.

18. If in the month of Pauṣa, when the moon passes through Pūrvabhādrapada there is a halo round the moon, and the day is accompanied by rains, lightning and thunder, the subsequent monsoon rains will be very good.

19. If on the 5th day of the bright half of Pauṣa, there is snowfall, the subsequent monsoon rains will be very good.

20. If on the 11th day of the bright half of Pauṣa, lightning, cloudiness and snowfall occur, and if the moon is in the asterism Rohiṇī on that day, the subsequent monsoon rains will be very good.

21. If lightning is seen on the 14th day of the bright half of Pauṣa, it is an auspicious sign and there will be plenty of rain in the dark half of Āṣāḍha.

22. The moon's presence in the asterism Svāti on the 7th day of the dark half of Pauṣa is indicative of prosperity. If on this day there is cloudiness, the monsoon rains will be moderate, and if there is rain on that day, the monsoon rains will be very good.

23. If on the 8th day of the dark half of Pauṣa there is no rain, there will be a spell of heavy rain when the sun traverses the asterism Ārdrā.

24. If in the month of Māgha, the five symptoms of conception are noticed with wind from east or north when the moon traverses the asterism Mūlā to Bharaṇī, there will be rain when the sun moves through Ārdrā to Viśākhā, i.e., if the symptoms occur when the moon is in Mūlā, there will be rain when the sun moves through Ārdrā. If they occur when the moon is in Pūrvāṣāḍhā, there will be rain when the sun moves through Punarvasu.

25. If there is rain on the 7th day of the bright half of Māgha, there will be a spell of heavy rain in the month of Āṣāḍha. If, on the other hand, there is no rain on the 7th day but rain on the 8th of the dark half of Māgha, the monsoon rains will be more than normal.

26. If during the month of Phālguna there is cloudiness on many days without rain, it indicates the healthy condition of the rain foetuses and the subsequent rainy season will yield ample rainfall.

27. On the *pūrṇimā* day of Phālguna, if there is wind from the east it will give above normal monsoon rainfall, if it is from the north, crops prosper, if it is from the west, moderate rainfall will occur during the subsequent monsoon season and if it is from the south, there will be a distress condition in the region.

28. If on the 2nd day of the dark half of Phālguna, there are no clouds of lightning and if there is wind from all directions, there will be good rain in the months of Śrāvaṇa and Bhādrapada.

29. If on the 5th, 9th and 13th days of the dark half of Phālguna,

lightning occurs and if there are symptoms of conception, the monsoon rains will be affected.

30. If there is rain in the month of Caitra when the sun moves through the asterism Revatī, and if there is no rain in the subsequent ten days it is to be taken that miscarriage of the rain foetuses has taken place and therefore the monsoon rainfall will be poor.

31. If rain occurs during the period from the first to the eighth day of the bright half of the month of Caitra, and if there is lightning on the 9th day, the monsoon will be poor in that region.

32. If during the bright half of Caitra, wind from the west and south blows continuously for two days, the subsequent monsoon will be failure.

33. If there is rain or lightning or even thunder on the 5th, 7th and 13th days of the bright half of the month of Caitra, there will be total failure of the subsequent monsoon.

34. If on the 2nd, 3rd, 4th and 5th days of the dark half of Caitra, there is rain with wind from the east, the monsoon rainfall will be poor.

35. Wind from the south without rain during the period when the moon moves from Mūlā to Bharaṇī in the dark half of Caitra is indicative of good monsoon rainfall in the year.

36. The 3rd day of the bright half of Vaiśākha is called Akṣaya Tṛtīyā, and events on that day have great importance in forecasting future events. The direction of the wind on that day bears a relation to the performance of the monsoon. Wind from the west favours good monsoon performance.

37. If there is rain on the 11th, 12th and 13th days of the bright half of Vaiśākha, it foretells distress conditions later. If there is no rain, there will be prosperity.

38. Thunderstorms in Vaiśākha are indicative of a good monsoon later.

39. The events in the month of Jyeṣṭha destroy the rain foetuses and are important for determining the rainfall of the ensuing monsoon season.

40. Thunder in the right half of Jyeṣṭha destroys the rain foetuses. Frequent occurrence of thunder results in poor rains in the months of Śrāvaṇa and Bhādrapada.

41. If there is cloudiness on the day when the moon is in the asterism Rohiṇī in the bright half of Jyeṣṭha, the monsoon will be good, and if there is no cloudiness will be bad.

42. The conjunction of the sun and the moon in the star Rohiṇī is extremely bad. There will be distress conditions in the region.

43. The moon is in the asterism Ārdrā on the 3rd day of the bright half of Jyeṣṭha and if there is rain, the subsequent monsoon will be a failure.

44. Wind from the east, north and west on the 5th day of the bright half of Jyeṣṭha portends prosperity, but the wind from the north is conducive to locust attack.

45. The examination of wind direction on four days commencing from the 8th day of the bright half of Jyestha is important for forecasting purposes. If the winds are light and pleasant they foretell prosperous conditions. If on these days lightning, and a halo around the sun and the moon also occur, they augur a good period ahead.

46. If there are no clouds on the nine days commencing from the day the moon is in Ārdrā in the bright half of Jyeṣṭha, there will be good rainfall later. If clouds appear, the monsoon will be poor. Also if rain occurs when the moon moves through Svāti, Viśākhā, Anuarādhā and Jyeṣṭhā, it portends total failure of monsoon.

47. Forecast of the quantities of rainfall during the monsoon season is based on observations during the 27-day period commencing from the *pūrṇimā* day of the bright half of Jyeṣṭha. There is a tendency for rainfall to follow a 27-day

cycle during the monsoon season, i.e., if it occurs when the moon returns to the same asterism after about 27 days. The following table shows the expected quantity of rainfall during the season if the initial showers occur when the moon is in the various asterisms shown on the left side:

Name of the Asterism	*Expected Quantity of rainfall for the season*
Dhaniṣṭhā, Revatī, Citrā, Hastā, Purvāṣādhā Mṛgaśīrṣā	16 *droṇas*
Svāti, Jyeṣṭhā and Śatabhiṣā	4 *droṇas*
Maghā, Anurādhā, Bharaṇī, Śrāvaṇa and Mūlā	14 *droṇas*
Uttarāṣāḍhā, Punarvasu and Viśākhā	20 *droṇas*
Kṛttikā	10 *droṇas*
Uttarabhādarapadā, Rohiṇī, Pūrvaphālgunī and Uttarāphālgunī	25 *droṇas*
Āśleṣā	13 *droṇas*
Puṣyā and Pūrvabhādrapadā	15 *droṇas*
Ārdrā	18 *droṇas*
Āśvinī	12 *droṇas*

The above forecasts are valid it unfavourable situation do not develop during the period.

48. If on the third day of the bright half of Āṣāḍha, easterlies prevail and clouds moves from east to west, there will be good rainfall in the month of Bhādrapada.

49. If on the second day of the bright half of Āṣāḍha, the first showers occur on the third day, easterlies appear giving rise to dark and large clouds on the fourth day. If the Wind from the south and clouds from the wind that appear, and on the fifth day northerlies blow and high clouds from the east appear, then in that year there will be good rains for four months

commencing from Śrāvaṇa.

50. The total amount of clouds that appear on the four days commencing from the fifth day of the bright half of Āṣāḍha is a measure of the quantity of rainfall during the ensuing entire monsoon season.

51. A clear sky on the *pūrṇimā* day of Āṣāḍha is indicative of distress conditions due to poor monsoon.

52. If there is a lunar eclipse on the Āṣāḍha *pūrṇimā* day, things will become very clear in the next four and a half months.

53. If there is rain on the fifth day of the dark half of Āṣāḍha, the ensuing monsoon will be good.

54. If at dawn and sunset the clouds look yellow in colour on the 4th, 5th and 6th days of the bright half of Āṣāḍha, they eventually become dark and bring rains.

55. If the sun is in the constellation Siṁha in the bright half of Śrāvaṇa, there is generally a break in monsoon rains and rainfall is confined to sea coast areas.

56. If clouds appear on the west on the 1st, 7th, 12th, 13th and *pūrṇimā* days of Bhādrapada, they portend good rainfall.

57. If it is not very cold in the month of Māgha, no winds in Phālguna, no clouds in Caitra, hailstorms in Vaiśākha and very hot weather in the month of Jyeṣṭha, there will be scanty rain during the monsoon season.

58. If there are no clouds in Māgha, if it rains in Caitra, and there is no thunder on *Akṣaya Tṛtīyā* day, then there will be scanty rain in the rainy season.

59. If it is warm in Māgha, subnormal temperatures in Jyeṣṭha and cool breeze in the month of Śrāvana, there will be scanty rain in the rainy season.

60. If there is no lightning in the month of Caitra, some rain occurs in the beginning of Vaiśākha, very hot in Jyeṣṭha, there will be very good rainfall in the rainy season.

61. Cold conditions in Caitra, hailstorms in Vaiśākha and clear skies in Jyeṣṭha foretell good monsoon rains.

62. If it is warm in Pauṣa, and cold in Vaiśākha, there will be some rains in Āṣāḍha and no rains in Śrāvaṇa and Bhādrapada.

63. Some rains when the sun enters Kṛttikā, hot weather when the sun is in Rohiṇī, some showers and light wind when the sun is in Ārdrā and absence of wind when the sun is in Punarvasu are all indicative of prosperous conditions.

64. Clearly the sky and hot weather when the sun moves through the asterism Rohinī is indicative of good rainfall during the subsequent monsoon season.

65. Jupiter, Venus, Moon and Mercury are auspicious planets. Saturn, Mārs and Sun are ferocious planets. Venus always favours rainfall. Mārs acts against rainfall. Principally these two determine the rainfall at a place. The other planets aid either of them. By nature, Mercury and Saturn produce winds, Venus and Jupiter produce water and Mārs and Sun produce heat.

66. Saturn moving through the asterism Hastā, Svāti, Bharaṇī, Ārdrā Śrāvaṇa and Pūrvāphālgunī brings rains but produce scanty rains when moving through Āśleṣā, Śatabhiṣaj, Jyeṣṭhā, Mūlā, Revatī and Uttarābhādrapadā. It stops rain when moving through Citrā, Viśākhā, Anurādhā and Puṣyā.

67. Jupiter moving through Bhādrapadā, Āśleṣā, Pusyā and Punarvasu brings in drought, moving through Kṛttikā, Rohiṇī, Viśākhā and Anurādhā brings in moderate rain, and moving through Maghā, Hastā and Ārdrā brings in good rains.

68. Venus moving in the northern *vīthī*s produces lot of rains and moving in the southern *vīthī*s.

69. During the rainy season if Mārs moves ahead of the sun, there will be drought if Venus is ahead of the sun there will be rains if Jupiter is ahead of the sun, the weather will be hot and if Mercury is ahead of the sun, winds will occur.

70. Conjunctions of the sun and Mārs, Saturn and Mārs, Jupiter and Mārs result in drought. Conjunctions of Mercury and Venus and Jupiter and Mercury give rains.

71. Venus, Mercury and Jupiter in conjunction and uninfluenced by other planets is indicative of abnormally heavy rain.

72. Equal volumes of water from well, tank and river at a place are weighted on the Āṣāḍha *pūrṇimā* day.

73. Four pots filled with water are placed in the four directions beginning with north and are named after the months beginning with Śrāvaṇa in the dextral order on the day the moon passes through the asterism Rohinī in the dark half of Āsāḍha. The amount of rain in the various months will have to be guessed from the quantity of water left in the pots at the end of fifteen days.

Many of all the above rules have been taken out from the collection presented by Madhusūdan Ojhā. Some of these have been extracted directly from the original text. Ojhā a noted scholar of Jaipur has presented in an orderly way hundreds of these rules in his book *Kadambiri* after collecting them from many an original text. The author has verified many of them with the original texts available to him.

6

Advaita and Science*

European logic owes its origin to Aristotle and is based on the syllogism, the most common example of which is:

All men are mortal
Socrates is a man
Socrates is mortal

There can of course be more complicated syllogisms, some of which can be very difficult to analyse in the above manner. As a matter of fact, because of this reason, much of Aristotle was found to be wrong. During the last century, logic was completely algebraised by Boole making the analysis of syllogisms fool-proof. In my paper on "Foundations of Scientific Thought", I have described how Boole was able to algebraise logic. The logic of Boole is one of formality of sentence structures, and succeeds well as a part of mathematics.

Aristotle's logic restricts itself to a proposition, being either true or false and there is nothing in between. However in recent times three-valued logic has been developed in which a proposition can be true, false or intermediate. In such logic we get the situation that 2 + 2 = 4 is either true or intermediate and 2 + 2 = 5 is either intermediate or false. The words true, false have a special meaning in language, but in general one can say they are merely two distinct possibilities. In three-valued logic the intermediate position becomes the third possibility. An example of

---

*Thanks to Rājā Ramaṇa for his articles published in *The Hindu* dated 7-9-1984.

three-valued logic in *Vedānta* is the definition of the supreme *Brahman* "It is this or it is that or it can be anything".

One can further generalise and assume there are between true and false many values and such logic has been developed and is known as many-valued logic. With all these developments it is to be expected that strange new conclusions are possible and this is what has happened in modern mathematical logic.

Towards the end of the last century the great German mathematician Cantor showed that there are many kinds of infinites depending on the way the method of counting is carried out. For integers 1, 2, 3, etc. we have what is known as the countable infinity. If, however, we count for example all the points on a continuous line, it can be shown quite simply and exceedingly elegantly that there are not enough numbers in the countable infinity to account for all the points on a continuous line. There must therefore, be a higher infinity. This is not all. Cantor could also demonstrate constructions to show that there are an infinite numbers of such infinites but only two of them seem to have any physical significance. Following similar lines of arguments it has been shown by Godel that it is possible to transfer all mathematical statement uniquely into numbers and show that there are many statements in mathematics which are true but can never be proved. In other words, mathematical logic leads to the situation when one can say "Truth is greater than proof"; it also leads to greater paradoxes of the type whether a statement of the type 'I am a liar' cannot ever be classified as either true or false.

My reference to modern mathematical logic is only to show that even in such a strictly defined departments as mathematics, unresolvable paradoxes are unavoidable. It is only to be expected that in a wider field of knowledge when the role of human consciousness plays a greater part and words do not have a one-to-one meaning but a one-to-many mapping, the possibilities of confused thinking and reasoning is great and this is what Śaṅkara warns us of all the time.

Schools of logic have existed in India for a long time and various tests of the validity of arguments have been specified. We now comment on some of the statements of the *Nyāya-Vaiśeṣika* theories as given in the *Tarkasaṁgraha* by the Indian logician Annambhaṭṭa and *Bhāsa-Pariccheda* by Viśvanātha.

After describing various categories into which things can be classified such as substances, quality action, etc. the work devotes itself to a penetrating discussion on perception, inference and comprehension. It is the chapter on inference that is of particular interest to us. It exposes the difference of approach between Indian and European logic and indicates how logic as defined in the West is restricted in scope. This is best explained in the extract from Benedetto Croce's celebrated book *Logic as the Science of Pure Concept*.

> The error, which appeared very early in our western world has spread during the centuries and yet dominates many minds so true is this that logic is usually understood to mean illogic or formalist logic. We say our western world, because if Greece created and passed on the doctrine of logical forms, which was a mixture of thoughts materialised in words and of words became rigid in thoughts, another logic is known which as it seems, developed outside the influence of Greek thought and remained immune from the formalistic error. This is Indian logic, which is notably antiverbalist... Indian logic studies the naturalistic syllogism in itself, as internal thought, distinguishing it from the syllogism for others, that is to say from the more or less usual, but always extrinsic and accidental form of communication and dispute. It has not even a suspicion of the extravagant idea of a truth which is merely syllogistic and formalist and which may be false in fact. It takes no account of the judgement or rather it considers what is called judgement, and what is really the proposition as a verbal clothing of knowledge; it does not make the verbal distinction of subject copula and predicate; it does not admit classes of categorical and hypothetical, of affirmative and negative judgements. All these are extraneous to logic, whose object is the constant 'knowledge considered in itself'.

Indian logic with reference to interference has its own form of syllogism, and stars with a major statement which is some sort of a generalisation from which by reasoning we arrive at something particular. This inference may be different for oneself and for others. All leading schools of Indian philosophy assume that generalisation is the ground work of inference — an assumption of great importance in understanding *advaita*. It is only the materialistic school of the Cāvākas who object to this and claim that from generalisation nothing can be obtained which is new.

As an example of logical analysis we give a *śloka* from Annambhaṭṭa; "The five members of a syllogism are: (1) the thesis set down, (2) the reason, (3) the examplification (4) the subsumptive correlation, and (5) conclusion; e.g., The mountain has fire — this is the thesis. 'For it has smoke' — this is the reason. 'Whichever has smoke has fire, as a hearth' — this is the exemplification. 'And so is this' — this is the subsumptive correlation. 'Therefore it is such' — this is the conclusion.

In passing, it would also be useful to reflect on the *śloka* from *Bhāsapariccheda* where an attempt is made to define distance and nearness in the most generalised way. The definition, certainly the idea of sets, the complete theory of which was developed mathematically only a 100 years ago by Cantor.

> Distance and nearness are described as being of two kinds, viz., spatial as also temporal. The spatial kind abides only in limited things. Distance arises from a notion of the preponderance of the conjunction of limited things, and nearness is said to arise from a notion of its meagreness.

We will now recall a few of the established facts from the developments of science in modern times.

It is clear that as science progresses, more facts observed on the structure of the universe will be explained in a unified way. In other words, a few laws and generalisation should be sufficient to explain all aspects of nature that we can observe in the physical sense.

This has been constantly happening in science. The work of Galileo and Newton, unified astronomy and mechanics, the electromagnetic theory, unified electricity, magnetism and light and more recently it seems that just three laws are required to explain everything in nature and efforts are in progress to unify even these three laws as well. In the process of unification, the laws of nature are now expressed as symmetries of various types, be it the geometric symmetry of the crystal, or the symmetry of interactions or symmetry in quantum behaviour. It is ultimately the symmetry of the process that becomes the law of physics. Obviously if there is to be a total unification of physical laws, it has to lead up to some very highly complex degree of symmetry. If further, we are made of atoms and molecules, these symmetries must be such as to include even human consciousness. It will mean a hypersuper symmetry of some sort.

Sometimes the physical laws appear not as pure symmetries of a process but as a result of a break in the symmetry. Much of fundamental physics is based on broken symmetries. We shall see this is of some relevance to Śaṅkara's *Advaita*, in the sense that if the supreme *Brahman* were to break from this symmetry, *Māyā* would be the cause of the real world. While essentially we are made of atoms, due to the complexity of the combinations, something like consciousness appears nearly in all living beings. It is so highly developed in man that he can ask questions about himself and even control nature. If, however, all this has to remain within the regime of physics, only a supreme symmetry and/or a departure from it can explain the real world.

It is a well-known fact that physical entities which are identical from the molecular and atomic point of view, exhibit phases of existence and transformations from one phase to the other. An example of this is 'water' which appears as ice, water and steam. The physical laws which hold for one do not necessarily hold for the other. I stress the importance of the existence of different phases in physical structure because as we see in discussing *Advaita*, consciousness can also appear in different phases in the brain each having its own region of validity.

Super Symmetry

I have referred to the fact that we are all made of atoms and molecules, and we must also take note of the fact that the sub-structure of atoms and molecules is so complicated that one has to give up the idea of a particle as such, and think in terms of interactions and fields as more important entities. This appearance in physics of quantities like wave function, quarks, etc. which are not even observable directly brings us closer to many abstract philosophical ideas which hitherto had no support from science. Now science itself is forcing these ideas on philosophy.

It is difficult to get directly from the writings of Śaṅkara the true meaning of *Advaita* as it requires a very thorough understanding of the subtle meaning of Sanskrit words. I will use the works of V. Subramania Iyer for examining the importance of *Advaita* in Modern science on which he has written many essays. I will also quote a few verses from some of the works of Śaṅkara where the meaning is clear to give an example of his deep insight. His detractors in earlier times especially from the West did not truly understand him as they themselves were not aware of the way science was progressing.

Śaṅkara says all knowledge can be comprehended if we assume that consciousness has three phases of existence:

(1) the waking condition

(2) the dream state

(3) the dreamless state.

The first of these refers to the stage in which all observations are made through our senses like the eyes, ears, nose, touch, etc. and all of science is based on this principle. We also cannot ignore the fact that some sort of consciousness is opening even when one is asleep. The thoughts in a dream may be just residues of what has happened during the day; or they may be illusions as a result of maloperation of the bodily systems but we make note of the fact that several mathematicians, physicists, and artists have received inspiration during this phase. Bertrand Russell has said when writing his famous work *Principia Mathematica* that while at the end of the day, he was unable to prove any of the conjecture theorems, in the morning within few minutes of starting, he had the answers to all of them. The brain must have been active all night while he was asleep. Many poets have been inspired in the same manner. Modern psychologists may not accept the dream state as another phase in human consciousness, but the fact remains that the brain is active while the rest of the body is in a transformed phase. Says Śaṅkara in *Vivekacūḍāmaṇi*:

> Just as in dream the universe existing on one's own self is seen as if, it were external, so be it known that even in the waking state, this universe exists within and appears to be external.
>
> In dream things appear by the light of one's own self. There is, then indeed no other light. The wise, have concluded that the case is just the same even in waking.
>
> Both waking and dreaming are subject to the illusion, that intellect imposes on us. In this respect there is no difference between them

The third and last phase is more difficult to follow because very few people have actually experienced it. In Indian philosophy, this phase is called *suṣupti,* a dreamless sleep which a man can work himself into where consciousness is totally separated from the body. Here there are no ideas of contradictions and objects in the working and other states do not bind it.

What is important to note is that each state has its only validity and relevance for that particular state. That Śaṅkara was not being merely mystical in this thinking is clear from the *śloka* in *Vivekacūḍāmaṇi*:

> The universe does not exist apart from the senses. The sense perception of its separateness is false like the quality of blueness of the sky. Has a superimposed attribute any meaning apart from its substratum? It is the substratum which appears like that through delusion.

We now come to the final part of our enquiry and that is the elucidation of truth and reality transcending our states of consciousness and with the full force of logic. To go into details would be beyond the scope of this article but we attempt to summarise the standpoint of Śaṅkara as to what is absolute truth and reality. We differentiate between absolute truth and relative truth, in that the latter refers to that which we observe in the waking and dream state of consciousness and is an of ephemeral nature.

It seems strange that these days anybody should worry about truth relative or absolute. Even in better times *sāvant*s have observed the following:

> The world is naturally averse to all the truth it sees or hears, but swallows nonsense and lies with greediness and gluttony. Truth has no hold on mankind. Every man seeks for truth, but God alone knows who has found it. Truth is always in a well.

But for some strange reason, there has always been an intense desire in man to seek truth and in the process define it. Śaṅkara more than anybody else has made attempts to define it with all his skill as a logician. The results are strange and disconcerting.

Purely for the sake of general argument let us admit that our states of consciousness have different states of existence, not necessarily as enumerated by Śaṅkara under name Avastraya, but enough to accept the waking state and *samādhi* as the two limiting states of consciousness. In between, there may be many others. If we define truth as something that cannot be contradicted and remains invariant in space and time etc. the laws of physics can claim to be the absolute truth in as long as we perceive it in the waking state of consciousness. But what of the other states, where time and relative measures of things are different. For example, in the dream state the mystical associations may dominate. In the final state of *suṣupti*, it is considered as the one in which no ideas exist and there is no thought of anything regarding which a contradiction or doubt may ever be conceived to exist.

In these various states, there must be something which is common to all of them in as far as truth is concerned. The nature of absolute truth is also such as not to admit of any contradiction and also be independent of time and space. Where can we find a situation where there can be no contradiction and things remain invariant in space and time involving all knowledge? It can only be in pure state of absolute supreme symmetry, i.e., the state of *suṣupti*. This according to Śaṅkara can be the only absolute truth and reality and none else is possible. This state can be called by several names depending on the various states of enlightenment the person finds himself in. It can be God, absolute *Brahman*, super symmetric state and so forth. Some people claim that it is possible to experience this state and return to lower states but by the very nature of things and definition they can never describe where they have been.

In trying to find an intersection between the various states, we have arrived at an all-embracing state difficult to define. Translating this into the terms of the language of set theory we started with a set of states of consciousness and looked for their intersection to get the truth component, but we have arrived at a stage where intersection and union merged into one at some absolute infinite level.

We will now put all this in the form of an Indian syllogism:

(a) *Pratijñā 1* (*Thesis 1*): There are various states of consciousness varying from the waking state.

(b) *Reason*: These have been observed depending on the state of enlightenment concerned.

(c) *Pratijñā 2* (*Thesis 2*): There are various forms of truth mostly relative to the state of enlightenment, but absolute truth, i.e., one which has no contradictions and is invariant in time and spae is common to all states in varying degrees.

Example: The laws of physics satisfy this condition in the waking state.

(d) *Thesis 3*: The entire universe has the structure of a super symmetry, the departure from which gives rise to the observable world. *Māyā* and super symmetry are perceivable only in the state of dreamless sleep.

(e) *Subsumptive correlation*: We thus have a state in which all is nothing, but the absolute truth, and its very existence is the cause of the universe.

Conclusion: Therefore, the only absolute truth and

reality is the super symmetrical state.

This is the final result of Śaṅkara's analysis which we arrive at after many an explanation.

Is this convincing for our times? Has Śaṅkara fallen into the same box of paradoxes as did Cantor's theory of sets when dealing with infinite sets or was that purely a restriction of mathematics? Even Rāmānuja does not accept Śaṅkara's analysis He prefers other modified solutions leading to an undefinable state.

The conclusion, however leads up to some sort of a sterile void and one would like to ask why use all this logic to lead up to a single supreme symmetry and call it *Advaita*. It could as well have been called the great one state of all.

The term *Advaita* is of great significance as it is a result of considering the totality of all knowledge and not merely a single state of consciousness. The best way to figure this out is by analogy to the term 'limit' in calculus. Through a point on a curve, many lines can be drawn, but only one of the lines is of significance, i.e., the tangent at the point because it is determined by another point or set of points infinitesimally close to it. The position of supreme symmetry or absolute truth is determined by all knowledge that goes behind it. It leads to the Supreme One, but because of all that has gone before it, it is neither one, nor two but it is not-two *Advaita*. It is not an independent unit, it is a pinnacle of all that has gone behind it.

7

Determinism

With the progress of knowledge, the sacred history related in Hinduism and the elaborate theology of the ancient and mediaeval temples have become less important than formerly to most religious-minded men and women. Religious criticism, in addition to science, has made it difficult to believe that every word of the religion is true; everyone now knows for instance that Genesis contains two different and inconsistent accounts of the creation by two different authors. Such matters, it is now held, are inessential. But there are three central doctrines — God, immortality and freedom — which are felt to constitute what is of most importance to all religions, insofar as it is not connected with historical events. These doctrines belong to what is called 'natural religion' in the opinion of Thomas Aquinas, and of many modern philosophers they can be proved to be true without the help of revelation by means of human reason alone. It is therefore important to inquire what science has to say as regards these three doctrines. My own belief is that science cannot either prove or disprove anything. I think, however, that there are scientific arguments which bear on their probability. This is especially true as regards freedom and its opposite, determinism, which we are to consider in the present chapter.

Of the history of determinism and free will something has already been said. We have seen that determinism found its strongest ally in physics, which seemed to have discovered laws regulating all the movements of matter and making them theoretically predictable. Oddly enough, the strongest argument against determinism in the present-day is equally derived from physics. But before considering it, let us try to define the issue as clearly as we can.

Determinism has a twofold character; on the one hand, it is a practical maxim for the guidance of scientific investigators; on the other hand, it is a general doctrine as to the nature of the universe. The practical maxim may be sound even if the general doctrine is untrue. Let us begin with the maxim and proceed afterwards to the doctrine.

The maxim advises men to seek causal laws, that is to say, rules connecting events at one time with events at another. In everyday life, we guide our conduct by rules of this sort, but the rules that we use purchase simplicity at the expense of accuraccy. If I press the switch, the electric light will come on — unless it is fused; if I strike a match, it will burn — unless the head flies off; if I ask for a number on the telephone I shall get it — unless I get the wrong number. Such rules will not do for science, which wants something invariable. Its ideal was fixed by Newtonian astronomy, where by means of the law of gravitation, the past and future positions of the planets can be calculated throughout periods of indefinite vastness. The search for laws governing them in relation to the orbits of the planets, because elsewhere there is a greater complexity of causes of different kinds, and a smaller degree of regularity of periodic recurrence. Nevertheless, causal laws have been discovered in chemistry, in electromagnetism, in biology, and even in economics. The discovery of causal laws is the essence of science and therefore there can be no doubt that scientific men do right to look for him. If there is any region where there are no causal laws, that region is inaccessible to science. But the maxim that men of science should seek causal laws is as obvious as the maxim that a man who wants to gather mushroom should visit a mushroom garden.

Causal laws, in themselves, do not necessarily invlove a complete determination of the future by the past. It is a causal law that the sons of white people are also white, but if this is where the only law of heredity is known, we should not be able to predict much about the sons of white parents. Determinism as a general doctrine asserts that complete determination of the future by the past is always possible, theoretically, if we know enough about the past and about causal laws.

The investigator, observing some phenomenon to find previous circumstance based on the principle and the causal laws, which together made the phenomenon inevitable. And, having discovered the laws, he should be able, when he observes similar circumstances, to infer that a similar phenomenon is going to occur.

It is difficult, if not impossible, to state this doctrine precisely. When we try to do so, we find ourselves asserting that this or that 'theoretically' means. It is of no use to assert that 'there are' laws which determine the future, unless we add that we hope to find them out. The future obviously will be what it will be, and in that sense is already determined; an omniscient God, such as the orthodox believe in must now know the whole course of the future; there is therefore, if an omniscient God exists, a present fact —namely his foreknowledge — from which the future could be inferred. This, however, lies outside what can be scientifically tested. If the doctrine of determinism is to assert anything that can be made probable or improbable by evidence it must be stated in relation to our human powers. Otherwise we run a risk of sharing the fate of the devils in *Paradise Lost* who

> reason'd high
> of providence, foreknowledge, will, and fate,
> Fixt rate, free will, foreknowledge absolute,
> And found no end, in wandring mazes lost.

If we are to have a doctrine that can be tested, it is not enough to say that the whole course of nature must be determined by causal laws. This might be true, and yet undiscoverable — for example, if what is more distant had more effect that what is nearer, for we should then need a detailed knowledge of the most distant stars before we could foresee what was going to happen on earth. If we are to be able to test our doctrine, we must be able to state it in relation to a finite part of the universe, and the laws must be sufficiently simple for us to be able to make calculations by their means. We cannot know the whole universe, and we cannot test laws which are so complicated as to require more skill than we can hope to possess for the working out of their consequences. The powers of calculation involved may exceed what is possible at the moment, but not what may probably be acquired before long. This point is fairly obvious, but there is more difficulty in stating our principle so as to be applicable when our date is confined to a finite part of the universe. Sometimes a new star appears in the heavens, and these appearances cannot be predicted from data confined to the solar system. And as nothing travels faster than light, there is no way, by which we can get an advance message telling us that a new star is going to appear.

We can attempt to escape from this difficulty in the following manner. Let us suppose that we know everything that is happening at the beginning of 1936 within a certain sphere of which we occupy the centre. We will assume, for the sake of definiteness that the sphere is so large that it takes just a year for light to travel from the circumference to the centre. Then, since nothing travels faster than light everything that happens at the centre of the sphere during the year 1936 must, if determinism is true, be dependent only on what was inside, the sphere at the beginning of the year, since more distant things would take more than a year to have any effect at the centre. We shall not really be able to have all our supposed data till the year is over, because it will take that length of time for light to reach from the circumference; but when the year is over we can investigate, retrospectively, whether the data we now have together with known causal laws, accounts for everything that happened on the earth during that year.

We can therefore now state the hypothesis of determinism, though I am afraid the statement is rather complicated. The hypothesis is as follows:

> There are discoverable causal laws such that given sufficient powers of calculation, a man who knows all that is happening within a certain sphere at a certain time can predict all that will happen at the centre of the sphere during the time it takes light to travel from the circumference of the sphere to the centre.

I want it to be clearly understood that I am not asserting this principle to be true; I am only asserting that it is what must be meant by 'determinism' if there is to be any evidence either for or against it. I do not know whether the principle is true, and no more does anybody else. It may be regarded as an ideal which science has held before itself, but it cannot be regarded, unless on some *a priori* ground, as either certainly true or certainly false. Perhaps when we come to examine the arguments, that have been used for and against determinism, we shall find that what people have had in mind was something rather less definite than the principle at which we have arrived.

For the first time in history, determinism is now being challenged by men of science on scientific grounds. The challenge has come through the study of the atom by the new methods of quantum mechanics. The leader of the attack has been Arthur Eddington, and although some of the best physicists do not agree with his views on this matter, his argument is a powerful one, and we must examine it as far as it is possible without technicalities.

According to quantum mechanics, it cannot be known what an atom will do in given circumstances. There are a definite set of alternatives open to it, and it chooses sometimes one, sometimes another. We know in what proportion of cases, one choice will be made, in what proportion a second or a third, and so on. We are in the same position as to argue against the determinism derived from the behaviour of atoms since it rests wholly on our present ignorance, and may be refuted tomorrow by the discovery of a new law. Up to a point this is true. Our detailed knowledge of atoms is very recent, and there is every reason to suppose that it will increase. No one can deny that laws may be disovered which will show why an atom chooses one possibility on one occasion and another on another. At present, we know of no relevant difference in the antecedents of the two different choices, but some such difference may be found any day. If we have any strong reason to believe in determinism this argument would carry great weight.

Unfortunately for the determinists, there is a further step in the modern doctrine of atomic caprice. We had or so we thought — a great mass of evidence from ordinary physics, tending to prove that bodies always move in accordance with laws which completely determine what they will do. It now appears that all these laws may be merely statistical. The atom chooses among possibilities in certain proportions and they are so numerous that the result, as regards bodies large enough to be observed by old fashioned methods, has an appearance of complete regularity. Suppose you were a giant who could not see individual men and never became aware of an aggregate of less than a million of them. You would notice that India contains more matter by day than by night, but you could not possibly be aware of the fact that on a given day Mr. X was ill in bed and did not take his usual train. You would therefore believe the movement of matter into India in the morning and out of it in the evening to be a much more regular affair than it is. You would no doubt attribute it to some peculiar force in the sun, a hypothesis which would be confined by the observation that the movement is retarded in foggy weather.

If, later, you became able to observe individual men, you would find that there is less regularity than you had supposed. One day Mr. Y is ill, and another, Mr. Z; the statistial average is not affected, and to large-scale observation there is no difference. You would find that all the regularity you had previously observed could be accounted for by the statistial law of large numbers, without supposing that Mr. Y and Mr. Z had any reason beyond caprice for their occasional failure to go to India for their work in the morning. This is exactly the situation at which physics has arrived in regard to atoms. It does not know of any laws completely determining their behaviour and the statistical laws which it has discovered are sufficient to account for the observed regularity in the motions of large bodies; and as the case for determining has rested on these, it seems to have broken down.

To this argument the determinist may attempt to reply in two different ways. He may argue that, in the past occurrences which, at first, seemed not subject to law, have afterwards been shown to follow some rule, and that, where this has not yet occurred the great complication of the subject-matter affords a sufficient explanation. If, as many philosophers have believed, there were *a priori* reasons for believing in the reign of law, this would be a good argument if these are no such reasons, the argument is exposed to a very effective retort. The regularity of large-sale occurrences results from the laws of probability, without the need of assuming regularity in the doings of individual atoms. What quantum theory assumes as regards individual atoms is a law of probability of possible choices open to the atom, there is a known probability of one, another known probability of a second and so on. From this law of probability, it can be inferred that large bodies are almost certain to behave as traditional mechanics expect. The observed regularity of large bodies therefore, is only probable and approximate, and affords no inductive ground for expecting a perfect regularity in the doings of individual atoms.

Long before quantum mechanics were invented, statistical laws already played an important part in physics. For instance, a gas consists of a vast number of molecules moving at random in all directions with varying speeds. When the average speed is great, the gas is hot; when it is small, the gas is cold. When all the molecules stand still the temperature of the gas is the absolute zero. Owing to the fact that the molecules are constantly bumping into each other, those that are moving faster than the average get slowed down and those that are moving slower get speeded up. That is why, if two gases at different temperatures are in contact, the colder one gets warmer and the warmer one gets colder until they reach the same temperature. But all this is only probable. It might happen that in a room originally at an even temperature all the fast-moving particles got to one side, and all the slow moving ones to the other; in that case, without any outside cause one side of the room would get cold and the other hot. It might even happen that all the air got into one half of the room and left the other half empty. This is vastly more improbable than the run of 100 heads, because the number of molecules is very great, but it is not strictly speaking impossible.

What is new in quantum mechanics is not the occurrence of statistical laws, but the suggestion that they are ultimate, instead of being derived from laws governing individual occurrences. This is a very difficult conception — more difficult. I think, than its supporters realize. It has been observed that of the different things an atom may do it does each in a certain proportion of cases. But if the single atom is lawless, why should there be this regularity as regards large numbers? There must, one would suppose, be something that makes the rare transitions depend upon some unusual set of circumstances. We may take an analogy which is really rather close. In a swimming bath, one finds steps which enable a diver to dive from any height that he may perfer. If the steps go up to a great height, the highest will only be chosen by divers of exceptional excellence. If you compare one season with another, there will be a fair degree of regularity in the proportion of divers who choose the different steps; and if there were billions of divers we may suppose the regularity would be greater. But it is difficult to see why this regularity should exist if the separate divers had no motive for their choice. It would seem as if some men must choose the high divers, in order to keep up the right proportion; but that would no longer be pure caprice.

The theory of probability is in a very unsatisfactory state, both logically and mathematically; and I do not believe that there is any alchemy by which it can produce regularity in large numbers out of pure caprice in each single case. If the coin really chose by caprice whether to fall heads or tails, have we any reason to say that it would choose one about as often as the other? Might not caprice lead just as well always to the same choice? This is no more than a suggestion since the subject is too obscure for dogmatic statements. But if it has any validity, we cannot accept the view that the ultimate regularities in the world have to do with a large number of cases, and we shall have to suppose that the statistical laws of atomic behaviour are derived from hitherto undiscovered laws of individual behaviour.

In order to arrive at emotionally agreeable conclusions from the freedom of the atom, assuming this to be a fact — Eddington is compelled to make a supposition which he admits is at present no more than a bare hypothesis. He wishes to safeguard human free will, which, if it is to have any importance, must have the power of causing large scale bodily movements other than those resulting from the laws of large-scale mechanics. Now the laws of large-scale mechanics, as we have seen are unchanged by the new theories as to the atom; the only difference is that they now state overwhelming probabilities instead of certainties. It is possible to imagine these probabilities counteracted by some peculiar kind of instability owing to which a very small force might produce a very large effect. Eddington imagines that this sort of instability may exist in living matter, and more particularly in the brain. An act of volition may lead one atom to this choice rather than that, which may upset some very delicate balances and so produce a large-scale result such as saying one thing rather than another. It cannot be denied that this is abstractly possible, but that is the most that can be conceded. It is also a possibility, and to my mind a much more probable one, that new laws will be discovered which will abolish the supposed freedom of the atom. And even granting the freedom of the atom, there is no empirical evidence that large-scale movements of human bodies are exempt from the process of averaging which makes traditional mechanics applicable to the movements of other bodies of appreciable size. Eddington's attempt to reconcile human free-will with physics therefore, though interesting and not strictly refutable, does not seem to me sufficiently plausible to demand a change in the theories on the subject which were held before the rise of quantum mechanics.

Psychology and physiology, insofar as they bear upon the question of free will tend to make it improbable. Work on internal secretions, increased knowledge of the functions of different parts of the brain, Pavlov's investigation of conditioned reflexes and the psycho-analytic study of the effects of repressed memories and desires have all contributed to the discovery of causal laws governing mental phenomena. None of them of course, have disproved the possibility of free-will, but they have made it highly probable that, if uncaused volitions do ever occur, they are very rare.

The emotional importance supposed to belong to free-will seems to me to rest mainly upon certain confusions of thought. People imagine that if the will has causes, they may be compelled to do things that they do not wish to do. This of course is a mistake, the wish is the cause of action even if the wish itself has causes. We cannot do what we would rather not do, but it seems unreasonable to complain of this limitation. It is unpleasant when our wishes are thwarted, but this is no more likely to happen if they are caused than if they are uncaused. Nor does determinism warrant the feeling that we are impotent. Power consists in being able to have intended effects and this is neither increased nor diminished by the discovering of causes of our intentions.

Believers in free-will always, in another mental compartment, believe simultaneously that volitions have causes. They think for example, that virtue can be inculcated by a good upbringing, and that religious education is very useful to morals. They believe that sermons do good, and that moral exhortation may be beneficial. Now it is obvious that if virtuous volitions are uncaused, we cannot do anything whatsoever to promote them. To the extent to which a man believes that it is in his power, or in any man's power to promote desirable behaviour in others, to that extent he believes in psychological causation and not in free-will. In practice, the whole of our dealings with each other are based upon the assumption that men's actions result from antecedent circumstances. Political propaganda, the criminal law, the writing of books urging this or that line of action would all lose their *raison d'être* if they had no effect upon what people do. The implications of the free-will doctrine are not realised by those who hold it. We say 'why did you do it'? and expect the answer to mention beliefs and desires which caused action. When a man does not himself know why acted as he did, we may search his unconscious for a cause but it never occurs to us that there may have been no cause.

It is said that introspection makes us immediately aware of free-will. Insofar as this is taken in a sense which precludes causation, it is a mere mistake. What we know is that, when we have made a choice we could have chosen otherwise—if we had wanted to do so. But we cannot know by mere introspection whether there were or were not causes of our wanting to do what we did. In the case of actions which are very rational, we may know their causes. When we take legal or medical or financial advice and act upon it, we know that the advice is the cause of our action.

It should be said, further, that the notion of 'will' is very obscure, and is probably one which would disappear from a scientific psychology. Most of our actions are not preceded by anything that feels like an act of will; it is a form of mental disease, to be unable to do simple things without a previous decision. We may, for instance, decided to walk to a certain place and then if we know the way, the putting of one foot before another until we arrive. It is only the original decision that is felt to involve, 'will'. When we decide after deliberation two or more possibilities have been in our minds, each or less attractive and perhaps also each more or less repulsive; in the end, one has proved the most attractive and has overpowered the others. When one tries to discover volition by introspection one finds a sense of muscular tenseness, and sometimes an emphatic sentence; 'I will do this'. But I, for one, cannot find in myself any specific kind of mental occurrence that I could call 'will'.

In fact, both absolute metaphysical doctrines, go beyond what is scientifically ascertainable. The search for causal laws, as we saw is the essence of science, and therefore, in a purely practical sense, the man of science must always assume determinism as a working hypothesis. But he is not bound to assert that there are causal laws except where he has actually found them; indeed he is unwise if he does so. But he is still more unwise if he asserts positively that he knows of a region where causal laws do not operate. This assertion has lack of wisdom at once theoretical and practical-theoretical, beause our knowledge can never be sufficient to warrant such an assertion; and practical because the belief that there are no causal laws in a certain province discourages investigation, and may prevent laws from being discovered. This double lack of wisdom seems to me to belong both to those who assert that changes in atoms are not completely deterministic, and to those who dogmatically assert free will. Faced with such opposite dogmatisms, science should remain purely empirical, carrying neither assertion nor denial beyond the point warranted by actual evidence.

Perennial controversies, such as that between determinism and free-will, arise from the conflict of two strong logically irreconciliable passions. Determinism has the advantage that power arises through the discovery of causal laws; science in spite of its conflict with theological prejudice has been accepted because it gave power. Belief that the course of nature is regular also gives a sense of security; it enables us, up to a point to foresee the future and to prevent unpleasant occurrences. When illnesses and storms were attributed to capricious diabolical agencies, they were much more terrifying than they are now. All these motives lead men to like determinism. But while they like to have power over nature, they do not like nature to have power over them. If they are obliged to believe that, before the human race existed, laws were at work which by a kind of blind necessity, produced not only men and women in general, but oneself with all one's idiosyncrasies, saying and doing at this moment whatever one is saying and doing — they feel robbed of personality, futile, unimportant, the slaves of circumstance, unable to vary in the slightest degree the part assigned to them by nature from the very beginning. From this dilemma, some men seek to escape by assuming freedom in human beings and determinism everywhere else, others by ingeniously sophistical attempts at a logical reconciliation of freedom with determinism. In fact, we have no reason to adopt either alternative, but we also have no reason to suppose that the truth, whatever it may be is such as to combine the agreeable features of both or is in any degree determinable by relation to our desires.

8

Soul and Body

Of all the more important departments of scientific knowledge, the least advanced is psychology. According to its derivation, 'psychology' should mean 'the theory of the soul' but the soul though familiar to theologians, can hardly be regarded as a scientific concept. No psychologists would say that the subject-matter of his study is the soul, but when asked to say what it is, he would not find it easy to answer. Some would say that psychology is concerned with mental phenomena, but they would be puzzled if they were required to state in what respect 'mental' phenomena differ from those which provide the data of physics. Fundamental psychological questions quickly take us into regions of philosophical uncertainly and it is more difficult than in other sciences to avoid fundamental questions, because of the paucity of exact experimental knowledge. Nevertheless, something has been achieved and much ancient error has been discarded. Much of this ancient error was associated with theology either as cause or as effect. But the connection was not, as in the matters we have hitherto discussed with particular texts.

The 'soul' as it first appeared in Greek thought, had a religious though not a Christian origin. It seems, so far as Greece was concerned to have originated in the teaching of the Pythagoreans, who believed in transmigration, and aimed at an ultimate salvation which was to consists of liberation from the bondage to matter which the soul must suffer so long as it is attached to a body. The Pythagoreans influenced Plato and Plato influenced the Fathers of the Church; in this way the doctrine of the soul as something distinct from the body because part of

Christian doctrine. Other influences entered in, notably that of Aristotle and that of the Stoics but Plantonism, particularly in its later forms, was the most important pagan element in patristic philosophy. "Be assured Socrates," says a character in the Republic,"that when a man is nearly persuaded that he is going to die, he feels alarmed and concerned about things which never affected him before. Till then he has laughed at those stories about the departed which tell us that he who had done wrong here must suffer for it in the other world; but now his mind is tormented with a fear, we learn that "the blessings which Musaesus and his son Eumolupus represent the gods as bestowing upon the just, are still more delectable than these (i.e., riches here on earth): "for they being them to the abode of Hades, and describe them as reclining on couches at a banquet of the pious, and with garlands on their heads spending all eternity in wine-bibbing." It appears that Musaesus and Orpheus succeeded in "persuading not individuals merely, but whole cities, also that men may be absolved and purified from crimes, otherwhile they are still alive and even after their decease, by means of certain sacrifices and pleasurable amusements which they call Mysteries which deliver us from the torments of the other world, which, is neglected to them is punished by an awful doom". Socrates himself, in the Republic holds that the next life should be represented as pleasant in order to encourage valour in battle; but he does not say whether he believes this to be the truth.

Soul and body, in the scholastic philosophy (which is still that of Rome) are both substances. 'Substances' is a notion derived from syntax, and syntax is derived from the more or less unconscious metaphysic of the primitive races who determine the structure of our languages. Sentences are analysed into subject and predicate, and it is thought that, while some words may occur either as subject or as predicate, and it is thought that while some words may occur either as conjunction or injunction, there are others which can only occur as subjects; these words — of which proper names are the best example — presuppose to denote 'substances'. The popular word for the same idea is 'thing' or 'person' when applied to human beings. The metaphysical conception of substance is only an attempt to give precision to what common sense means by a thing or a person. Let us take an example. We may say "Socrates taught Plato" and so on; in all these statements, we attribute different attributes to Socrates. In another statement "Socrates was wise". The word 'Socrates' has exactly the same meaning in all these sentences; the man Socrates is thus something different from his attributes, something in which the attributes said to 'inhere'. Natural knowledge only enables us to recognise a thing by its attributes; if Socrates had a twin with exactly the same attributes, we should not be able to tell them apart. Nevertheless a substance is something other than the sum of its attributes. This appears most clearly from the doctrine of the Eucharist. In transubstantiation, the attributes of the bread remain, but the substance becomes that of the Body of Christ. In the period of the rise of modern philosophy, all the innovators from Descartes to Leibnitz, Vyāsa to Śaṅkarācārya took great pains to prove that their doctrines were consistent with transubstantiation; that authorities hesitated for a long time, but finally decided that safety was only to be found in scholasticism.

It thus appeared that, apart from revelation, we never could be sure whether a thing or person seen at one time was or was not identical with a similar thing or person seen at another time; we were in fact exposed to the risk of a perpetual comedy of errors. Under Locke's influence, his followers took a step upon which he did not venture; they denied the whole utility of the notion of substance. Socrates, they said, insofar as we can know anything about him, is known by his attributes. When you have said where and when he lived, what he looked like, what he did, and so on, you have said all that there is to say about him; there is no need to suppose an entirely unknowable core, in which his attributes inhere like pins in a pin-cushion. What is absolutely and essentially unknowable cannot even be known to exist, and there is no point in supposing that it does.

The conception of substance, as something having attributes but distinct from any and all of them was retained by Descartes, Spinoza, and Leibnitz; also, though with greatly diminished emphasis, by Locke. It was however, rejected by Hume, and has gradually been extruded both from psychology and from physics. As to the way in which this has happened, more will be said presently; for the moment, the theological implication of the doctrine and the difficulties resulting from its rejection must concern us.

Take first the body. So long as the conception substance was retained, the resurrection of the body meant the reassembling of the actual substance which had composed it when alive on earth. The substance might have passed through many transofmrations, but had retained its identity. If, however, a piece of matter is nothing but the assemblage of its attributes, its identity is lost when the attributes, change, and there will be no sense in saying that the heavenly body, after the resurrection, is the same 'thing' that was once an earthly bodie. This oddly enough, is exactly paralleled in modern physics. An atom with its attendant elections, is liable to sudden transformations, and the electrons which appear after a transformation cannot be identified, with those that had appeared before. Each is only a way of grouping observable phenomena, and has not the sort of 'reality' required for the preservation of identity through change.

The result of the abandonment of 'substance' were even more serious as regards the soul than as regards the body. They showed themsleves, however, very gradually because various attenuated forms of the old doctrine were, for a time, thought to be still defensible. First the word 'mind' was substituted for the word 'soul' in order to seem to avoid theological implications. Then the word 'subject' was substituted and this word still survives particularly in the supposed contrast of 'subjective' and 'objective'. A few words must, therefore be said about the 'subject'.

Kant, who undertook to answer Hume thought he had found a way out, which was considered profound because of its obscurity. In sensation, he said, things act upon us, but our nature compells us to perceive; not the things as they are in themselves, but something else, which results from our having made various subjective additions. The most notable of these additions are time and space. Things-in-themselves, according to Kant, are not in time or in space, though our nature obliges us to see things as if they were. The ego or soul as a thing in itself, is also not in time or space, though as an observable phenomenon it appears to be in both. What we can observe in perception is a relation of a phenomenal self to a phenomenal object, but behind both there is a real self and a real thing-in-itself, neither of which can exist or ever be observed. Why, then, assume that they exist? Because this is necessary for religion and morals. Although we cannot by scientific means, know anything about the real self, we know that it has free will, that it can be virtuous or sinful, that it is immortal, and that the apparent injustice of the sufferings of the good here on earth must be redressed by the joys of heaven. On such grounds, Kant, who held that pure reason cannot prove the existence of God, thought that this was possible for practical reason, since it was a necessary consequence of what we intuitively know in the sphere of morals.

It was impossible for philosophy to rest long in such a half-way house, and the sceptical parts of Kant's doctrine proved of more lasting value than those in which he tried to rescue orthodoxy. It was soon seen that there was no need to assume the existence of the thing-in-itself which was merely the old substance with its unknowability emphasised. In Kant's theory, 'phenomena' which can be observed, are only apparent and the reality behind them is something of which we should know only the bare existence if it were not for the postulates of ethics. To his successors — after the line of thought which he suggested had reached a culmination in Hegel — it became evident that 'phenomena' have whatever reality we can know of, and that there is no need to assume a superior brand of reality belonging to what cannot be perceived. There may, of course, be such a superior brand of reality, but the arrangements proving that must be invalid, and the possibility, therefore, is merely one of those countless bare possibilities which should be ignored because they lie outside the realm of what is known or may be known thereafter. And within the realm of what can be known there is no room for the conception of substance, or for its modification in the form of subject and object. The primary facts which we can observe have no such dualism, and give no reason for regarding either 'things' as anything but a collection of phenomena.

In considering the relations of soul and body, it was not only the conception of substance that was found difficult to reconcile with modern philosophy; there were equal difficulties as regards causality.

The conception of cause entered into theology chiefly in connection with sin. Sin was an attribute of the will, and the will was not itself the result of antecedent causes, since, if it were, we should not be responsible for our actions; in order to safeguard the notion of sin, therefore, it was equally necessary that the will should be uncaused, and that it should be a cause. This entailed a number of propositions both as to analysis of mental occurrences, and as to the relations of mind, and body, and some of these propositions, as time went on became very difficult to maintain.

The first difficulty arose through the discovery of the laws of mechanics. During the seventeenth century, it became apparent that the laws which experiment seemed to show to be true all the motions of matter. No reason appeared for making an exception in favour of the bodies of animals or men. Descartes drew the inference that animals are automata, but still thought that in men the will could cause bodily movements. The progress of physics quickly showed his conclusion to be impossible and his followers abandoned the view that mind could have any effect on mind. This led them to the theory of two parallel series, mental and physical, each with its own laws. When you meet a man and decide to say 'how do you do' your decision belongs to the mental series; but the movements of lips and tongue and larynx which seem to result from it really have purely mechanical causes. They compared mind and body to two clocks which both keep perfect time; when one reaches the hour both strike; through the one has no influence on the other. If you could see one of the clocks, but only knew the other through its strike, you would think that the one you could see caused the strike.

This theory, besides being difficult to believe, had the disadvantage that it could not save free will. There was supposed to be a strict correspondence between states of body and states of mind, so that when either was known, the other could theoretically be inferred. The man who knew the laws of this correspondence, and also the laws of physics, could, if he had enough knowledge and skill predict mental occurrences as well as physical ones. In any case, the mental volitions were useless if no physical manifestations followed. The laws of physics determined when you would say 'how do you do' since this is a physical action; and it would be small consolation to believe that you could will to say 'good bye' if it was foreordained that you should in fact say the opposite.

If it is not surprising, therefore, that the Cartesian doctrine gave place, in eighteenth century France, to pure materialism in which man is treated as wholly governed by the laws of physics. Will no longer has any place in this philosophy, and the concept of sin disappears. There is no soul and therefore there is no immortality except that of the separate atoms which are temporarily joined together in the human body. This philosophy which was supposed to have contributed to the excesses of the French Revolution became an object of horror, after the Reign of Terror, first to all who were at war with France, and then, after 1814 to all Frenchman who supported the government. England relapsed into orthodoxy; Germany adopted the idealistic philosophy of Kant's successors. Then came the romantic movement which liked emotions and would not hear of the control of human actions by mathematical formulae.

In human physiology, meanwhile those who disliked materialism took refuge either in mystery or in the vital force; some thought that science could never understand the human body, others declared that it could only do so by invoking principles other than those of chemistry and physics. Neither of these views has now much popularity among biologists, though the latter still has a few supporters. The work which has been done in embryology in bio-chemistry, and in the artificial production of organic compounds makes it more and more probable that the charateristics of living matter are wholly explicable in terms of chemistry and physics, and the theory of evolution has, of course, made it impossible to suppose that principles applicable to animal bodies are not applicable to those of human beings.

To return to psychology and the theory of will; it was always obvious that many, perhaps most, of our volitions have causes; but orthodox philosophers maintained that these causes, unlike those in the physical world, do not necessitate their effects. It is always possible, so they maintained, to resist even the most powerful desires by a sheer act of will. Thus it came to be thought that when we are guided by passion, our acts are not free, since they have causes, but that there is a faculty sometimes called 'reason' and sometimes 'conscience' which when we follow its guidance, gives us real freedom. Thus 'true' freedom, as opposed to mere caprice, was identified with obedience to the moral law. The Hegelians took a further step, and identified the moral law with the law of the state, so that true freedom consisted in obeying the police. This doctrine was much liked by the Governments. The theory that the will is sometimes uncaused was, however, very difficult to maintain. It cannot be said that even the most virtuous acts are unmotived. A man may wish to please God, to win his neighbours approval or his own to see others happy or to alleviate pain. Any one of these desires may cause a good action, but unless some good desires exists in a man he will not do the things of which the moral law approves. We know much more than we knew formerly as to the causes of desires. Sometimes they are to be found in the working of the ductless glands, sometimes in early education, sometimes in forgotten experiences, sometimes in the desire for approval and so on. In most cases, a number of different sources enter into the causation of a desire. And it is clear that, when we make desire at the result of some desire, though there may at the same time be other desires pulling us in a contrary direction. In such cases, as Hobbes said, the idea of will is 'the last appetite' in deliberation. The idea of a wholly uncaused act of volition is thus not defensible. With the results of this in ethics we shall be concerned in a later chapter.

As psychology and physics become more scientific, the traditional concepts of both give way increasingly to new concepts capable of greater accuracy. Physics until very recently, was content with matter and motion in philosophical moments, as technically substance in the medieval sense. Matter and motion have now been found inadequate even technically, and the procedure of theoretical physicists has come much more into line with the demands of scientific philosophy. Psychology in like manner, is finding it necessary to give up such concepts as 'perception' and 'consciousness', because it is found that they are incapable of precision. To make this plain, a few words about each will be necessary.

'Perception' seems at first sight perfectly straightforward. We 'perceive' the sun and moon, the words we hear spoken, the hardness of the things we touch, the smell of a rotten egg or the taste of mustard.

There is no doubt about the occurrences of which we give this description; it is only the description that is questionable. When we 'perceive' the sun, there has been a long causal process, first in the 93,000,000 miles of intervening space then in the eye, the optic nerve, the brain. The final 'mental' event which we call seeing the sun cannot be supposed to bear such resemblance to the sun itself. The sun, like Kant's thing-in-itself remains outside our experience, and only to be known, if at all by a difficult inference from the experience which we call 'seeing the sun'. We suppose that the sun has an existence because many people see it at once, and because all sorts of things, such as the light of the moon, are most simply explained by assuming that the sun has effects in places where there are no observers. But we certainly do not 'perceive' the sun in the direct and simple sense in which we seem to do so before we have realised the elaborate physical causation of sensations.

We can say, in a loose sense, that we 'perceive' an object when something happens to us of which that object is the main cause and which is of such a nature as to allow us to make inferences as to the object. When we hear a person speaking the difference in what we hear corresponds to differences in what he says; the effect of the intervening medium is roughly constant, and may therefore be more or less ignored. Similarly when we see a patch of blue side by side, we have a right to assume some difference between the places from which the red and blue light comes through. This difference cannot be supposed to resemble the difference between the sensation of red and the sensation of blue. In this way, we may attempt to save the concept of perception but we shall never succeed in giving it accuracy. The intervening medium always has some distorting effect; the red place may look red because of the effect of intervening mist or the blue place blue because we are wearing coloured glasses. To make inferences as to the object from the sort of experience which we naturally call a 'perception', we must know physics and the physiology of the sense-organs and we must have exhaustive information about what is in the intervening space between us and the object. Given all this information and assuming the reality of the external world we can derive some highly abstract information, and immediately the implication in the word 'perception' will have vanished in this process of inference by means of difficult mathematical formulae. In the case of distant objects, like the sun, this is not difficult to see. But it is equally true of what we touch and smell and taste, since our preception of such things is due to elaborate processes which travel along the nerves to the brain. The question of 'consciousness' is perhaps rather more difficult. We say that we are conscious, but that sticks and stones are not; we say that we are 'conscious' when awake but not when asleep.We certainly mean something when we say this, and we mean something that is true. But to express with any accuracy what it is that is true is a difficult matter, and requires a change of language.

When we say we are 'conscious', we mean two things. On the one hand, that we react in a certain way to our environment, on the other hand that we seem to find, on looking within some quality in our thoughts and feelings which we do not find in inanimate objects.

As regards our reaction to the environment, this consists in investigation by psychical research. I have not sufficient knowledge on this subject myself to judge of the evidence already available, but it is clear that there could be evidence which would convince reasonable men, and this was elaborately discussed in a later analysis of Hinduism with a new look at soul and body. To this, however, certain provisos must be added. In the first place, the evidence at best, would only prove that we survive death, not that we survive for ever. In the second place, where the philosophy of desire is involved, and it is very difficult to accept the testimony, even the habitual evidence, of accruing persons; of this there was much evidence during the war, and in all times of great excitement. In the third place, if on other grounds it seems unlikely that our personality does not die with the body, we shall require much stronger evidence of survival than we should if we thought that the hypothesis believer in spiritualism could pretend to have as much evidence of survival as historians can adduce to prove that witched did bodily homage to Satan, yet hardly anyone now regards the evidence of such occurrences as even worth examining.

The difficulty, for science arises from the fact that there does not seem to be such an entity as the soul or self. As we saw, it is no longer possible to regard soul and body as two substances, having that endurance through time which metaphysicians regarded as logically bound up with the reason, in psychology, to assume a subject which, in perception, is brought into contact with an object. Until recently it was thought that matter is immortal, but this is no longer assumed by the technique of physics. An atom is now merely a convenient (up to a point to think of the atom as a nucleus with attendant electrons) but the electrons at one time cannot be identified with those at another, and in any case no modern physicist thinks of them as 'real'. While there was still material substance which was supposed to be eternal it was easy to argue that minds must be equally eternal; but this argument, which was never a very strong one, can now no longer be used. For sufficient reasons, physicists have reduced the atom to a series of events; for equally good reasons, psychologists find that a mind has not the identity of a single continuing thing but is a certain series of occurrences bound together by certain intimate relations. The question of immortality, therefore, has become the question whether these intimate relations exist between occurrences which take place after that body is dead.

We must first decide, before we can attempt to answer this question, what are the relations which bind certain events together in such a way as to make them the mental life of one person. Obviously the most important of these is memory; that I can remember something else. It might be objected that two people may remember the same event, but that would be an error; no two people ever see exactly the same thing, because of differences in their positions. No more can they have precisely the same experiences of hearing or smelling or touching or tasting. My experience may closely resemble another person's but always differs from it in a greater degree. Each person's experience is private to himself, and when one's experience consists in recollecting another, the two are said to belong to the same person.

There is another, less psychological, definition of personality, which derives from the body. The definition of what makes the identity of a living body at different times would be complicated, but for the moment we will take it for granted. We will also take it for granted that every mental experience known to us is connected with some living body. We can then define a person as the series of mental occurrences connected with a given body.

These two ways of defining a 'person' conflict in cases in being conscious 'of' something. If you shout 'Hi!', people look round, but stones do not. You know that when you yourself look round in such a case, it is because you have heard a noise. So long as it could be supposed that one perceives things in the outer world, one could say that, in perception, one was 'conscious' of them. Now we can only say that the stimuli to which they react are fewer. So far, therefore, as eternal 'perception' is concerned, the difference between us and a stone is only one of degree.

The more important parts of the notion of 'consciousness' is concerned with what we discover by introspection. We not only react to external objects, but we know that we react. The stone, we think does not know when it reacts, but if it does, it has consciousness here also; on analysis the difference will be found to be one of degree. To know that we see something is not really a new piece of knowledge, over and above the seeing, unless it is a memory. If, we first see something and then, immediately afterwards, reflect that we saw it, the reflection, which seems introspective, in as immediate memory. Memory, it may be said, is something distinctively, 'mental', but this again may be denied. Memory is a form of habit, and habit is characteristic of nervous tissue, though it may occur elsewhere, for example, in a roll of paper which rolls itself up again if it is unwound. I do not suggest that the above is a complete analysis of what we vaguely call 'consciousness' the question is a large one, and would require a volume. I mean only to suggest that what at first sight seems a precise concept is really quite the opposite and a different terminology is required by scientific psychologists.

Finally, it should be said that the old distinction between soul and body has evaporated quite as much, because 'matter' has lost its old solidity and because 'mind' has lost its spirituality. It is sometimes still thought, and is used to be thought universally, that the data of physics are public, in the sense that they are public in the sense that they are visible to anyone, whereas those of psychology are private, being obtained by introspection. This difference however is only one of degree. No two people can perceive exactly the same object at the same time, because of the difference in what they see. The data of physics when closely examined are seen to have the same kind of privacy as those of psychology and such quasi-publicity as they possess is not wholly impossible in psychology.

The facts which form the starting-point of the two sciences are, at least in part, identical. The patch of colour that we see is a datum for physics and psychology equally. Physics proceeds to one set of inferences in one sort of context, psychology to another set in another sort of context. One might say, though this would be putting it too crudely, that physics is concerned with causal relations outside the brain and psychology with causal relations inside the brain-excluding, in the latter case, those which are discovered by the external observation of the physiologist inspecting the brain. The data for both physics and psychology are events, which in some sense, happen in the brain. They have a chain of external causes, which are investigated by physics and a chain of internal effects — memories and a chain of habits which are investigated by psychology. But there is no evidence of any fundamental difference between the constitutents of the physical and the psychological world. We know less than was formerly thought, but we know enough to be fairly sure that neither 'soul' nor 'body' can find a place in modern science.

What science has to say on the subject of immortality is not very definite. There is, indeed, one line of argument in favour of survival after death, which is, at least in intention, completely scientific — I mean the line of argument associated with the phenomena of what is called dual personality. In such cases, what seem to outside observation to be one person, is subjectively split into two; sometimes neither knows anything of the other, sometimes one knows the other, but not *vice versa*. In cases where neither knows anything of the other, there are two persons if memory is used as the definition, but only one if the body is used. There is a regular gradation to the extreme of dual personality, through absent-mindedness, hypnosis, and sleep-walking. This creates difficulty in using memory as the definition of personality. But it appears that lost memories can be recovered by hypnotism, or in the course of psycho analysis; thus perhaps the difficulty is not insuperable.

In addition to actual recollection, various other elements, more or less analogous to memory, enter into personality habits, for instance, which have been formed as a result of past experience. It is because where there is life, events can form habits that an 'experience' differs from a mere occurrence. An animal and still more a man is formed by experiences in a way that dead matter is not. If an event is causally related to another in that peculiar way which has to do with habit-formation, then the two events belong to the same person. This is a wider definition than that by memory alone, including all that the memory-definition included and a good deal more. If we are to believe in the survival personality after the death of the body, we must suppose that there is continuity of memories or at least of habits, since otherwise there is no reason to suppose that the same person is continuing, but at this point physiology makes difficulties. Habit and memory are both due to effects on the body, especially the brain; the formation of a habit may be thought as analogous to the formation of a water-course. Now the effects on the body, which give rise to habits and memories, are obliterated by death and decay, and it is difficult to see how, short of a miracle, they can be transferred to a new body such as may be supposed to inhabit in the next life. If we are to be disembodied spirits, the difficulty is only increased. Matter is only a certain way of grouping events, and therefore where there are events, there is matter. The continuity of a person throughout the life of his body, if, is I contend, it dependent upon the continuity of the body. It would be as easy to transfer a water-course to heaven without loss of identity as it would be to transfer a person.

Personality is essentially a matter of organisation. Certain events, grouped together by means of certain relations, form a person. The grouping is effected by means of causal laws connected with habit-formation, which includes memory — and the causal laws concerned depend upon the body. If this is true — and there are strong scientific grounds for thinking that it is — to expect a personality to survive for thinking that it is — is to expect a personality to survive the disintegration of the brain.

In Hinduism, the soul plays an important role. It may be recalled that soul is one of the main fundamental units for the development of Hinduism. On the postualte of religion, there is so much diversity of views as on the soul. This is because the soul eludes all attempts to discover it, showing itself everywhere and nowhere. It is in conjunction with various things itself, but eclipses this important entity. While in conjunction with the body, the soul gives it life and makes it move. The body and its motion are seen, but the soul is not seen. In conjunction with the mind, it desires and thinks. The acts are attributed to the mind, and the soul is lost in it. As a result of Āṇavic construction, it gets such feelings as pride, anger and lust, which are identified with the body, the mind, and the empirical ego, and have been regarded as a physical or superphysical substance. On the other extreme, it has been identified with the highest entity, God. This is because, like God and on account of the gifts of God, it has love, light and lordship. The soul is like the captain of a ship who is not seen by those outside it, though the ship itself is seen and also the sailors. This elusiveness of the soul has given rise to various theories regarding its nature.

One class of psychologists identify what we call the soul with the mind, and speak of the mind as some mysterious form of cerebral activity. They thus ignore the soul and make a mystery of the mind. Certain classes of philosophers conceive the soul as possessing unlimited energy in addition to the abilities to know, to desire, and to do. With them, the soul is a perfect being by itself, and the imperfection is due to its body and mind. This theory is untenable on several grounds. If the tools are so defective, such a perfect being as the soul is believed to be, would not have chosen it; neither could it have been thrust on it by a higher and beneficent being if it had no choice. Secondly, there is nothing inherent in the tools to confound such a perfect being, if it had no choice of perfect being. This theory does not also explain the possibility of a soul sometimes doing right deeds, and at other times doing wrong deeds. Besides, the body, instead of assisting the soul, is presumed to be a means of doing harm to the soul. There is nothing in the body or in the mind to lead a perfect being to wrong-doing.

Another class of philosophers attributes every kind of perfection to the soul, but tacks on to it a freewill. They credit the soul with full power to do what is right, but attribute wrong-doing to free-will which may direct it to do right or wrong. Why, at one time it directs the soul to do right and at another to do wrong, is not explained. This view is also untenable. A whimsical power is not amenable to any kind of control or improvement, and gives no scope for evolution. There would then no goal, no progress, no system. A theory that would lead to such ends can find no place in scientific investigation. On the other hand, the theory of free-will is the formation and justification for punishment in the sense of penalties. According to this view, it is quite possible for the murderer, the robber and the incendiarist to have avoided the respective offences.

These and similar conceptions would make the soul a composite entity. As most of the components such as the intellect and the will are subject to change, the qualities that would be attributed to the soul would also be of a changing character. This would take the conception which is necessary for the formulation of a theory of life. Compositeness is always a bar to the evolution of knowledge. For example, if a body has various accelerated velocities, very little can be known of it if only its resultant velocity at an instant is known. On the other hand, if each velocity is separately known, it will be possible to give a full history of the body's motion. Laws get more accurate as analysis becomes more and more exhaustive. Therefore, if it is possible to isolate the soul from the intellect and other tools, it would be unscientific to consider the soul and its tools as forming a single entity. The soul is therefore conceived in Hindu philosophy as an entity which has the abilities to know, to desire, and to do. Then it cannot be further analysed in Advaitic philosophy.

We have already seen that the soul has only the abilities to know, to desire, and to do. But we also see that it knows, desires, and does. This shows that the soul has also the ability to act when it is provided with the necessary energy and tools. It is this ability which makes its evolution possible. It increases its knowledge and power till they become perfect. The soul may be compared to an engineer and the abilities to the steam engine. We know that the speed, and the direction, though neither the engineer nor the engine may undergo any appreciable change. The changes are caused by the quantity of steam that is supplied through so while the soul and its abilities remain unchanged, its activities change as a result of the change in the quantity of the energy supplied and the quality of the tools.

We seldom find two men or two other living beings occupying

identical situations. There is a great difference in the righteousness of men. Some are saintly and some others utterly destitute of the moral sense. The cause of this difference cannot be found in the soul themselves. We have seen that two things can differ only in the quality of their components. But souls are not components. Therefore they must be all alike. If they are all alike, the difference that we notice must be due to extraneous influences. The only permanent extraneous influence is *āṇava*, as *māyā* comes and goes and so does action. Therefore, the difference in the state of souls can be due only to the amount of construction maintained by *āṇava*. This construction must be different in different souls. If the construction is different now, it must have been different in the whole past. Souls are, therefore at different points in the path of evolution and will continue to be interpreted differently by of scholars till the end, i.e., till they reach the goal. In the path of evolution, the speed at any point must be the same for all because the same best facilities are afforded for the progress of all souls. Souls are therefore like people who start from different points of a path but travel in exactly similar vehicles to the same destination. But, though we do not see two living beings exactly alike, it does not allow that they cannot be exactly in the same position; it is not impossible that a number of souls are exactly in the same condition and reach the goal at the same time. All that we are sure of is that the condition of all souls is not the same.

The first activity of the soul is knowing. Knowledge is obtained by experience and reasoning. Experience may be either one's own or that of the other obtained by communication. The conditions of other lands are made known to us by those who have seen them. One's own experience may be either of events or of pain and pleasure. The experience of events is ordinarily obtained through the senses. But it is claimed that the mind is not limited by space, and can see things beyond the reach of the senses. It is also believed that, in its last stages of evolution, the soul more or less gets out of its restrictions and can see things in their absolute form with the help of the divine light given by God. Every kind of knowledge except the one obtained by the last means is liable to error, as a result of various imperfections such as those in the senses, in memory, and in the method of reasoning.

The next activity of the soul is desiring. To desire is to form a judgement that a certain thing is useful and to attach oneself to it. Before I first desire to have a mango, I form the judgement that it is useful to me, and then attach my *manas* to it. If the desire for the mango has got strengthened by repetition, it arises even when it is known to be injurious. The expectation of its well-known pleasure blinds the intellect for the time being, and goads the *manas* on to it. The *manas* is ever active, and this is often a source of great inconvenience, as when we have to check it from its usual wanderings and attach it to something new.

The energy necessary for the activities of the soul come freely from *māyā*. *Āṇava* constricts the abilities, but its efforts are counteracted by *vidyā*, *rāga*, and *kalā*, which force these energies in, according to the needs of the soul. The energy of knowing passes on to the intellect. It forms judgements and decisions, the correctness and righteousness of which depend upon the available part of its knowledge. Similarly the energies to desire and to do reach respectively the *manas* and the will, and cause desire and the initiation of action. The organs of senses and actions are ordinarily put in motion by the will. The tools in the physical body obey the behest of the inner organ according to the amount of physical energy available to the tools. A man may like to read for five hours at a stretch, but if the brain is not prepared to spare the necessary energy, he will not be able to read as long as he likes. If when a man wishes to run three miles the body does not possess the necessary energy, he will have to stop short of the distance. Thus, the actual activity of man depends partly on the energy supplied by the abilities of the soul, and as far as the energy in the work turned out by the person is concerned, it seems to depend entirely on the body. The mental organs seem to depend for energy on the *śuddhamāyā*, and the supply determines the quality of the work that is done. The greater the energy to know, the more extensive is the knowledge and more accurate is the thinking.

Repetition effects great saving of energy. We require great effort to write a difficult letter of the alphabet for the first time. After a number of repetitions, we are able to write it with almost no effort. The sum of two numbers, say 10 and 11, is at first not easily got but after practice much longer additions are done with very little exertion of the brain. We sometimes read page after page with the mind busy with something else. We are able to get through a chain of actions without our being quite aware of them. If it were not for such economy, life would be almost intolerable. But this economy is often as mischievous as it is beneficial. Unkind words are sometimes said, and evil deeds are done as the result of this economy leading to very painful consequences. A large percentage of the crimes and of praiseworthy acts that are done by us are due to the influence of repetition which is called habit. When habits get crystallised, they almost ignore the intellect and the will and in the very process of labour saving they weaken them and even control them, especially in the performance of wrong deeds.

Besides repetition, instincts are also a means of saving energy. These are the results of repetitions, not in the present body, but in previous bodies in the course of physical evolution. These often assert themselves before the soul can make full use of the intellect and the will, sometimes incapacitate the brain, shut out the intellect, and assume a dictatorial control over human conduct. Both habits and instincts, while saving the labour of the intellect and the will, also disregard them and even subjugate them.

On the other hand, the will and the intellect can, in certain circumstances, gain mastery over instincts and habits. The problem is entirely a matter of relative strength and efficiency. The supremacy of the instinct is possible if the will is weak and has been allowed to degenerate. But if the soul's powers of knowing and doing are great, the intellect and the will which are fed by them also become powerful, and may not be overruled by instinct or habit. This requires a habit of considerable action under the stimulus of habit or instinct. Then man is said to acquire self-control. When the will is further strengthened, it is able to exercise control over beings, as man, beast and even animate objects. If a soul has gained self-control, the intellect assumes sovereign power and is able to dispense with the services of the senses for acquiring information. The senses can only transmit knowledge of objects that are within their reach at a given time. But the sovereign intellect sees the events of all times and of all places.

The immediate purpose of one's activity is the supply of one's needs. But the ultimate purpose is the attainment of perfection or freedom from *āṇava*. Perfection can be attained only by practice. Every act of practice, till perfection is reached, must necessarily be imperfect. It is imperfect acts, therefore that lead to a perfect act. If a perfect act is called a right act, an imperfect act can be called a wrong act. Thus wrong acts lead to right acts and are therefore as useful as right acts. Every activity of a living being, whether right or wrong, leads it to perfection and freedom from *āṇava*. When it has reached perfection, it no longer worries itself with things of the world, but attaches itself to God and becomes divine.

The progress that the average man makes in his upward march during his lifetime seems to be infinitesimally small. His life is an alternation of right acts and wrong acts. His real character, his power of avoiding wrong deeds, does not undergo much change during a lifetime. If the gain in a single birth is so insignificant, and a soul is so far away from perfection it follows that the soul must pass through an indefinitely large number of births before it can attain the goal. This is called the doctrine of rebirth. A lifetime can be regarded only as an instance in the period of a soul's evolution. The change of the body makes no more difference to a soul than a change of house makes to an embodied soul. The soul does not, therefore view, with much concern any change of body. All the real knowledge that the soul has acquired and the tendency towards righteousness that its power of desiring has gained, remain for ever with the soul. This accounts for some men being born as saints and geniuses and others as criminals and dullards.

When a body no longer serves the purpose of the soul, it is separated from it, and its place is taken by a fresh body. This new body is the one most helpful to the soul from that instant. Its individual characteristics coupled with those of the family, and the species to which it belongs are just the tools with which the soul is qualified to work from that instance for its self-expression and for the experience of the fruits of certain past actions.

Just as a prince who was living in a palace may have to lodge in an uncomfortable tent in the forest, so a soul which has been using a human body may receive a non-human body. The body of an animal may be particularly suited to do certain kinds of actions and for experiencing the fruits of certain kinds of past actions. There are authentic stories of animal who have shown greater gentleness and goodness than animals. These are probably more advanced souls than these men, and might have been human beings in previous births. Say Manikavachakar:

> Grass was I, shrub was I worm, tree,
> Full many a kind of beast, bird, snake,
> Stone, man and demon. 'Midst thy hosts I served
> The form of might *asuras*, ascetics, gods I bore
> Within these immobile and mobile forms of life

In every species born, weary I've grown, great Lord. The soul has thus to pass through an indefinitely large number of births to remove Āṇavic constriction, and to get full knowledge and on attaining full knowledge, the purpose of its birth ceases. The soul gets divine illumination and merges in God.

There are an infinite number of souls which being simple, cannot die, and most therefore be separate from *prakṛti* which in itself changes and manifests all these phenomena, and the soul, according to the *Sāṁkhyas*, is inactive. It is a simple by itself, and *prakṛti* works out all these phenomena for the liberation of the soul, and liberation consists in the soul's discriminating that it is not nature. At the same time we have seen that the *Sāṁkhyas* were bound to admit that every soul was omnipresent. Being simple the soul cannot be limited, because all limitations come either through time, space or causation. The soul being entirely beyond these cannot have any limitation. To have limitation one must be in space, which means that it must have a body, and that which has a body must be in *prakṛti*. If the soul had form, it would be identified with *prakṛti*; therefore the soul is formless, and that which is formless cannot be said to exist here, there or anywhere. It must be omnipresent. Beyond this, the *Sāṁkhya* philosophy does not go.

The first argument of the Vedāntists against this is that this analysis is not a perfect one. If this *prakṛti* be simple, and the soul is also simple, then there will be two simples, and all the arguments that apply in the case of the soul to show that it is omnipresent, will apply equally in the case of *prakṛti*, and that too will be beyond all time, space and causation, and as the result, there will be no change or manifestation. Then will come the difficulty of having two simples which is impossible. What is the solution of the Vedāntist? His solution is that, it requires some sentient being as the motive power behind, to make the mind think and *prakṛti* work, because *prakṛti* in all its modifications from gross matter up to *mahat* is simply insentient. Now, says the Vedāntist, this sentient being which is behind the whole universe is what we call God, and consequently this universe is not different from Him. It is He Himself who has become this universe. He not only is the instrumental cause of this universe, but also the material cause. Cause is never different from effect, the effect is but the cause reproduced in another form. We see that everyday. So this Being is the cause of *prakṛti*. All the forms and phases of *Vedānta*, either dualistic or monistic first take this position — that God is not only the instrumental but also the efficient cause of thus universe, that everything which exists is he. The second step in *Vedānta* is that these souls are also a part of God, one spark of that infinite fire. As from a mass of fire millions of small particles fly, even so from this ancient one, have come all these souls. So far so good, but it does not yet satisfy. What is meant by a part of the infinite? The infinite is indivisible; there cannot be parts of the infinite. The absolute cannot be divided. What is meant therefore by the expression that all these sparks are from him? The Advaitist, the non-dualistic Vedāntist, solves the problem by maintaining that there is really no part; that each soul is really not a part of the Infinite, but actually is the infinite *Brahman*. Then how can there be so many souls? The sun reflected from millions of globules of water appears to be millions of suns, and in each globule is a miniature picture of the sun; so all these souls are but reflections and not real. They are not the real 'I' which is the God of this universe, the one undivided being of the universe and so all these little different beings — men, animals, etc. are but reflections, and not real. They are simply illusory reflections upon *prakṛti*. There is but one infinite Being in the universe and that Being appears as 'you' and as 'I', but this appearance of division is after all delusion. He has not been divided, but only appears to be divided. This apparent division is caused by looking at Him through the network of time, space and causation. When I look at God through the network of time, space and causation, I see Him as the material world. When I look at Him as the higher place, yet through the same network, I see Him as an animal; a little higher as a man, a little higher as a god. Yet He is the one infinite being of the universe, and that Being we are. I am that, and you are that. Not parts of it, but the whole of it. It is the eternal knowers standing behind the whole phenomena. He himself is the phenomena. He is both the subject and the object. He is the I and the you. How is this? How to know the knower? The knower cannot know himself. I see everything but cannot see myself. The self, the knower, the Lord of all, the Real Being is the cause of all the visions that are in the universe, but it is impossible for him to see himself or know himself except through reflection. You cannot see its own nature until it is reflected, the self cannot and this whole universe therefore is the self trying to realise itself. This reflection is thrown back first from the protoplasm, then from plants, and animals, and so on and on from better and better reflectors, until the best reflection — the perfect man — is reached. A man wanting to see his face, looks first in a little pool of muddy water, and sees just an outline. Then he comes to clearer water, and sees a better image, then to a piece of shining metal, and sees a better image, and at last to a looking-glass, and sees himself reflected as he is. Therefcre the perfect man is the highest reflection of that Being, who is both subject and object. You now find why man instinctively worships everything, and how perfect men are instinctively worshipped as God in every country. They are much higher than all the conceptions of God that you or I can make. A perfect man is much higher than such conceptions. In him, the circle becomes complete; the subject and the object become one. In him, all delusions go away and in their place comes the realisation that he has always been that perfect being. How came this bondage then? How was it possible for the perfect Being to degenerate into the imperfect? How was it possible that the free became bound? The Advaitists says he was never bound, but was always free. Various clouds of various colours come before the sky. They remain there a minute and then pass away. It is the same eternal blue sky stretching there for ever. The sky never changes; it is the cloud that is changing. So you are always perfect, eternally perfect. Nothing ever changes your nature or your will. All these ideas — I am imperfect, I am a man or a women or a sinner or I am the mind, I have thought, I will think — are all hallucinations; you never think, never had a body; you never were imperfect. You are the blessed Lord of this universe, the one almighty ruler of everything that is the universe and ever will be, the one mighty ruler of these suns and stars and moons and earths and plants, and all the little bits of our universe. It is through you the sun shines, and the stars shed their lustre, and the earth becomes beautiful. It is through your blessedness that they all love and are attracted to each other. You are in all, and you are all. Whom to avoid, and whom to take? You are the all in all. When this knowledge comes, delusion immediately vanishes.

When a man has reached that state it is called *jīvan-mukta*, 'living-free' — free even while living. The aim and end in this life for the *jñāna yogī* is to become this *jīvan-mukta,* or attain the state of 'living freedom', — he is *jīvan-mukta* who can live in this world without being attached. He is like the lotus leaves in water, which are never wet by the water. He is *jīvan-mukta* who can live in this world without being attached. He is the highest human being, nay, the highest of all beings, for he has realised his identity with the Absolute — he has realised that he is one with God. So long as you think you have the least difference from God, fear will seize you, but when you have known that you are He, that there is no difference, entirely no difference between you and Him, that you are all of Him and the whole of Him all fear ceases. There who sees whom? Who worships whom? Who talks to whom? Who fears whom? Where one sees another, where one talks to another, where one hears another, it is in law. Where none sees none, where none speaks to none, that is the highest, that is the great; that is the *Brahman*. Being That you are always That. What will become of the world then? What good shall we do to the world? Such questions do not arise. What becomes of my ginger beard if I become old? says the baby. What becomes of my marbles if I grow? So I will not grow, says the boy. What will become of my dolls if I grow old? — says the little child. It is the same question in connection with this world; it has no existence in the past, present and future. If we have known the *ātman*, as it is if we have known that there is nothing else but this *ātman*, that everything else is but a dream with no existence in reality, then this world with its properties, its miseries, its wickedness and its goodness will cease to disturb us. If they do not exist, for him and for what shall we take trouble? This is what the *jñāna yogīs* teach. Therefore dare to be free, dare to go as far as your thought lead, and dare to carry that out in your life. It is very hard to come *jñānam*. It is for the bravest and most daring who dare to smash all idols, not only intellectual, but also of the senses.

The body is not I; it must go. All sorts of curious things may come out of these teachings. I have neither birth nor death; father or mother I never had; friends and foes I have none, because they are all I; I am my own friend and I am my own enemy; I am Existence-Knowledge-Bliss Absolute; I am He, I am He. If in a thousand bodies I am healthy. If in a thousand bodies I am starving, in another thousand bodies, I am feasting. If in thousand of bodies I am suffering from misery, in thousand of Bodies, I am happy. Who shall blame whom, who praise whom? Whom to see, whom to avoid? I seek none, nor avoid any, for I am the universe. I praise myself, I blame myself, I suffer for myself, I am happy at my own will, I am free. This is the *jñānī*, brave and daring. Let the whole universe tumble down; he smiles and says — it never existed it was all hallucination. Thus he sees the universe really disappear before his eyes and questions, wondering — where was it? Whither has it melted away?

Before going into the practical part we will take up one more intellectual question. So far the logic is tremendously rigorous. If a man reasons, there is no place for him to stand until he comes to this, that there is but one existence, that everything else is nothing. There is no other way left for rational mankind but to take this view. But now it is that what is infinite, ever perfect ever blessed, existence knowledge-bliss, Absolute has come under these delusions? It is the same question that has been asked all the world over in all times. How did sin come into this world? This is the most vulgar and sensuous form of the question, and the same. The same question has been asked in various grades and fashions, but in its lower forms it finds no solution, because the stories of apples, and serpents and women do not give the explanation. In that state, the question is childish and so is the answer. But the question has assumed very high proportions now. How did this illusion come? And the answer is as fine. The answer is that we cannot expect any answer to an impossible question. The very question is that impossible in terms. You have no right to ask that question. Why? What is perfection? That which is beyond time, space and causation. That is perfect. Then you ask how the perfect became imperfect. In logical language, the question may be put in this form — how did that which is beyond causation become caused? You contradict yourself. You first admit it is beyond causation, and then ask what causes it. Questions can only be asked within the limits of causation. As far as time and space and causation extend, so far can this question be asked. But beyond that it will be nonsense to ask it, because the question is illogical. Within time, space and causation, it can never be answered, and what answer may lie beyond these limits can only be known when we have transcended them; therefore the wise will let this question rest. When a man is ill, he devotes himself to curing his disease without insisting that he must first learn how he came to have it.

There is another form of this question, a little lower but more practical and illustrative. What produced this delusion? Can any reality produce delusion? Certainly not. We see that one delusion produces another, and so on. It is delusion always that produces delusion. It is disease that produces disease, and not health that produces disease. The wave is the same thing as the water. The effect is the cause in another form. The effect is delusion, and therefore the cause must be delusion. What produced this delusion? Another delusion. And so on without beginning. The only question that remains for you to ask is — Does not this admission break your monism, because you get two existences in the universe — one your self, and the other the delusion? The answer is — delusion cannot be called existence. Thousands of dreams come into your life, but do not form any part of your life. Dreams come and they have no existence; to call delusion existence will be sophistry. Therefore there is only one individual existence in the universe — ever free and ever blessed, and that is what you are. This is the last conclusion reached by the Advaitists. It may then be asked, what becomes of all these various forms of worship? They will remain; they are simply groping in the dark for light, and through this groping light will come. We have just seen that the self cannot see itself. All our knowledge is within the network of *māyā* and beyond this is freedom. Within the network, there is slavery, it is all under law. Beyond that there is no law. So far as the universe is concerned, existence is ruled by law, and beyond that is freedom. As long as you are in the network of time, space and causation, to say you are free is non-law-sequence and consequence. To say that the will is free is sheer nonsense. It is only when the infinite existence comes as it were into this network of *māyā* that it takes the form of will. Will is a portion of that being, caught in the network of *māyā*, and therefore free-will is a misnomer. It means nothing-sheer nonsense. So is all this talk about freedom. There is no freedom in *māyā*. Everyone is bound in thought, word, dead and mind, a piece of stone of this table. That I talk to you now is as rigorously in causation so that you listen to me. There is no freedom until you go beyond *māyā*. That is the real freedom of the soul. Men, however sharp and intellectual, however clearly they see the force of the logic that nothing here can be free are all compelled to think they are free, they cannot help. It means that the freedom we talk about is the glimpse of the blue sky through the clouds, and that the real freedom — the blue sky itself — is behind. True freedom exists in the midst of this delusion, this hallucination, this universe of the senses, body and mind. All these dreams without beginning or end, uncontrolled and uncontrollable, ill-adjusted, broken inharmonious, form our idea of this universe. In a dream, when you see a giant with 24 heads chasing you, and you are flying from him, you do not think it inharmonious; you think it is proper and right. So is this law. All that you call law is simply chance without meaning. In this dream state you call it law. Within *māyā*, so far as this law of time, space and causation exists, there is no freedom and all these various forms of worship are within this *māyā*. The idea of God, and the ideas of a brute and man are within this *māyā*; and such equally hallucinations; all of them are dreams. But you must take care not to argue like some extraordinary men of whom we hear at the present time. They say that the idea of God is a delusion, but the idea of this world is true. Both ideas stand or fall by the same logic. He alone has the right to be an atheist who denies this world as well as the other. The same argument is for both. The same mass of delusion extends from God to the lowest animals; from a blade of grass to the creator. They stand or fall by the same logic. The same person who sees falsity in the idea of God ought also to see who sees, and see it in the idea of his own body or his own mind. When God vanishes, then also vanish the body and mind. There the eyes cannot go nor the speech, nor the mind. We cannot see it, neither know it. And we now understand that so far as speech and thought and knowledge and intellect go, it is all within this *māyā,* within bondage. Beyond that is Reality. There neither thought, nor mind, nor speech can reach.

So far it is intellectually all right, but then comes the practice. The real work in these classes is the practice. Are any practices necessary to realise this oneness? Most decidedly it is not that you become this *Brahman*. You are already that. It is not that you become God or perfect; you are already perfect, and whenever you think you are not, it is a delusion. The delusion which says that you are Mr. so and so or Mrs. so and so can be got rid of by another delusion, and that is practice. Fire will eat fire, and you use one delusion to conquer another delusion. One cloud will come and brush away another cloud, and then both will go away. What are these practices them? We must always bear in mind that we are not going to be free, but are free already. Every idea that we are bound is a delusion. Every idea that we are happy or unhappy, is a tremendous delusion; and another delusion will come that we shall have to work and worship and struggle to be free, and this will chase out the first delusion, and then both will stop.

The first question is — who are fit to become *jñāna yogīs*? Those who are equipped with these requisites. First renunciation of all fruits of work and of all enjoyments in this life or another life. If you are the creator of this universe, whatever you desire you will have, because you will create it for yourself. It is only a question of time. Some get it immediately; with others the past *saṁskāra*s stand in the way of getting their desires. We give the first place to desire for enjoyment, either in this or another life. Deny there is any life at all, because life is only another name for death. Deny that you are a living being. Who cares for life? Life is one of these hallucinations and death is its counterpart. Joy is one part of these hallucinations and misery the other part, and so on. What have you to do with life or death? These are all creations of the mind. This is called giving up desires of enjoyments, either in this life or the other.

Then comes controlling the mind, claiming it so that it will not break into waves and have all sorts of desires; holding the mind steady, not allowing it to get into waves from external or internal cause; controlling the mind perfectly just by the power of will. The *jñāna yogī* does not take any of this physical help. Simply, philosophic reasoning, knowledge and his own will — these are the instrumentalities he believes in. Next comes *titikṣā* bearing all miseries without murmuring, without complaining. When an injury comes, do not mind it. *Titikṣā* means to bear everything, not to complain of anything. I myself have seen men who say, "I am the soul; what is the universe to me? Neither pleasure, nor pain, nor virtue, nor vice, nor heat, nor cold is anything to me". That is *titkṣhā*; not running after the enjoyments of the body.

The ultimate goal is becoming one with God. The soul has no power of its own, but has the ability to use any power it receives. Its activities depend upon the amount of power that it receives. This power gradually increases and illumines the soul. At the goal, the soul is once for all free from the hold of *āṇava,* and is filled with and enveloped in the love of God. It is then indistinguishable from God, just as a crystal pillar in the rays of the noon-day sun cannot be distinguished from the light. It has then none of the activities of knowing, desiring or doing. It enjoys the inexpressible bliss which knows no change, and which knows no change, and in which all thought of lover, love, and the beloved is absent.

Bibliography

Raja Ramanna, *Advaita and Science.*

Anthony, H.D., *Science and its Background.*

Basham, A.L., *The Wonder That Was India.*

Chakraborty, Shanti, *Weather Forecast in Ancient India.*

Chattopadhya, Aditya, *Statistical Methodology in Ancient India.*

Dutta, Bibuti Bhushan, *The Scope and Development of the Hindu Ganita.*

Lunia, B.N., *Evolution of Indian Culture.*

Majumdar, R.C., *Scientific Spirit in Ancient India.*

Manson, S.F., *Main Currents of Scientific Thought.*

Matraux, G.S. and Crouzet F., *Studies in the Cultural History of India.*

Misra, S.D., *Technical Terms Related to Yantras.*

Pandit, M.D., *Mathematical Concepts in the Rig Veda.*

Radhakrishnan, S., *Indian Philosophy.*

Rani, Vijaya, *A Study of the Wave Theory of Sound and Light.*

Sarkar, B.K., *Hind Achievement.*

Sarkar, B.K., *Hindu Achievements in Exact Science.*

Sartaon, G., *Introduction to the History of Science.*

Subbarayappa, B.V., *India's Contribution to the History of Science.*

Taylor, P.S., *A History of Science and Scientific Thought.*

Vartak, P.V., *The Theory of Birth of Universe from Nasadiya Sukta in Comparison with that of Modern Science.*

Wadekar Mukund, L., *The Unnoticed Devala : Exposition of Comets.*

Glossary

Abduda : One crore

Abhradhruva : The 11th and 13th day of Kārttika month, when there will be heavy rain.

Ācārya : Preceptor.

Adhakas : The amount of rain received per year.

Ādhibhūta : Matter. Matter is defined to be that which is limited, and spirit to be that which is limitless.

Ādhidaiva : The illumining principle which unifies the spirit and matter.

Adhvaryu : One who performs the sacrifice. The *Adhvaryu* who is instrumental in all sacrificial activities belongs to the *Yajurveda*.

Adhyātma : The spirit of two kinds. They are pure and impure. The pure spirit is that portion of the spirit which lies behind the range of the matter while the impure spirit is the portion of the supreme spirit.

Advaita : Non-duality. The most popular philosophy in India today. "*Brahman* alone is real, the phenomenal world is an illusion, and the individual soul is none other than the Supreme Reality" is the essence of *Advaita*.

Adri : Rock.

Agni : Fire-god. There were 85 Agni gods in Hindu Mythology.

Ahaṁkāra : Egoism. This is not pride, but the simple feeling of agency in action, like "I am doing", "I am eating", etc.

Ahorātra : One crore. Ṛgvedic method of calculation.

Ajastringe : Odina Pinnat.

Aitareya Upaniṣad : One of the *Upaniṣads* that discusses the spiritual character.

Ākāśa : Sky.

Akṣara : Imperishable thing.

Alinda : A type of wood used for the construction of palaces.

Amāvasyā : New Moon Day.

Āṇava : Egoism. When the egoism leaves the body, then the body becomes free.

Anekāntavāda : The doctrine of existence and non-existence of a matter.

Anna : Food.

Antaḥkaraṇa : The four types of senses, particularly, mind, *cit,* intellect and ego.

Antaḥkaraṇas : The combination of organs with internal instrument.

Antardhām : The number system which is followed in *Yajurveda*. The designated number of this is 10 followed by 11 zeros.

Anumāna : Involvement in a particular activity.

Ap / Āpa : Water.

Apām-Napāt : Water god. The Naighaṇṭuka mentions his name among the territorial deities. His name is mentioned 30 times in the *Ṛgveda*.

Apa : Liquid form.

Apamarg : Achayrcuthus aspera.

Ātmā : Soul.

Apsu-Jit : Water conqueror.

Aratu : Colavsauthus Indica.

Āṣāḍhā : Star.

Asuras : Demon. The *asuras* and *rakṣasas* are very old demi-gods. The *Nirukta* says that the word *asura* implies a cauldron that sprinkles water.

Asvattha : Ficus Regligiossa.

Aṭaka : Big size of *śālā*.

Avavasthā : Conclusion.

Avyaktam : Nature which has 3 forces — one of which is called *sattva*, the second, *rajas* and the third, *tamas*.

Ayuta : The number system which is followed in *Yajūrveda*. The designated number for this is 10 followed by 5 zeros.

Bhādrapadā : Asterism.

Bharaṇī : Star — one of the 27 constellations measured by the daily march of the moon. This name is assigned to a star in the sky along the zodiac and the milky-way.

Bhujya : Zero.

Bhūmi : Earth.

Bhūtas : The grossest elements, which is composed of fine materials.

Brāhmaṇa : The first of the four castes, the category of people who are sober, refined, intellectual, learned and devoted.

Brahmāṇḍa : Big globe.

Buddhi : The power of the intellect.

Caitra : Month (March-April). In the month of *Caitra* westerlies continue, temperatures slowly build up and the first thunderstorms occur and decrease the haze.

Caturadha : The method of division. In particular, three methods were practised by the Ṛgvedic people.

Catuṣka : A kind of wood used for palace construction.

Citta : State of mind.

Dānastutis : Gods worshipped for wealth during the Vedic period.

Daśa-sahasra : Ten thousand.

Daśa-śate : Ten hundred.

Devas : The heavenly bodies from the order of satellites to the order of Indra star.

Dhṛtavrata : The upholder about the movement of luminary bodies.

Divya-yuga : 1200 divine years.

Droṇa : Village.

Dvāparayuga : The second of the four Hindu time-cycles. A period of 8,64,000 years during which only two quarters of *Dharma* reigns.

Dva-sahasra : Two hundred. The method of calculation which was adopted by the Vedic people. This method was used by the Ṛgvedic people.

Dvī-janman : Rebirth. Two-fold division of the Universe.

Gaṇita : Mathematics.

Garbhagṛha : The place where the deity was kept in the temple. Only priests were allowed to enter it.

Ghaṭikā : 60 *Vighaṭikā*s.

Ghī : Wood.

Giri : Mountain.

Grāma : Village.

*Guṇa*s : Character.

Hara : God of destroyer.

*Indriya*s : Organ.

Īśa-sṛṣṭi : God's creation.

Jaḍa : Insentient.

Jagati : The movement of sun in the southernmost track.

Janaḥ : *Loka* (world). This world is situated above the earth.

Jīvan-mukta : Bodily salvation.

Jñāna-yogī : Method of free living to attain the end of life.

Jyeṣṭha : Older than all. The infinite is That which was even before the very concept of space came into existence. The term is the superlative degree of the Aged.

Kāla : Time.

Kālavādin : Doctrine which discusses the periodical destruction of the world and its creation.

Kaliyuga : The last of the four Hindu time-cycles — the current one — of duration 4,32,000 years when only one quarter of *Dharma* reigns.

Kalpa : A time-cycle of 4,32,000,000 years; one of the *Vedāṅgas* — the authority on religious rites.

Karma : All expressions of activity, by thought, word or deed; the first of the two Doctrines on which Hindu religion and philosophy are based; the Law of Causality in the spiritual world; the theory that every action has a reaction and that none can escape it.

Karma-kāṇḍa : Musical note.

Kathā : Story.

Khadira : Acacea catechu.

Khetaka : Village designed according to the king's advice.

Koṭi Brahmāṇḍa Nāyaka : The lord of the innumerable cosmic big globe.

Krayvāda : Flame form of Agni.

Kṛṣṇa-pakṣa : 15 days after full moon day.

Kṛta-yuga : Also called *Satya-yuga* — the first of the four Hindu time-cycles — of a duration of 17,28,000 years when *Dharma* reigns in full. It is said that in this period, the word *Satya* will be unknown.

Kṛttikā : Star.

Kṣatriya : An individual belonging to the ruling caste, a person devoted to righteous conduct and protection of others' honour and property, when they deserve it.

Kustha : Castus specius.

Liṅga-Śarīra : Subtle body of a man.

Lokāyata : The world is permanent. No method can destroy it.

Madamba : Village.

Mādhyamika : The intermediate appearance of an object in the world.

Mahaḥ: *Loka* (world). This world is situated above the earth.

Mahāpralaya : Great cataclysm.

Mahat: The movement of the particle.

Mahāyugas : Also called *Caturyuga*. The four *yugas* or the time-cycles put together — duration 43,20,000 years.

Marutvant : The Maruts occupy a prominent place in the *Ṛgveda*, 33 hymns being addressed to them. They are sons of Rudras and Cow *Pṛṣṇī*.

Māsa : Month.

Māyā : Unreality.

Mīmāṁsaka : Science of sentence interpretation. The *Mīmāṁsā* helps man to have a correct perspective of *Dharma* through teaching of mortality and immortality of the object.

Mṛtyubandha : Regarding death as a relation. In the *Ṛgveda,* it is specified only twice.

Muktakoṇa : During the Vedic period, the palaces were constructed using this eight-corner method.

Nadyavārtā : Dance.

Nagara : Town.

Nakṣatras : Stars. From the spiritual points the stars are called *Devas* and Gods, and from the material points they are called *Lokas*. They are 27 in number. They are believed to be held up and sustained in space by the force of air.

Nāsadīya : No non-existence.

Nirukta : Book.

Nitatuti : Solsmum nigrun.

Niyuta : Ten thousand.

Oṣadhis : Cereals. It is derived from food. It is born from *Pṛthivī*.

Pakaras : The outer space inside the temple.

Pakṣas : 15 *ahorātras*.

Pañcīkaraṇa : The mixture of 5 elements, particularly, the air, water, earth, fire and ether.

Parabrahman : Almighty who can be attained by meditation.

Paramāṇus : The smallest form of particle, which is invisible.

Paramātman : Almighty who can attained by meditation.

Parārdham : Month.

Pauṣa : Month.

Pāśa : The way of movement of the star.

Prakṛti : The word *prakṛti* literally means Nature or the automatic outcome of the action of mixture of any kind or the last natural state of matter to which it returns in the end, and from which it manifests in the beginning of the cycle.

Pralaya : The word *pralaya* is taken to mean the burning of the bodies into ashes. But it is not so. It is rather the absorption of the heavenly bodies into their primaries.

Prāṇas : Vital air for human beings.

Pratijñā : Thesis.

Pratyakṣa : Intellectuality which can be obtained by deep meditation.

Prayuta : The number system which is followed in *Yajurveda*. This is designated as 10 followed by 5 zeros, i.e., 1000000 (10 lakhs).

Pr̥thivī : Nature.

Purohita : Priest.

Puruṣa : *Brahman*. One who completes and fulfils the Existence everywhere.

Pūrvāṣāḍhā : Asterism.

Rāga : Songs.

Ṛgveda : The *Ṛgveda* mainly consists of hymns of praise and is believed to be the earliest collection of the knowledge of the Āryans. It is believed to be the oldest book known to man.

Ṛtvij : The sacrifice performed for god Agni.

Rohiṇī : Star — One of the 27 constellations measured by the daily march of the moon. It is found in the milky way.

Ṛṣis : The word *r̥ṣi* according to the *Nirukta* means the rays of the sun and these are said to be 7 in number. The *Satapatha Brāhmaṇa* considers the *r̥ṣis* as breaths and says, "Inasmuch as before all this universe, they, desiring this universe, were worn out with toil and austerity, therefore they are *r̥ṣi*."

Ṛta : Season.

Rūpa : Not the real form, but the transient form and deceptive appearance.

Sādhanā : Achievement.

Sahasra : The number system which is followed in *Yajurveda*. The designated number of this is 10 followed by 2 zeros.

Śaiva : The doctrine of Śiva followed by certain groups of peoples called Śaivites.

Śaiva-Siddhānta : The doctrine based on the origin and efficient cause of the universe.

Śāla : A kind of wood used for constructing palaces and other types of household buildings.

Samādhi : Cremating place for the dead.

Saṁhitā : The name *Saṁhitā* (collection) first occurs in the so-called *Āraṇyaka*s or supplements to *Brāhmaṇa*s, and in the *Sūtra*s.

Sāṁkhya : The oldest system of Indian philosophy attained the position of a full-fledged system before any other *āstika* thought. The literature available is very little.

Samudra : Digit. There are 9 *samudra*s, which begin with 53 digit and end with 60th digit. The names are *Daśa, Śata, Sahasra, Daśa Sahasra, Mahā, Daśa Mahā* (i.e. 1 x 53 zeros).

Sapta Sūryasya Raśmayaḥ : Seven types of rays (said to refer to the 'Vibgyor').

Saptanām Sapta Ṛṣṭayaḥ : Seven members on each side.

Sarvam Khalvidam Brahman : The world is under the control of *Brahman*.

Sat : The Existence in all things and beings is the same ever, and is all-pervading.

Satkāryavāda : The pre-existence effect in the case of a thing which may lead to *māyā*.

Sattva : Seventh.

Satyam : Truth.

Siddhānta : Successful. One who has achieved all that has to be achieved, as He Himself is the final goal for all.

Siddhiyar : God for success.

Siṁha : The Lion. Due to His great exploits in fighting the negative forces during His various incarnations, He is indicated as the Lion among beings in the Universe.

Śiva-Jñāna-Bodham : The cosmic factor which discusses the origin of the Universe.

Śloka : Hymn.

Somapa : *Soma*-drinker. Indra is known to be a *soma*-drinker.

Śrāvaṇa : Month (October-November).

Śrīvatsa : Main hall in the palace.

Śukla-pakṣa : 15 days after New Moon days.

Sūktas : Songs.

Suṣupati : A dreamless sleep.

Svarga : Heven.

Svastika : Symbol.

Śūdra : The working or the serving class — with a preponderance of Tāmasic qualities on Rājasic base — who contribute the labour for the welfare of the society.

Syādvāda : The world comes out of nothing.

Tamas : One of the three *guṇas*, marked by inertia, inactivity and ignorance.

Tanmātras : *Mantras* dedicated to wealth.

Tapaḥ : Meditation.

Tapas : Meditation.

Titikṣā : To beam everything, not to complain of anything.

Tredhā : The method of division (three methods, in particular, were practised by the Ṛgvedic people).

Tretāyuga : The third of four Hindu time-cycles. A period of 1,296,000 years during which only two quarters of *Dharma* reigns.

Tridha : The method of division (three methods, in particular, were practised by the Ṛgvedic people).

Tri-karaṇī : One who perform three types of actions. In the mathematical sense, it is the value of Pi — calculated to be 1.732.

Udaya-kalpa : 1000 *divya yuga*.

Udumbe : Ficus glomarata.

Upaniṣads : The word *Upaniṣad* is constructed of three syllables which together mean "Near-below-sit".

Upavana-Vinoda : Magical method of curing the disease of a plant.

Uṣas : Goddess of Dawn. The Naighaṇṭuka mentions the name of Uṣas in the list of celestial as well as aerial deities.

Vāhanālaya : Type of temple.

Vaiśākha : Month (April-May). During this month temperature will increase and the sky will be clear.

Vaiśeṣika : Month. The 3rd day of the bright half of *Vaiśeṣika* is called *Akṣaya Tṛtīyā*.

Vardhamāna : Type of palace.

Vāyu : Wind.

Vāyu-vāta : Wind destroyer.

Vedāṅga : The limbs of the *Veda*s — Phonetics, Grammar, Vedic glossary, Religious rites, Prosody and Astronomy.

Vedānta : The end of the *Veda*s, which can mean either the concluding portion of the *Veda*s or the end or goal of the *Veda*s.

Vidyā : Master.

Vidyut : Lightning spread over the sky.

Vighaṭikā : 6 *prāṇa*s.

Viṁśatim-śata : 20 group of one hundred.

Vipra : The sacrifice which is performed for god Agni.

Vithis : Pathway for star movement. For example, when Venus moves in the northern direction, it produces a lot of rains and when it moves in the southern direction, it destroys the crops.

Vṛtti : Development.

Yajus : It is sacrifice or combustion of the atoms of the combustible matter of the 3 *guṇa*s.

Yantras : Mechanical device. There were two machines, and they are static and moveable.

Yāska : Composer of songs.

Yogī : Sage and man of wisdom.

Index